PLURAL PREDICATION

Plural Predication

THOMAS J. MCKAY

CLARENDON PRESS · OXFORD

OXFORD

UNIVERSITY PRESS

Great Clarendon Street, Oxford OX2 6DP

Oxford University Press is a department of the University of Oxford.
It furthers the University's objective of excellence in research, scholarship,
and education by publishing worldwide in
Oxford New York
Auckland Cape Town Dar es Salaam Hong Kong Karachi
Kuala Lumpur Madrid Melbourne Mexico City Nairobi
New Delhi Shanghai Taipei Toronto

With offices in
Argentina Austria Brazil Chile Czech Republic France Greece
Guatemala Hungary Italy Japan Poland Portugal Singapore
South Korea Switzerland Thailand Turkey Ukraine Vietnam

Oxford is a registered trademark of Oxford University Press
in the UK and in certain other countries

Published in the United States
by Oxford University Press Inc., New York

© Thomas J. McKay 2006

British Library Cataloguing in Publication Data
Data available

Library of Congress Cataloging in Publication Data
McKay, Thomas J.
Plural Predication / Thomas J. McKay.
p. cm.
Includes bibliographical references and index.
ISBN-13: 978–0–19–927814–5 (alk. paper)
ISBN-10: 0–19–927814–8 (alk. paper)
1.   Semantics (Philosophy)   2.   Language and language – Philosophy.   3.   Predicate (Logic)
4.   Grammar, Comparative and general – Number.   5.   Logic.   I.   Title.
B840.M435 2006   160 – dc22   2006007429

Typeset by Laserwords Private Limited, Chennai, India
Printed in Great Britain
on acid-free paper by
Biddles Ltd., King's Lynn, Norfolk

ISBN 0–19–927814–8   978–0–19–927814–5

1 3 5 7 9 10 8 6 4 2

Contents

Introduction   1

1. A Formal Language with Non-distributive Plurals:
   Preliminary Considerations   5
   Non-distributive Predication   5
   Distributive and non-distributive plurals: some basics   9
   Conjoined predicates and argument-place distinctions   11
   Non-distributive relations   13
   Plurals in philosophy   17

2. Against Singularism   19
   The multiple relations idea   19
   Singularism   22
   Singularist prejudice displayed   27
   Mereology   33
   Can one thing be many?   36
   Composition relations   42
   The plurally plural?   46
   Martian perplurals   51
   A linguistic argument for singularism   53
   The peculiarity of singularism   54

3. Semantics   55
   Metalinguistic resources   56
   Terms   57
   Quantifiers   58
   The formal language   59
   Semantics   60
   Specific quantifiers   70
   Existence entailments   71
   Dual quantifiers   74

4. Natural Language Issues 78

    Distributive correlates 78
    'at least', 'at most', and 'exactly' 79
    Marking distributive predication 81
    Distribution: A better approach 83
    Intermediate distributions and collective objects? 88
    Multiple quantification 92
    Cumulative readings of multiple quantification 93
    Relationship between singular and plural
        quantification 96
    A problem with conjoined terms 97

5. Set Theoretic Semantics 103

    Set theoretic representation of non-distributive
        predication 103
    Quantifiers 107
    Proportional quantifiers 110
    The formal language and semantics 111
    Relationship between singular and plural
        quantification 113
    The set theoretic approach and the goal of semantics 114

6. *Among* 119

    The elimination of singular variables 120
    Axioms for "*Among* Theory" 121
    Theorems 124
    Principles of sameness ($\approx$) 127
    Adding other predicates 128
    The identity schema 128
    Comprehension 129
    Consequences of comprehension 130
    Terms 132
    One of 135
    Perplurals 137
    Relationship to second-order logic 139
    Criticisms of plurals 143
    Williamson on everything, plurals and second-order
        logic 147
    Relationship to set theory 154

Further relationship to set theory 156
Is *among* a logical constant? 160

7. *THE*: The Basic Logic 162

Plural 'the' 162
'All of the A' 166
Improper plural descriptions 167
Peculiar definite descriptions 170
The singular definite description 171
Comparison with mass quantifiers 173
Plural *de re* 177
Relationship to Scha's discussion of definite
    descriptions 181

8. *THE*: Context Sensitivity 185

Predicate supplementation and domain restriction 186
Problem 1: lack of unique specification 187
Problem 2: multiple domains 189
Problem 1 reconsidered 194
"Psychologism" 196
Definite descriptions as existentials 198
A problem for another proposal 203
Events 203
A problem for the maximality account 204

9. Pronouns 207

Uses for pronouns 208
Pronouns as bound variables 209
Referential pronouns 212
E-type pronouns 213
Donkey sentences 216
Relative reference 218
Caveats 222
A continuum of linguistic information 231
Categories of pronouns again 233

10. Plurals and Events 240

Distributive ambiguity and events 241
Events and Paradox 245

Unscoped quantification again 246
Schein's complex examples 247
Landman's objection to the multiple role approach 250
All 252

Bibliography 256
Index 261

Introduction

The codification, interpretation and development of first-order logic constitute one of the great intellectual achievements of the last 150 years. However, the standard formalization of that language does not provide adequate resources for properly representing many ordinary things that we say.[1] For example, any of these predicates might be true of some people without being true of any one of them:

They are shipmates (classmates, fraternity brothers)
They are meeting together
They lifted a piano
They are surrounding a building
They come from many different countries
They weigh over 500 pounds

Such predications are a routine part of ordinary language use, yet standard systems of first-order logic provide no place for such non-distributive predication.

Work on plurals and non-distributive predication has led me to the conclusion that we should extend first-order logic to allow for the representation of non-distributive plural predication. Philosophers often employ first-order logic as a basis for regimenting claims, assessing inferences, and developing their thoughts. Enriching first-order logic

---

[1] Gerald Massey's exposition (Massey 1976) of these problems is probably the best known. George Boolos explored related themes (Boolos 1984, 1985) in his discussion of plural quantification as an alternative to a set-theoretic understanding of second-order logic. Landman 2000 is the most extensive systematic development of the semantics of plurals in English. Many who have approached this topic have succumbed to the *singularist* bias, assuming that the semantics for plurals must make reference to single entities: groups, sets or mereological sums (see Chapter 2). Notably, Boolos has avoided this singularist bias, and, in recent work, so have Hossack, Yi, Rayo, and Oliver and Smiley. Yi 1999, 2002, and 2005, and Oliver and Smiley 2001 argue against singularism in ways that overlap significantly with considerations to be developed in this work.

with a clear semantics for non-distributive plurals can provide us with a better tool with a wider range of applicability in philosophy and other disciplines.

The use of non-distributive plurals in metaphysics has become common in the discussions of when some things compose a single thing, for example. Also, when a metaphysician proposes to say "Everything is identical with itself," she often refuses to concede that this can be said only of some restricted domain, less than everything. Timothy Williamson has formulated a very general version of Russell's paradox and argued that the metaphysician must adopt second-order logic in order to support such a universalist position. I argue (in Chapter 6) that a plural first-order approach can do as well in defusing the paradox and allowing us to speak of everything.

Linguists have already done much towards the difficult task of accounting systematically for the expression of non-distributive predication and plural quantification in natural language.[2] Linguists who might wish to explore questions about natural language in a formal language with a clear semantics and without singularist assumptions will still find this discussion to be a valuable resource. I think that the simplicity of the semantics and some success in accounting for the semantics of many difficult examples from natural language should help to make a case that using a plural, first-order, non-singularist metalanguage might make our semantic theories simpler. We will also see some considerations in favor of the conclusion that such a metalanguage provides a more accurate semantics by allowing us to assign semantic roles to the correct individuals rather than to set-theoretic surrogates. I also argue more specifically (Chapter 10) that we do not need to introduce events in order to give a successful semantic account of the core phenomena of plurality (even if there are other reasons to introduce events into semantics).

---

[2] Landman 2000 is an especially rich source, both for the account it develops of the semantics for English and for its exposition of earlier work. Several linguists and philosophers exploring plurality, including Landman, do so within the context of a semantics that follows Donald Davidson and Terence Parsons in taking events as fundamental to semantics. I believe that the core phenomena of non-distributive predication and plural quantification are independent of that aspect of the semantics. By exploring these phenomena without giving a fundamental role to events, I think that this work will make a case for that independence. However, this should not be taken as an argument that events are not important to semantics. The consideration of adverbs provides strong arguments for an event-based semantics. (See Landman 2000, esp. pp. 1–25, and Parsons 1990, esp. 3–19 and Davidson 1967.) See Ch. 10 for further discussion of this issue.

There is also potential value for mathematicians and philosophers studying the foundations of mathematics, since the language of plurals provides some of the expressive power of set theory but is not subject to the paradoxes that we find in naïve set theory or the coping mechanisms that we find in non-naïve set theory. It also has the fundamental expressive power of monadic second-order logic, though it is first-order—predication and quantification involve the individuals of the domain and nothing else. Results concerning monadic second-order logic transfer to a first-order plural logic.

Chapter 1 presents some preliminary considerations in favor of taking non-distributive predication seriously, introduces key concepts, and indicates some of the issues that need to be worked out in order to have a successful treatment of non-distributive predication, plural quantification with a full range of quantifiers, and compound plural terms.

Chapter 2 presents a fuller set of arguments against singularist (set-theoretic and mereological) approaches to the semantics of plurals and non-distributive predication.

Chapter 3 codifies a formal language of plurals and presents a full semantics. The language allows non-distributive predication and a full range of quantifier concepts.

Chapter 4 connects the formal language more explicitly with some problems in the formal representation of English sentences. This should enable readers to get a better understanding of the formal apparatus, and it also indicates the direction of some applications in the semantics of natural language. Using quantifiers as the basis for representing distributive predication is a central development here.

Chapter 5 indicates how to develop the semantics within a set-theoretic context. Although I hope that Chapters 1–3 will have made the case that a set-theoretic semantics is not needed, some readers will probably find this more familiar approach to be useful, and having it may facilitate comparison with some other work. It also provides a base for reconsidering limitations of the set-theoretic approach.

Chapter 6 explores the fundamental semantic concept *among* and discusses the relationship of the work here to set theory, to mereology and to second-order logic. Axioms for the concept make some of these relationships especially clear. This chapter is suggestive concerning the role that a logic with non-distributive predication might play in the foundations of mathematics. With the formal apparatus in place, we can also present the plural, first-order alternative to Williamson's second-order language for speaking of everything.

Chapter 7 develops a formal treatment of definite descriptions indicating how the singular and plural descriptions are related and exactly how they differ from (and are analogous to) mass descriptions. The formal theory is applied to produce a natural solution to a puzzle about plurals due to Philip Bricker.

Chapter 8 considers the significance of the context sensitivity of definite descriptions (singular and plural) and suggests some ways of understanding it.

Chapter 9 indicates what significance the account of descriptions has for the development of a theory of English pronouns, especially E-type pronouns.

Chapter 10 shows how to use the material developed here to deal with some of the principal puzzles that have led people to the conclusion that the introduction of events into the semantics of English is important to understanding plurals. While events may be important to the semantics of English for other reasons, we can deal with the core issues involving plurals without giving a central role to events.

I thank Mark Barber, José Benardete, Hanoch Ben-Yami, Mark Brown, Dean Buckner, Michael Fara, Gregory Fowler, Martina Gracanin, Delia Graff, Allen Hazen, Harold Hodes, Brendan Jackson, Pat Kenny, Jaklin Kornfilt, Manfred Krifka, David Lewis, Øystein Linnebo, Peter Ludlow, Ishani Maitra, Kris McDaniel, Daniel Nolan, Agustín Rayo, Adam Sennett, John Shoemaker, Ted Sider, Kora Smith Gould, Joshua Spencer, Mark Steen, Zoltan Gendler Szabo, Christopher Tillman, Gabriel Uzquiano, Megan Wallace, Brian Weatherson, Yoad Winter, Byeong-Uk Yi and several anonymous readers for their helpful comments on drafts of material related to portions of this work. Yi, Linnebo, and Uzquiano have been especially helpful with their comments on elements of this work. With this many, there is a good chance that some might even agree with some of the things I say.

1

A Formal Language with Non-distributive Plurals: Preliminary Considerations

NON-DISTRIBUTIVE PREDICATION

Standard first-order logic does not provide adequate resources for properly representing many ordinary things that we say.

(1) Arnie, Bob and Carlos are shipmates.[1]

This is something true of the three of them together. We cannot say

Arnie is a shipmate

except perhaps as elliptical for something that connects Arnie to others. (Arnie is a shipmate *of someone*.) Many predicates can be true of some things without being true of any one of them. For example:

They are shipmates (classmates, fraternity brothers)
They are meeting together
They lifted a piano
They are surrounding a building
They come from many different countries
They weigh over 500 pounds

Standard systems of logic provide no place for such predication.

Let's say that a predicate F is *distributive*[2] if the following condition holds in virtue of the meaning of the predicate F:

Whenever some things are F, each one of them is F.

---

[1] The predicate 'are shipmates' is the principal example in Massey 1976.

[2] Unfortunately, the word 'distributive' has been used for a wide variety of different things in discussions in logic and metaphysics. In using it here, though, I am following an established usage, not introducing a new one.

For example:

Whenever some things are baboons, each one of them is a baboon. In standard first-order logic, every predicate is distributive. The concept of a single individual satisfying a predicate is fundamental; saying that some individuals satisfy a predicate can only mean that each of them satisfies it. Ordinary quantification is built on this. The formulas:

$\exists x \, Fx$

$\forall x \, Fx$

are true just when at least one individual (each individual) satisfies 'Fx'. We can always look at individuals in the domain separately in deciding what satisfies the predicate.

Although restricted quantification has many advantages over standard unrestricted quantification,[3] it has usually been limited in the same way to distributive predication.

$[\exists x : Fx] \, Gx$ (Some F are G)

$[\forall x : Fx] \, Gx$ (Every F is G)

These are true when at least one (each) thing that satisfies 'Fx' also satisfies 'Gx'. We look at each individual separately to determine whether the predicates are satisfied. There is no provision for non-distributive predication.

As our examples illustrate, though, many ordinary predicates are not distributive. When some people surround a building, they satisfy the predicate '. . . are surrounding the building' together, not separately. The principal goal of this work is to explore the semantics of non-distributive predication and to look at the consequences of extending ordinary first-order logic to allow for such predication.[4] We will develop the semantics

---

[3] See Barwise and Cooper 1981, Neale 1990 or Brown 1984 for some accounts of the advantages of restricted quantification. Neale 1990, 38–44, is a very useful brief discussion of restricted quantification. McKay 1989 (revised 2005) presents an elementary introduction to restricted quantification (Ch. 10).

[4] Byeong-Uk Yi's work has developed the semantics for plural predication and quantification within a system of unrestricted quantification. See esp. his 2005, "The Logic and Meaning of Plurals". His work is full of valuable insights. My work initially developed independently of his, but it is largely consistent with his approach, though my work develops a language with restricted quantification, and, accordingly, a larger range of quantifiers and a more immediate link with natural language. Hossack 2000 also develops plural quantification within a framework that employs only unrestricted quantification. In linguistics, the work of Scha, Link, Landman, Schwarzschild and Lasersohn (among others) also contains many ideas that are important to developing a semantics for plural predication and quantification.

for a language with restricted quantification. This enables us to do a better job of modeling the features of English sentences that include such predicates. It also allows us to consider a full set of quantifier concepts, including *several, many, most,* and cardinal quantifiers (*exactly n, at least n,* etc.), in addition to universals and existentials.[5] We will look at the way that both conjoined noun phrases and quantifier phrases combine with such predicates to form sentences.

In addition to distributivity, there is another limitation on the predicates of traditional systems of logic. In traditional logic, all predicates are *cumulative*:[6]

> A monadic predicate F is cumulative iff the meaning of the predicate requires that whenever some things X are F and some things Y are F, then X and Y together are F.[7]

For example, if Alice, Betty and Carla are students, and Dave, Ernie and Frank are students, then Alice, Betty, Carla, Dave, Ernie and Frank are students. Many (though not all) non-distributive predicates are also non-cumulative. For example, even if Alice, Betty and Carla are classmates, and Dave, Ernie and Frank are classmates, it does not follow that Alice, Betty, Carla, Dave, Ernie and Frank are classmates. And even if some students X are sitting in a circle and some students Y are sitting in a circle, it does not follow that X and Y together are sitting in a circle.[8] There are also some predicates that are distributive and not cumulative, for example:

> They are fewer than four in number.
> They are a minority.
> They are of just one gender.
> They are odd in number.

---

[5] Agustín Rayo (2002) has also proposed a semantics for generalized quantifiers, but his treatment does not take account of a problem for proportional quantifiers that introduces semantic anomaly. This problem will be discussed in Ch. 3.

[6] Schwarzschild 1996, 11 introduces this use of the term *cumulativity*, with some indication of its relation to earlier uses of *cumulative* (in Landman 1989 and Quine 1960) and also to a contrasting use of the term in Scha 1984.

[7] For general applicability to infinite domains, we need a slightly different definition: a monadic predicate F is cumulative iff the meaning of F requires that for any things X, if whenever some things Y are properly among X, Y are F, then X are F.

[8] Tyler Burge 1977 presents a theory of aggregates to deal with non-distributive plural predication, but his account will not give the right results for non-cumulative predicates. (Cf. the "analog to set-abstraction" on p. 100 of Burge 1977.)

Extending ordinary first-order logic to allow for such non-distributive and non-cumulative predication will give us resources for representing a wider range of arguments, resources for expressing some philosophical theories in ways that make their ontological claims clearer, and resources that might be useful in developing natural language semantics.

Because of the relative rarity of non-cumulative predicates that are distributive, I will usually refer to our task as the task of accommodating non-distributive predication. That can be taken as shorthand for *non-distributive and non-cumulative* predication.[9] Really what we want is a notion of joint satisfaction of a predicate, contrasted with individual satisfaction.[10]

We will develop this formal language with ordinary language in mind, as a guide to what can be said and so might be incorporated.[11] Some predicates allow for both distributive and non-distributive satisfaction, producing ambiguous sentences. ("They weigh 500 pounds" for example.) We will see that there are two ways to think of this: we can regard the argument position as the locus of the ambiguity, or we can identify an implicit (unexpressed) "distributing universal" in the distributive sentence as the source of the ambiguity. (Linguists have differed about the locus of the ambiguity, about whether it is in predicates or singular terms, and our work provides an alternative approach.) We will identify "distributive correlates" of non-distributive predicates that sometimes mislead us in considering examples. We will find that we need to distinguish between two very different universal quantifiers in connection with quantification with non-distributive predicates. We will also need to

[9] For completeness, we also note that there are predicates that are cumulative and not distributive, such as "They are more than four in number," "They are a majority of the students," "They come from more than seven countries," etc.

[10] One might also define a concept of strong distributivity: whenever some things X are F, if Y are among X, then Y are F. The predicate 'X are odd in number' is distributive but not strongly distributive, given our definitions. Such predicates are in any case non-cumulative, so the differentiation is of little significance.

Another definition of distribution is also current. Let's say that a predicate F is distributive* if and only if the following holds: some things are F if and only if each of them is F. (This is an adaptation of Oliver and Smiley's definition of distribution.) A predicate is distributive* if an only if it is distributive and cumulative. My separation of the two highlights cumulativity, a property of some independent interest.

[11] My goals may contrast with the goals of many linguists. I plan to enrich predicate logic with new expressive resources, and I will look at many interesting examples from ordinary language to illustrate the use of these new resources. The linguist must say in general how what can be said with such resources is said in natural language, and give a systematic theory of the connection. My illustrations provide suggestions, but not a full linguistic theory.

make a distinction among quantifiers, between the proportional and the non-proportional, and we will recognize a source of semantic anomaly in the use of proportional quantifiers that has not been widely recognized before.[12] In providing a semantics and avoiding "singularism" (see Ch. 2), we will make it clear that using plural pronouns and quantifiers and non-distributive predicates in our semantics can expand the expressive scope of our formal language in an important way.[13]

DISTRIBUTIVE AND NON-DISTRIBUTIVE PLURALS: SOME BASICS

Many plural sentences, those involving only distributive, cumulative predicates, have seemed unproblematic from the standpoint of standard systems of logic.

(2) Arnie, Bob and Carlos are students (read, live in New York City).

(3) (a) Some students read.
    (b) All students read.

Within the logical tradition, we have generally represented sentences like (2) as conjunctions, viewing (2) as an ellipsis for:

(2′) Arnie is a student, Bob is a student, and Carlos is a student.

---

[12] There are many things that this work will not accomplish. The intent is to develop a formal language with non-distributive predication and quantification. We will not deal with every issue of interest concerning plurals in natural language. For example, David Dowty has considered some similar issues concerning non-distributive predication, but his principal goal was to understand the varying uses of *all*. I will present some semantic considerations that may help with the foundations of that particular project. In particular, the recognition of two distinct universals, the systematic treatment of the difference between distributive and non-distributive argument places, and the explicit representation of distributing universals provide us with resources for the analysis of natural language quantifiers. I will not, however, attempt to account for the full variety of uses of *all* in English in this discussion. Another example: I will provide a way of representing so-called "cumulative readings" of multiply quantified sentences (in Ch. 4), but I will not answer the (perhaps pragmatic) question of how, precisely, the use of quantifier expressions in English can produce such an interpretation as the principal interpretation of a sentence.

[13] I make the usual logicians' assumption that a common noun like 'student' in 'All students' is to be represented in terms of the predicate 'x is a student'. There are reasons to treat the common noun as something that differs from a true predicate and to see such predicates as requiring analysis in terms of the common noun, rather than vice versa. That is an issue that is, I think, independent of any issue involving plurals, and I continue with the standard logicians' assumption for simplicity in exposition.

Since the predicate 'are students' is distributive, (2) and (2′) must be equivalent. No such ellipsis is at work in (1), however.

(1*) *Arnie is a shipmate, Bob is a shipmate, and Carlos is a shipmate.

Similarly, the representation of (3) in ordinary first-order logic (with restricted quantifiers) is the following:[14]

(4) (a) [∃x: Sx] Rx (Some x such that x is a student satisfies this condition, x reads)
(b) [∀x: Sx] Rx (Every x such that x is a student satisfies this condition, x reads)

Although these are singular and the English is plural, these seem to capture adequately the sense of the English. Clearly, though, no such logical formulas can capture the sense of sentences involving non-distributive predicates.

(5) Some students surrounded Adams Hall.
(6) All students in my class are shipmates.

No single student satisfies the predicate 'x surrounded the building' (at least in the typical situation) or 'x is a shipmate', and so nothing like (4) will work in representing these sentences.

Sentences like (5) and (6) have another feature of importance. They involve connecting a distributive predication ("are students") with a non-distributive predication ("are surrounding Adams Hall" and "are shipmates"). It seems that a single (plural) variable can have both distributive and non-distributive occurrences within a sentence. Our ultimate theory will need to reflect this in some way.

Our goal might be described as the development of a formal language that can be a framework for the general understanding of plurals, of plural quantification, of non-distributive and non-cumulative predications, and of non-distributive or plural argument positions in predicates and relations. We need to fit all of these together.

---

[14] This example could also be represented with unrestricted quantification.

(3U) ∃x (Sx ∧ Rx) (Some x is such that x is a student and x reads books)
∀x (Sx ⊃ Rx) (Every x is such that if x is a student then x reads books)

We employ restricted quantification because it provides the resources for a fuller set of quantifiers (*most* and *many*, for example, in addition to the universal and existential).

CONJOINED PREDICATES AND ARGUMENT-PLACE DISTINCTIONS

The problem of providing a place for non-distributive plurals also calls into question the treatment of other plurals as conjunctions. If we regard (2) as fundamentally a conjunction, then we treat the subject terms in (1) and (2) in different ways.[15] However, we can conjoin the predicates in (1) and (2) to produce a sentence in which they have the same plural term as subject:

(7) Arnie, Bob and Carlos are students and are shipmates.
(8) Arnie, Bob and Carlos are shipmates who are students.

So it appears that we must after all have a unified account of plural terms that allows for distributive and non-distributive satisfaction of predicates.[16] That suggests that we should look for a unified account of plural terms.

The treatment of this is complicated by the fact that sometimes predicates can take either singular or plural subjects, creating an ambiguity that must also be accounted for.

(9) Alicia, Betty and Carla lifted the table.
(10) Seven students lifted the table.

These sentences are made true either by multiple individual achievements or by a single lifting by a group of people. If given as an answer to the question "Which students lifted the table?" (9) would be unclear

---

[15] In what follows we are arguing against Frege (among others), who favored this disparity of treatment. Frege 1914, 227–8:

> If we say 'Schiller and Goethe are poets', we are not really connecting the proper names by 'and', but the sentences 'Schiller is a poet' and 'Goethe is a poet', which have been telescoped into one. It is different with the sentence 'Siemens and Halske have built the first major telegraph network'. Here we don't have a telescoped form of two sentences, but 'Siemens and Halske' designates a compound object about which a statement is made, and the word 'and' is used to help form the sign for this object.

[16] Massey, 1976, 103, Dowty 1986, 98, Schwarzschild 1996, 14–15, Oliver and Similey 2001, 294, and Yi 2002, 25–6 (among others) present similar arguments. (We shouldn't expect this argument to take us too far, though. Some compound NPs are clearly related to compound sentences: *Arnie, Bob or Carlos will stand watch tonight*. It would be a stretch to think that what is possible for 'or' is not possible for 'and'.) This issue brings with it further complications that will be discussed in Ch. 4.

about whether the lifting was collective or distributive. English does not overtly mark distributivity or non-distributivity in (9) or in (10), and we use context, paraphrase or additional clarification to indicate whether the predication is distributive. It may be true that they lifted it together but not true that they lifted it individually (or vice versa), and so it seems that we must mark that distinction in the formal theory we develop, where we want to mark semantically and inferentially significant distinctions.[17] Although a single quantifier can be connected to variables that are in both distributive and non-distributive clauses, we must have a way to mark the difference between distributive and non-distributive interpretations of (10).

The problem becomes even more evident in the quantificational case.

Seven students stepped forward and lifted the table.

The same seven students are to be understood as the subject of 'X stepped forward' and 'X lifted the table' here. (This is not equivalent to "Seven students stepped forward and seven students lifted the table.") So it seems that a single quantifier must be connected to variables that are in both distributive and non-distributive clauses. At the same time, we must distinguish the distributive and non-distributive readings of (10), since it may be true non-distributively and yet false distributively (or vice versa).

The need for marking the distinction is reinforced when we consider other examples. Suppose that Max, Norman and Oscar each weigh 200 pounds. We can say any of these:

(11) Max, Norman and Oscar weigh 200 pounds.
(12) Max, Norman and Oscar weigh less than 210 pounds.
(13) Max, Norman and Oscar weigh 600 pounds.
(14) Max, Norman and Oscar weigh more than 500 pounds.

The continued coherence of ordinary numerical predications seems to require that we have a way of indicating that the predication is distributive in (11) and (12) and non-distributive in (13) and (14). Our formal language will incorporate a way of indicating this.

---

[17] Some have said that sentences like (9) and (10) have an ambiguity in the predicate, for example Dowty 1986, 98. But Moltmann 1997, 52, point outs that we cannot treat this distinction (between distributive and non-distributive readings of a predicate) as an ambiguity in the predicate because predicate ellipsis is readily available. The correct approach, in light of these facts, will be developed in Chs. 2 and 4.

NON-DISTRIBUTIVE RELATIONS

It is important to emphasize that relations can be non-distributively satisfied with respect to one or more argument places.

(15) John Wayne circled wagons 1–9 around the campfire.

(16) John Wayne circled some wagons around the campfire.

The natural way to take this seems to be to regard it as a three-place relation (_____ circled . . . around ***) that requires plurality in the second place. (Maybe 'requires' is too strong. He could circle a long rope around the campfire.) The first and third places also allow for plurality, if the encircling was a group effort or if several things are in the center. ("John, Buddy and Gabby circled some wagons around the campfire and the food items.")

In representing such relations, I will employ upper-case variables to indicate the possibility of plurality; for example, 'X circled Y around Z', and 'x is one of Y'.[18] With plural quantification, such variables will relate to plural pronouns in English in the way that lower case variables relate to the singular pronouns of English. Thus 'x is one of Y' is very much like 'it is one of them', but we have access to an infinite stock of different pronouns ('x', 'y', 'x_1', 'x_2', etc., 'X', 'Y', 'X_1', 'X_2', etc.) for making cross-reference relations clear.

All of this indicates that we should really be talking about the plural character of the various places in a relation. For example, when I provided the definition of a distributive predicate, I used a relation that is non-distributive in the second place: 'x is one of Y'. Nevertheless, for reasons of brevity, I will often simply use the phrase "non-distributive predicates," and that should be understood to make reference to predicates and relations that can be non-distributively or non-cumulatively satisfied relative to one or more argument positions.[19]

---

[18] Some others (e.g. Rayo, Linnebo and Williamson) use *xx* and *yy* (etc.) for the plural variables, instead of upper case letters. That notation seems to have originated in Burgess and Rosen 1997, 152. Yi uses '*xs*', '*ys*', (etc.). There is no significance in this difference of notation. We are all talking about a first-order plural language.

[19] Strictly speaking, we should now provide a new definition of *distributive*. Here is an informal version of that.

In an n-place relation R, place j is *distributive* iff the meaning of R requires that whenever Rt1 t2 . . . T . . . tn (with T in the jth place) is true and a is one of T, then Rt1 t2 . . . a . . . tn (i.e., with a term referring to a in the jth place) is true.

It will work out best in the long run if we take these "plural" variables to be neutral in number. That is:

$$[\exists X: FX]\ GX$$

will express the claim that one or more individuals that are F are G, where F and G are allowed to be non-distributive. For example:

Some students are surrounding Adams Hall today.

'X are surrounding Adams Hall' is non-distributive.

$$[\exists X: SX]\ X \text{ are surrounding Adams Hall}$$

In the case in which one student surrounds Adams Hall (in the story "Elasticman Goes to College" perhaps), this sentence will be judged true. If we wish to specify that we are talking about more than one student, we can specifically indicate that we require more than one.

$$[\exists X: SX \land X \text{ are more than one in number}]\ X \text{ are surrounding Adams Hall}$$

In fact, it may be useful to introduce a predicate

$$NX: X \text{ are more than one in number}$$

that we can use whenever we wish to rule out individual satisfiers of a predicate, as the plural in English might be thought to do.

$$[\exists X: SX \land NX]\ X \text{ are surrounding Adams Hall}^{[20]}$$

Similarly, we can define cumulativity relative to an argument place.

> In an n-place relation R, place j is *cumulative* iff the meaning of R requires that whenever Rt1 t2 . . . T . . . tn (with T in the jth place) is true and Rt1 t2 . . . T′ . . . tn (with T′ in the jth place) is true, then if T″ is a term non-distributively referring to the things among T together with the things among T′ (and only to those), then Rt1 t2 . . . T″ . . . tn (with T″ in the jth place) is true.

Here t1, t2, etc. may be any terms, singular or plural, variable or constant, T, T′, T″ are plural terms, and a is singular. For full generality, we would need to give a definition relative to an assignment to variables. For the definition of cumulativity, we also need a full account of term conjunction. These are elements of the language and semantics to be developed. (In a more formal treatment, we would also clearly differentiate object-language and metalanguage references.)

[20] I will not try to definitively resolve the question of whether non-distributive plural English sentences have plurality as an implication or at most as an implicature. In the former case, we would include 'NX' routinely as a part of the symbolization of English plurals, and in the latter case we would not. In our formal language we can do it either way, but we have to pick one. In dealing with illustrative examples, I will assume that plurality is an implicature only, and thus not include 'NX' in the formal representation on a routine basis.

We will eventually want to consider *among* as a fundamental relation (see Chapters 2 and 6). If we let 'YAX' stand for 'Y are among X', with the singular variant 'yAX' meaning 'y is one of X' (i.e., 'y is among X'), then we can define 'NX' in terms of *among* and *identity*. $NX = df \exists y \exists z (yAX \wedge zAX \wedge y \neq z)$.

Multiple quantifications are also possible, and indicate something else about the interaction of quantifiers and plurals:

(17) Some cowboys circled some wagons around a campfire.

(18) Each cowboy circled some wagons around a campfire.

(18) makes it evident that 'some wagons' is a full-blown quantifier phrase and not a referential expression. If the existential is read as subordinate to the universal in (18), 'some wagons' cannot somehow *refer* to a some particular wagons, because each cowboy's wagons can be distinct from those of the other cowboys.[21] Ultimately we must provide a semantics for plural predicates and plural quantification that allows for such quantifier embedding.

Also, once we allow non-distributive predicates, we will also have the resources for expressing other sentences that involve non-distributive plural predication even though all of the basic predicates in the surface English are distributive. For example, the "non-first-orderizable" Geach–Kaplan sentence:[22]

(21) Some critics admire only one another.

We can represent this in a plural, first-order language in the following ways:

(22) [$\exists X: X$ are critics] X admire only one another

(23) [$\exists X: X$ are critics] [$\forall y: y$ is one of X] [$\forall z: y$ admires z] (z is one of X and $z \neq y$)

This is first order because it quantifies with respect to only the basic individuals of the domain (people in this case) and it quantifies only

---

[21] This is why an approach taken in McKay 1994 cannot work. There it is suggested that we can treat each plural quantifier phrase as making reference to some things. But in sentence (13), that is evidently not possible for (the small scope reading of) the quantifier 'some wagons'. (For the same reason, a small-scope reading of 'a campfire' cannot be interpreted referentially in that sentence.)

[22] See Boolos 1984, 432–3 (56–7 in Boolos 1998) for a presentation of a proof, attributed to David Kaplan, that this is not representable in standard (singular) first-order logic.

into argument position. There is a non-distributive predicate in each of these representations:

'*X* admire only one another' in (22)
'*z* is one of *X*' in (23)

But the basic predicates that appear explicitly in the English sentence ('*X* are critics' and '*X* admire *y*') are distributive.

We can also represent the Peano induction axiom as a plural, first-order axiom:

$\forall X$ (if 0 is one of *X* and if [$\forall y$: *y* is one of *X*] the successor of *y* is one of *X*, then $\forall z$, *z* is one of *X*)

This also contains the non-distributive '*z* is one of *X*' (see Chs. 2 and 6 for further discussion).

George Boolos has argued that some second-order quantification can be understood as plural quantification.[23] Boolos's work has much to tell us about plurals, but it seems that he was not motivated by a general introduction of non-distributive predicates. The predicate '*x* is one of *Y*' is the only primitive non-distributive relation that he employed. He writes '*x* is one of *Y*' as '*Yx*', indicating the way in which he assimilates (monadic) second-order quantification to plural quantification involving that one non-distributive relation. But this provides no immediate way to represent the relationship between 'he lifted a piano' and 'they lifted a piano', where the same predicate is applied to an individual and, non-distributively, to some individuals.

Boolos's consideration of another example of non-distributive predication, in a discussion of the sentence "The rocks rained down" (1985b, 168 in Boolos 1998), is revealing. There he says:

If we have learned anything at all in philosophy, it is that it is almost certainly a waste of time to seek an analysis of "The rocks rained down" that reduces it to a first-order quantification over the rocks in question. It is highly probable that an adequate semantics for sentences like "They rained down" or "the sets possessing a rank exhaust the universe" would have to take as primitive a new sort of predication in which, for example, "rained down" would be predicated not of particular rocks such as this one or that one, but rather of these rocks or those. . . . The predication "they M" is probably completely intractable.

I take the last sentence to mean that such predication ("They rained down", for example) is intractable without accommodating non-distributive predication (as first-order predication) in a general way.

---

[23] Boolos 1984, 1985*a*. His arguments apply to monadic second-order logic.

I hope I am showing how to make that accommodation (without wasting our time).[24]

PLURALS IN PHILOSOPHY

In recent years, several philosophers have adopted the language of plurals and non-distributive predicates. For example, David Lewis uses non-distributive plurals and plural quantification in the language that is at the foundation of his reworking of the theory of classes.[25] Peter van Inwagen and others use the language of plurals with non-distributive predicates in posing and answering fundamental questions in metaphysics, such as the question of when some things constitute a single thing.[26] Keith Hossack has developed the language of plurals as a part of a defense of atomism (compositional nihilism).[27]

We cannot use ordinary first-order logical notation in representing what these philosophers say. All point out that plural language is widely used and understood in ordinary discourse. Nevertheless, I think that our exploration of the notation and the semantics for such a language will lead to some interesting insights and surprises. Certainly we should wish to make this as well understood as the more traditional, singularist first-order language, so as to provide a similar resource for sorting out ambiguities and making judgments about the validity of arguments.

Another reason to develop the semantics is to assure ourselves that the semantics of plurals does not itself need to rely on the resources of set theory or anything else that might be a problematic element in the foundation of the philosophical projects that employ such plural language. In Chapter 3 we will formulate the semantics without employing the resources of set theory (and without other singularist assumptions).

---

[24] Alex Oliver's review (Oliver 2000) of Boolos's collected articles is a helpful discussion of these and related issues, esp. pp. 871–2. Oliver concludes that "what is needed is a logic of plurals that offers uniform representation of singular and plural forms of a predicate and this is excluded by the hierarchical structure of second-order logic."

[25] Lewis 1991. See esp. 62–71 for his discussion of the role of plural quantification. See also Rayo and Uzquiano 1999 for another use of plurals in the development of set theory.

[26] *Material Beings*, van Inwagen 1990.

[27] Hossack 2000. Hossack develops the semantics for non-distributive plurals, and there are many points of contact with his paper. There are, however, significant differences in approach.

We can also make a positive use of our plural language in response to Timothy Williamson's arguments that plural language is not an adequate basis for the expression of propositions that are about everything.[28] A better understanding of the semantics of plurals is required if we are to evaluate his arguments. We will consider those arguments explicitly in Chapter 6 and argue that he has overlooked an important resource for talking about everything.

[28] Williamson 2003, esp. 455–8. See Ch. 6 for further discussion of this and the related issue of the connection between plurals and second-order logic.

2

Against Singularism

Because of the power and significance of first-order logic in its traditional form, restricted to distributive predication, it has been natural to try to express non-distributive plurals within that framework. Two approaches leap quickly to the mind of the student of standard first-order logic who is trying to come to terms with non-distributive plurals. The first is what I will call "the multiple relations idea." The second is the adoption of some variety of singularism, representing plurals by a single object that encompasses many.

In this Chapter I present some initial considerations for the case that it will ultimately be better to reconsider the underlying logic. We will return to further consideration of singularist arguments in Chapter 6, after we develop a formal semantics for plurals and a more detailed account of *among*.

THE MULTIPLE RELATIONS IDEA

In teaching first-order logic, it is natural to treat non-distributive predicates as relations of some sort, tying the individuals together in that way.

(1) David and Ed are meeting together.

cannot be represented as

(2) *David is (are) meeting together and Ed is (are) meeting together.

(3) * Md ∧ Me

But (1) can be represented as a relational sentence, with one dyadic relation Mxy (x and y are meeting together):

(4) Mde.

However, consider an attempt to use this relation to represent

(5) Arnie, Bob and Carlos are meeting together.

Perhaps one would try

(6) Mab ∧ Mac ∧ Mbc.

But (6) could be true even though (5) is false, if there were three separate meetings and no single meeting of Arnie, Bob and Carlos. We need a triadic relation, and a tetradic relation, etc. Following this approach, we find that *are meeting together* must have variable polyadicity – i.e., be many relations – since any number of individuals (greater than one) can meet together. Then we must also have a way to show that these many meeting relations are semantically related. Fundamentally, though, such an approach seems to be taking one thing, the property expressed by the predicative expression "are meeting together", and turning it into many, a family of relations, in order to meet the needs of a system that is just not adequate.

Consideration of other predicates should help to dispel thoughts of representing these sentences using families of predicates of varying polyadicity.

(7) Some students surrounded the administration building.
(8) They come from many different countries.

It seems very implausible to think that there is a family of *surround* relations or a family of *coming from many countries* relations with varying polyadicity.

The "variable polyadicity" approach is more than just implausible, though. It seems to be completely untenable when we try to deal with even simple sentences like (7), (8) and the following:

(9) They are meeting together.
(10) Some people are meeting together.

There is no unclarity in the English sentences (9) and (10), but they are impossible to represent in a suitably simple way if 'are meeting together' is represented by a family of predicates of different polyadicities, since there is no basis for picking one of these predicates (one polyadicity) rather than another. Note too that (10) follows from (1) and that (10) follows from (5) (given the additional premises that Arnie, Bob, Carlos, David and Ed are people). If (1) and (5) were represented as involving different relations, as the multiple polyadicity approach suggests, then there could be no single representation of (10) that follows from the representations of (1) and (5).[1] So this approach seems to be rather hopeless for the representation of the validity-producing characteristics of arguments.

The multiple relations idea is one interpretation of what some have meant by a "multi-grade relation" – really a family of relations expressed by predicates of differing polyadicity. However, some may have meant a different idea, the idea of a relation that can take a different number of referential terms (or names joined by 'and') in a single argument place.[2] It is difficult to see how to represent that within an ordinary first-order language. It seems that we must either introduce a way of representing plural reference and predication (our project here) or else introduce some singularizing device – talking of sets or mereological sums of individuals, for example. (We consider the singularizing approach in the next section of this chapter.)

There are still at least two more ideas that might go under the heading of "multi-grade relation." These share the doctrine that a single predicate might have a variable number of argument places, but the ideas differ in the role that these multiple argument places play. On one approach, each individual involved in a predication must have its own argument place, so 'are classmates', for example, can have any number of argument places greater than one, and 'lifted a table' can have any number of argument places greater than zero. This approach is a variation on the multiple predicates approach, but it at least superficially solves the problem of semantically uniting the various predications (by having the same predicate but varying the number of argument places). However, it still leaves us in the dark about how to represent cases (like (9) and (10)) with pronouns, demonstratives or quantifiers that are unspecified with respect to number (unless it is to turn into just a notational variation of the plural approach to be favored here).

The other phenomenon that might be called "multi-grade" is variation in the number of argument places of a predicate where each optional argument place represents a distinct semantic role. For example, we can say that Carla hit Doris, that Carla hit Doris with a dinner plate, that Carla hit Doris with a dinner plate on Tuesday, etc. Whatever reasons there are for this approach, however, are independent of issues

---

[1] See Yi 2005, section 2.2, for a fuller presentation of an argument like this.

[2] Oliver and Smiley 2004 includes considerable consideration of various approaches to the idea of multi-grade relations.

about plurals. The same issues arise whether we allow some things to play a semantic role together or not. Bob and Carla bought three bottles of wine, Bob and Carla bought three bottles of wine for Doris and Ed, Bob and Carla bought three bottles of wine for Doris and Ed at *Wine Shack* and *Quicker Liquor* on Tuesday, etc. So we will not be attending to this kind of "multi-grade" feature, since the issues surrounding it are independent of issues about plurality. Concerning this we make the usual simplifying assumption that predicates have a fixed number of argument places, corresponding to semantic roles. In 'Bob and Carla bought three bottles of wine', there are two argument places for the main verb, 'X bought Y', and in this sentence each is associated with a plural expression (either names joined by 'and' or a plural quantification). The project of developing a way of showing how that is semantically related to the other statements about their purchase is an interesting one, but not directly germane to our study here.

SINGULARISM

The second idea that is likely to leap to the mind of the student of first-order logic is that non-distributive predicates are predicates of sets of individuals.[3] Those with a dislike of sets and a taste for metaphysics might instead propose mereological sums as the objects. Non-distributive predicates like 'surround the building', 'are shipmates', etc., are then viewed as predicates applying to these aggregative objects. Such views make a *singularist* assumption, that every plural predication is based on a singular predication or is analyzable as a singular predication, thus making it possible to apply the framework of standard first-order logic.[4] Fundamentally, the problem with such approaches is that they have not taken plurality seriously. No set ever surrounds a building, though its members may. Singularist approaches distort the facts about the true subjects of predication in order to eliminate plural predication with non-distributive predicates from their favored language. The fact that some individuals are surrounding a building does not semantically imply that some single individual (of any kind) surrounds the building.

---

[3] This is defended in Resnik 1988. Discussion of his arguments follows. See also Lewis 1991, 65–7.

[4] Lewis 1999, 65–9, introduces the term 'singularist' for this semantic view.

A partisan of mereology might want to say that in the following argument, it is necessary that if the premise is true, then the conclusion is true.

A1   (11) 'Some students are surrounding the building' is true.
So, (12) some individual is such that it is surrounding the building.

But even if you think that mereology is necessarily true and guarantees that connection, you should still not allow that it is a matter of the meaning of terms that if the premise is true, then so is the conclusion.[5] Consider these claims:

(11) 'Some students are surrounding the building' is true.

(13) Some students are surrounding the building.

(14) 'Some individual is such that it is surrounding the building' is true.

(12) Some individual is such that it is surrounding the building.

A semantic theory, giving us the meanings of sentences, should have these as results:

(15) (11) iff (13)
(16) (14) iff (12).

Partisans of mereology will ordinarily want to say that this is a further necessary truth:

(17) If (13) then (14).

Such a view provides a way to the conclusion (a way from (11) to (12)), but there is no way based solely on the meanings of the terms.

One might use mereology or set theory in constructing a semantics for some plural language, where that semantics is intended to indicate something about inferential relations among sentences. But such a formal semantics will go beyond just giving meanings if it relies on a principle like (17). **A1** is not a logical, semantic or analytic entailment. It is not a part of the meaning of the premise (11) that the conclusion must be true. If there is a connection between premise and conclusion, it is a matter of metaphysics, not semantics.

---

[5] Yi presents arguments against singularism that look at inferences that cannot be represented if one adopts the singularist stance. (See section I.B of Yi 2005 or pp. 7–15 of Yi 2002.) Oliver and Smiley 2001 present related reasons for avoiding singularism (under the apt critical heading "changing the subject").

Similar remarks apply to set theory. Few will want to endorse the idea that a set is an individual that surrounds a building in any case.[6] A singularist who holds that plural sentences must be explicated in terms of singular sentences about sets will need to change the predicate as well as the subject.[7] The truth of 'The students are surrounding the building' is modeled by the fact that some single individual (a set or other composite individual) is surrounding* the building. Other examples may make the point more forcefully. The students are seventeen in number (we can imagine), but the set of students is one in number (though it is seventeen-membered, a very different property from being seventeen in number).

When our semantics changes the predicate, introducing a surrogate predicate that applies to a set, *is-surrounding** or *is-meeting-together**, we may still wonder which people are surrounding the building and which people are meeting together. We have an answer only to a rather different question, involving a different predicate. Furthermore, it seems that we can ask what makes it true that some set of students is-meeting-together*. The answer then, presumably, is that its members are meeting together, and the expression of that takes us back to plural, non-distributive predication. If we employ plural predication in the account of what it is for a set to meet together (meet-together*), plural predication must be separately understood anyway.

Contemplating predicates like 'surround' might lead one to think that mereological singularism is better off than set-theoretic singularism, that the introduction of new predicates is unnecessary because the mereological sum has a spatial location and can surround a building. But that would be an illusion created by the particular example. If we consider other predicates that can apply to some things, like 'are meeting together' or 'are three in number', I think that there should be little temptation to think that they can apply to some single individual (a mereological sum) whenever they apply to some things.[8] The mereological approach also requires the introduction of

---

[6] Some might try to use the idea of a set or class "as many" here, and if talking of a class "as many" is not a way of talking about a set that is an individual, then perhaps there is no disagreement with the plural approach. (See Ch. 6 for further discussion of classes "as many.")

[7] See Oliver and Smiley 2001, 295 ff for an exposition of some problems in changing the predicate.

[8] There is further discussion of predicates like 'are three in number' later in this chapter.

new predicates, like 'are-meeting-together*'. (It is difficult to even see how that can even get started with 'are three in number'.)

A semanticist might respond that the use of single individuals to semantically interpret plurals should not be taken to validate arguments like **A1**.[9] Semantics employs a metalanguage in which we refer to the objects that we need for the systematic interpretation of the object language; arguments like **A1** make the mistake of assuming that the entities of the semantic analysis are the referents of the original object language's expressions. The singularist no more needs to endorse **A1** than the possible worlds semanticist needs to endorse the following argument:

M1 (18) 'I could have had a martini' is true (though I didn't have a martini).

Therefore, (19) possible worlds exist.

My initial response to this is that I think that the semanticist who uses possible worlds in giving the *meaning* of modal claims is committed to the semantic validity of **M1**. One can give a formal semantic analysis of a language that uses objects of some unrelated kind simply to show that the analysis provides a consistent model for some claims. Marbles arranged in a certain way, with each marble associated with a particular set of sentences, might serve as a model for some modal claims. However, if we are really to give the meaning of the modal claims like (18), then the semantics must employ possibilities, not marbles.[10] The model with marbles might have other interpretations, taking the marbles to stand in for times, places, or doxastic states, for example. It is only when they are taken to indicate how the possibilities are that we can say that they are interpreting the premise of **M1** (rather than just providing the basis for a consistency proof, for example). But then the assertion of the premise and affirmation of the semantics in terms of possibilities commits one to the existence of those possibilities. Similarly, if the correct interpretation of 'These are more numerous than those' requires the existence of relations, then, as a matter of

---

[9] A comment from Delia Graff suggested this response to me. I am not sure to what extent she would endorse the position as I present it here. Stephen Yablo 2000 has a consideration of *a priori* knowledge that would support some skepticism about semantics as a source of knowledge of validity in cases like these. On the other hand, one might draw from Yablo's discussion only the moral that formal semantics should not be viewed as a source for *a priori* knowledge of meaning. These issues deserve further consideration.

[10] Cf. Plantinga 1974, 125–8, for similar comments about modality.

meaning, if the sentence is true then relations exist; and if the correct interpretation of 'John is walking slowly' requires the existence of events, then, as a matter of meaning, if the sentence is true, then events exist.

In the same way, the semanticist who employs sets or other single individuals in giving the meaning of plurals is committed to the idea that, as a matter of meaning, if the plural sentence is true, then the sets exist. If the sets (or other singular interpretants) are not just elements of an artificial model constructed for a formal consistency proof or some similar purpose, but rather are presented as what is needed to give the meaning of the plural, then the singularist must say that arguments like **A1** are semantically valid;[11] if the premise is true, the conclusion must be true as well, and that is a consequence of what the words mean. A plural interpretation, however, generates no need to accept the semantic validity of arguments like **A1**.

In the end, though, this point just comes to saying that sets and mereological sums are not required for the semantics of plurals. If you resist the idea that purely semantic principles can take you from the premise to the conclusion in **A1**, then perhaps that will be a source of some additional openness to a semantic approach that does not make singularist assumptions in the interpretation of plurals. That is what I will develop in Chapter 3.[12]

Semantic Roles

Fred Landman 2000 (165, for example) also supports a principle that is worth considering here, that semantics should associate the actual individuals who play roles with the various thematic (semantic) roles determined by the basic predicates in a sentence. It is individuals and not sets or mereological sums that are the agents of plural propositions: surrounding a building, being numerous, meeting together, being very different, being 37 in number.[13] So we should associate the thematic role with those individuals, not with some single surrogate.

---

[11] Or perhaps the variant **A1***, with the conclusion:

(12*) some individual is such that it is surrounding* the building.

[12] There is further discussion of these issues in Ch. 5.
[13] There is further discussion of this issue in Ch. 4.

Landman would not apply his principle to get this conclusion. His way of putting the principle presupposes a singularist position. For example, p. 165: "Basic predicates are predicates that have **thematic** commitment. If a basic, singular predicate applies to a certain argument, that argument fills a thematic role of that singular predication." However, if we properly distinguish the argument position in a sentence from the individual or individuals who satisfy the basic predicate or are referred to by the term in that position, then we should conclude that sentences like 'They surrounded the building', 'They are very different', 'They are numerous' and 'These are most of those' require some things (rather than some thing) as the interpretation of each plural term in argument position. There is no reason to restrict the principle to singular sentences. So we can say: If a basic predicate applies to some thing or things, that thing or those things fill a thematic role of that predication. No single thing satisfies such predicates as '. . . surrounded the building', '. . . are very different', '. . . are numerous' and '. . . are most of _____'.

SINGULARIST PREJUDICE DISPLAYED

Let's look again at the famous Geach–Kaplan sentence, and see how singularism can mislead.

(20) Some critics admire only one another.

We can represent this in the following ways:[14]

(21) [∃X: X are critics] X admire only one another

(22) [∃X: X are critics] [∀y: y is one of X] [∀z: y admires z] (z is one of X and $z \neq y$)[15]

Using (22) as the basis for an English paraphrase of (20), we would say:

(22a) Some critics are such that each one of them admires only other ones of them.

---

[14] Ultimately we will want to explicitly represent the distributive character of 'X are critics.' It will be '[∀y: y is one of X] y is a critic.' This is developed in Chs. 3 and 6.

[15] Here we write 'y is one of X', using both singular and plural variables ("It is one of them"). This relation can be viewed as a special case of the more general *among* relation, which could have either a singular or plural variable in the first argument position, i.e., an individual y is one of X iff y is among X. Some individuals Z are among X iff each one of Z is among (is one of) X.

Michael Resnik asks of such paraphrases of the Geach–Kaplan sentence[16]:

How else are we to understand the phrase 'one of them' other than as referring to some collection and as saying that the referent of 'one' belongs to it?

The answer is that we take 'it is one of them' as a two-place relation that is non-distributive in the second place. We can say that 'them' refers to some individuals, the critics under discussion, but that provides no reason to go on to say that there is some further thing, the set, collection, or sum of those individuals, that 'them' refers to. They are many; the grammar provides no basis for insisting that they are also one.

Resnik's rhetorical question exemplifies the singularist prejudice. His particular version is set-theoretic singularism: when some things are referred to, we must take that as a reference to a thing (the collection) that exists in addition to the things. I see no reason to fall in with this prejudice. And, as Boolos and Lewis point out, this does not even seem to be coherent, given the set-theoretic paradoxes that make it impossible to continue collecting without limit. Some sets are the non-self-membered sets, but there is no set of them.[17] We cannot require that all plural predications are really (or are reducible to) singular predications of sets. We just correctly predicated something (being such that there is no set of them) of the non-self-membered sets.

Even if we try to take such singularism to be more limited, applying only to sentences, like the Geach–Kaplan sentence, that have no first-order representation, Yi has noted that there is a serious difficulty in the implications of the singularist view.[18] The Geach–Kaplan sentence, (20), is implied by the following singular sentence:

(23) Ezra and Thomas are critics, Ezra ≠ Thomas, and Ezra and Thomas admire only each other.

[16] Resnik 1988, 77. He is criticizing Boolos, who presents a paraphrase like (22a).

[17] Lewis 1991, 68, and Boolos 1984, 64–6 in Boolos 1998. Boolos, Lewis, Yi, Oliver and Smiley 2001, and Rayo 2002 have developed arguments against singularism based on its leading to set-theoretical paradoxes. (Some sets are non-self-membered. They cannot be all and only the members of some set. My use of 'They' at the beginning of the last sentence therefore cannot refer to a set, and my use of 'some sets' at the beginning of the first sentence cannot be explicated in terms of a singular quantification involving sets.) Lewis has replied to Resnik's response to the argument. Rayo 2002 develops a very general version of this that indicates how there are similar difficulties for mereological singularism (my term, not his) and event approaches to the semantics for plurals.

[18] Yi 2005, section 2.2.

If (20) semantically implies that some set (or other composite entity) exists, then (23) must semantically imply the existence of such an entity. But (23) is a purely singular sentence, and (23) does not semantically imply that sets (or other composite entities) exist.

We can also see the role of singularism when we consider Øystein Linnebo's (2003) discussion of Boolos's plural statement of the numerical induction axiom:[19]

(I) Whenever there are *some natural numbers* such that 0 is one of *them* and for every natural number *n* that is one of *them*, *n* + 1 is one of them, then every natural number is one of *them*. [Italics are Linnebo's.]

Linnebo (2003, 77) discusses Charles Parsons' work:[20]

It is far from clear, Parsons claims, that when sentences such as [(I)] are uttered, the utterer cannot be said to have made a claim about *collections* or *pluralities* of natural numbers. It is very natural to regard the occurrences of 'them' as referring to an entity of this sort.

It is very natural to do that if one is in the grip of singularist prejudice. But it is really no more natural than it is to regard the sentence "They are surrounding the building" or "They come from many countries" as asserting that some single individual surrounds the building or comes from many countries. Once we allow non-distributive predication and recognize that ordinary plural pronouns don't refer to some single thing, what had seemed natural to some has no appeal at all.

Linnebo himself says that "these playings of intuitions against each other . . . don't carry much weight." Considering languages like the one being developed here that allow non-distributive predication, Linnebo has more to say, however. Calling such a language PFO+ (plural first-order + non-distributive predication), he says:[21]

When plural expressions in this way are allowed to occur as subjects of true non-distributive predications, it is particularly hard not to regard them as standing for entities. Moreover, in PFO+ we can introduce an identity predicate that

---

[19] Using 'XAY' for 'X are among Y' ('x is one of Y' in the singular), we can write:

$[\forall X: NX] ((0AX \wedge [\forall n : nAX](n + 1)AX) \rightarrow [\forall y : Ny] yAX)$. Also,

$[\forall X: NX] ((0AX \wedge [\forall n : nAX](n + 1)AX) \rightarrow [\forall Y : NY] YAX)$.

[20] There is discussion of Parsons' criticisms of Boolos's plural interpretation of second-order logic in Ch. 6.

[21] Linnebo 2003, 79.

holds between pluralities: $[X = Y \leftrightarrow \forall u \, (uAX \leftrightarrow uAY)]$.[22] This too indicates that reification has taken place.

The first sentence seems again to be a pure expression of singularist prejudice. What remains seems to require that the following is valid: "These are the same things as those; therefore, these are (constitute; are elements of) some single thing x and those are (constitute; are elements of) some single thing y such that $x = y$." There is no evident reason to credit that inference.

A2   The students in my class are the same individuals as the students who are philosophy majors.
       Therefore, the students in my class are (constitute; are elements of) some single thing x and the philosophy majors are (constitute; are elements of) some single thing y such that $x = y$.

Sometimes our use of sentences can carry unexpected semantic commitments. For example, it would be natural to think that "John is walking slowly" is committed only to the existence of the referent of 'John'. But Davidson and others have argued very persuasively that understanding the inferences that such a sentence is involved in will require that we understand the sentence as asserting that an event of walking exists.[23] Such arguments might make a case that what we see on the surface is not the whole story and that additional entities are required to give an adequate semantics.[24]

When one does not allow non-distributive predication, then much that he wishes to say must be replaced by surrogates involving sets or other aggregates. Instead of saying "They are three in number" or "They are surrounding the building," he must find some single thing that he can apply correlated predicates to. So he says, for example, that some set is three-membered (not three in number) or that some set of things bears some relationship (different from, but related to, surrounding) to a building.[25] Such paraphrases change the subject and change the

---

[22] Linnebo uses a different notation here, to the same effect: $xx = yy \leftrightarrow \forall u \, (u < xx \leftrightarrow u < yy)$.

[23] Connecting this to our earlier discussion of semantic commitments, we might expect the Davidsonian semanticist to accept the principle that if 'John is walking slowly' is true, then at least one event exists.

[24] In Ch. 10 we will consider the specific question of whether events are needed for the semantics of plurals in more detail.

[25] Exactly how such a paraphrase would go in the case of 'They are surrounding the building' is left as an exercise for committed singularists.

predicate, so that he can get by with only distributive predication. To justify this, one would need an argument (perhaps like Davidson's) to establish a need that does not show at the surface. As Resnik and Linnebo both recognize, the kinds of appeals to intuition that they make can't get us far in that discussion. However, neither Resnik nor Linnebo gives us any such arguments that sets (collections, pluralities, aggregates) are involved in the meanings of plural sentences of natural language.[26]

If we are in the context of an ordinary first-order logic that allows only distributive predicates, then we need to introduce sets or other "second-order" devices to interpret the Geach–Kaplan sentence or to define ancestral relations. But we have seen that there is good reason to take non-distributive predication seriously, and once we do that, one cannot use such examples to argue that there are no first-order plurals. We have an independent motivation for introducing plural predication and quantification in the consideration of sentences like 'They are numerous' and 'Some students are surrounding Adams Hall'. As a consequence of doing so, we can represent the Geach–Kaplan sentence and define ancestral relations without sets or other "second-order" devices. By allowing non-distributive predication, we avoid the immediate need for such surrogates for representing these sentences of ordinary language, and we are no longer forced to change the subject (from some critics to some set) in the formal representation of the Geach–Kaplan sentence.

One could also advance a case against our non-singularist approach by arguing that a set-theoretic or other singularist approach has greater over-all systematic or theoretical value; and the great mathematical power and success of set theory would then be a powerful consideration. However, any approach of this kind, that requires that all plurals refer to some single individual (like a set) that the basic individuals bear a relationship to (like membership) will have to face the problem of Russell's paradox.

> Some sets (or other items constituted by individuals) are the non-self-membered (or non-self-related) sets (or other). They are not enumerable.

---

[26] Resnik has arguments that relate mainly to Boolos's plural interpretation of second-order logic, but that is not the main task before us here. In so far as we take his comments to relate to the understanding of plurals themselves, the concerns raised are largely answered by the development of a semantics for plurals in general (Ch. 3) and a theory of *among* (Ch. 6).

The reference of 'the non-self-membered sets' (or 'non-self-related individual with individual constituents') and 'They' cannot be construed in the prescribed way (as a set of non-self-membered sets or as an individual constituted by all and only the non-self-related individuals), on pain of paradox.[27] George Boolos provides this kind of support for the plural understanding of plurals as a part of his defense of the plural understanding of (monadic) second-order logic:

Abandon, if one ever had it, the idea that use of plural forms must always be understood to commit one to the existence of sets (or "classes," "collections," or "totalities") of those things to which the corresponding singular forms apply. The idea is untenable in general in any event: There are some sets of which every member of a set that not a member of itself is one, but there is no set of which every set that is not a member of itself is a member, as the reader, understanding English and knowing some set theory, is doubtless prepared to agree.[28]

Set theory has had a century to develop an impressive non-paradoxical response to Russell's paradox. However, developing an alternative approach employing plurals will lay the groundwork for seeing how far we can go without taking on those problems. For metaphysics, for the foundations of mathematics, and for the semantics of ordinary language, it will be valuable to know whether singularism is really needed, and, if so, where. We are here involved in the preliminary development of a non-singularist language so that its power can be explored. There is nothing in this development that would prohibit us from speaking of sets when it actually becomes useful or important to do so.[29]

---

[27] See Boolos 1984 and Lewis 1991. Other presentations of general forms of the paradox are in Williamson 2003, Rayo 2002 and in Higginbotham 2000, 88–90. In Ch. 6 we consider a general form of the paradox that is based on Williamson's.

[28] Boolos 1984, Boolos 1998, 66. We consider the relationship of plurals to second-order logic in Ch. 6.

[29] My criticism of singularism has focused on making a place for non-distributive plural predication. This can be supplemented usefully by Richard Cartwright's arguments that we can quantify over some things without there being any single thing of which the things are members. Cartwright 1994, esp. 7–8. He criticizes the "All-in-One Principle" (p. 7): 'that to quantify over certain objects is to presuppose that those objects constitute a "collection," or a "completed collection" – some one thing of which those objects are members.'

He criticizes the idea that "we cannot speak of the cookies in the jar unless they constitute a set" (p.8):

[T]he needs of quantification are already served by there being simply the cookies in the jar, the natural numbers, the pure sets; no additional objects are required. . . . It is one thing for there to *be* certain objects; it is another for there to be a *set*, or set-like object, of which those objects are members.

MEREOLOGY

There is also a mereological version of singularism. According to this view, a plural reference is a reference to a single thing, a mereological fusion.[30] The difference, though, is that the mereological fusion is sometimes said not to be distinct from the individuals fused. It is a thing, but not an additional thing, because the individuals fused are parts of it. "It is nothing over and above its parts." [31]

One can adopt plural language without requiring that it have a singularist semantics and go on to adopt mereology as the appropriate metaphysics. David Lewis does this.[32] I will not try to argue against mereology as a metaphysical view. However, I think that it is important not to adopt mereology as a part of the semantic underpinning of plural language. The use of plural language does not require the acceptance of mereological singularism, and we should try to find a semantics that does not presuppose the truth of the basic mereological principle:

> <u>Unrestricted composition</u>: whenever some things exist, their fusion exists.[33]

Semantics should not depend on the truth of this principle. Even if it is true, it is, for example, students who are seventeen in number and making different plans, not their sum.

Some of the recent work on plurals and mereology might lead one to think that taking plurals seriously goes hand-in-hand with accepting mereological principles. For example, Lewis defends the use of plural quantification and the mereological principles, but it is important to notice that these are two separate elements in his discussion of a mereological approach to class theory. His defense of mereology plays no role in the defense of plural quantification with non-distributive predicates.

---

[30] Gerald Massey 1976 attempted a mereological account of plural predication. Tyler Burge's theory of aggregates (Burge 1977) has some affinity with mereology but more with the idea of "classes as many". In any case, that also is an attempt at a singularist account of plurality (see Chapter 6 for a discussion of "classes as many").

[31] Lewis 1991, 80. Godehard Link also endorses this, e.g., he cites Lewis and endorses the conclusion that "the process of taking fusions doesn't carry any ontological commitment beyond the commitment to those entitites we start from." Link 1998, 337. See also 318ff.

[32] Lewis 1991.

[33] Cf. Lewis 1991, 7 for the principle of *unrestricted composition*.

Nothing about the logic of plurals requires or directly supports the fundamental mereological principle, and it seems that only the singularist assumption could produce the idea that there is such a relationship.[34]

Godehard Link, though, who has done some important work on the semantics of non-distributive plurals, has taken the view that mereology is a part of the ontological basis of the semantics of plurals. He says that plural quantification "is both in need and capable of a theoretical explanation, which I submit is mereology."[35] This strong position on mereology would seem to mean that every sentence involving plurals must have a paraphrase in which no plurals occur. Let's call that the *singularist paraphrase principle* (SPP).

SPP requires mereological paraphrases that turn a plural sentence into a singular sentence.

(24) Some students are surrounding the building.

(24M) A student-fusion is surrounding the building.

In the case of students surrounding a building, this may seem untroublesome. A fusion of spatially located objects is (presumably) located where its parts are, and a single thing can surround a building, so a predication of *surrounding* something transfers easily from some individuals to their mereological sum. But this must be very artificial (if possible at all) for many other predicates.

(25) Eight students (in my class) are fraternity brothers.

(25M) ?A fusion of eight students is fraternity-brotherly.

(26) The students in my class were born in many different countries.

(26M) ?A fusion of the students in my class was born in many different countries.

(27) Whenever some individuals exist, their fusion exists.

(27M) ?? Whenever a fusion of individuals exists, it exists.

---

[34] Lewis defends the view that mereology is ontologically innocent, and so one might wonder at any reluctance to accept mereology. However, Yi 1999 provides some reasons why we should not accept the claim of ontological innocence. If one accepts mereology and accepts that a cat Tom and a mouse Jerry exist, then one must also accept that something that is neither a cat nor a mouse exists. That does not seem ontologically innocent. See also Higginbotham 2000, 97.

[35] Link 1998, 332. Massey 1976 also turned to mereology. Consideration of the use of quantifier expressions with mass terms ("Some water is cold") is a powerful impetus for a mereological approach, to unify uses of quantifier words. See Chs. 6 and 7 for discussion of this issue.

(28) The students in my class are numerous.

(28M) ?? The fusion of students in my class is numerous.

We can resort to the explicit language of parts to introduce the fusion into our sentence more smoothly:

(25′) An individual is the sum of eight parts that are fraternity brothers (and each part is a student).

(26′) An individual is the sum of students in my class and has parts that are from many different countries.

(27′) Whenever some individuals X exist, they are parts of an individual which has no parts that do not overlap (at least) one of X.

(28′) An individual is the fusion of the numerous students in my class.

But this is pointless from the point of view of giving a singularist semantics for plurals. Its motivation would have to be from metaphysics, not semantics, since it does not eliminate the plural predication. Plural predication stands as robust as ever in each of these paraphrases.

SPP is not a principle that I think can be endorsed. Several kinds of cases can be made against it. First is the case based on the awfulness, perhaps untenability, of the required paraphrases (just given). There is also a case based on the lack of a need to endorse SPP, a case made by satisfactory completion of our whole project of giving a semantics for plurals and non-distributive predication without accepting SPP. If we succeed, then even one who accepts the principles of mereology can conclude that mereological sums do not play a necessary role in the semantics of plurals. We will develop the semantics for plural predication and quantification without adopting the singularist assumptions of set theory or mereology. Plural noun phrases can refer to several things. We will not assume that they must then automatically also refer to one thing.[36] Plural sentences can be about students, critics or numbers without presupposing or implying that there are sets or mereological sums.

---

[36] Peter Simons also makes a case for plural reference and against singularism, in 1982*a*. However, he uses the singular term 'a manifold' in talking about many things, and thus at least invites singularist interpretation of what he says. (His 1982*a* and 1982*b* have valuable related discussions of the relationship of all this to work of Frege, Russell, Husserl, Cantor and Bernays.)

Sometimes unrestricted composition is combined with another thesis:

<u>Composition as identity</u>: a fusion is nothing over and above its parts.[37]

There is also a strong case against combining this position, that mereological composition is identity, with the position that mereological sums are needed for the semantics of plurals. In the next section we look first at some difficulties with the metaphysical thesis (composition as identity) and then at the problem in combining it with the semantic thesis that plurals require a mereological semantics.

CAN ONE THING BE MANY?

Link and Lewis endorse the idea that the mereological sum of some things is "nothing over and above"[38] those things. The most straightforward understanding of this is that the things are (jointly) identical to the sum, though Lewis eventually backs away from that position to the weaker position that there is an analogy to identity.[39] Given our insistence on the importance of plural predication, which allows for things to jointly (non-distributively) possess a property, the idea of joint identity might seem to be a congenial thought. However, there are difficulties with the idea that there can be such an identity between some things and a single thing. These difficulties magnify into an overwhelming obstacle when we combine this joint identity thesis (the "Composition as Identity" thesis,

It should also be noted that the formal theory of *among* (see Ch. 6) shares its core principles with formal mereology. See Simons 1987, 37–43 for an account of the features of a formal mereology. The fact that a formalization of *among* is a variant of a classical mereology may be the root of the drive towards mereological singularism in the discussion of plurals. However, nothing about this formal treatment of plurals requires the acceptance of singularism.

Nino Cochiarella (Cochiarella 2002) has developed a formal system that incorporates the idea of "sets as many." This formalizes the singularism that Simons' use of 'a manifold' invites. Rather than allowing non-distributive relations, such as *X are among Y*, it remains singularist, developing a distributive relation *x is a member of y*. The fact that *y* here cannot itself be a member of anything means that Cochiarella's work is closer to the approach to be taken here than ordinary set theory is. But if we allow non-distributive predication, then we do not need to accept even this weaker singularism (see Ch. 6 for further discussion of the idea of "classes as many".)

[37] Cf. Lewis 1991, 80–2 (among other places) for statements of the principle *composition as identity*.

[38] Ibid., 1991, 81.

[39] Ibid., 1991, 84ff.

hereafter 'CI') with a semantic explication thesis (SE), that plurals can be explicated in terms of these single individuals. These are the two views about mereological sums that I wish to argue cannot tenably combine.

> CI (composition as identity): whenever some things compose some single thing, their fusion or mereological sum, they are (jointly) identical to that sum individual.

> SE (semantic explication): the semantics of plurals can be given in terms of these mereological sums.

Plural (joint) identity claims are not problematic in themselves. For example, if Alice = Doris, then Alice, Bill and Carla ≈ Carla, Bill and Doris; also, Alice, Bill and Doris ≈ Alice and Bill; in addition, Alice ≈ Alice and Doris. I use a separate symbol for the "plural" identities, but there really is no need to do so. (In Chapter 6, I will define '=' for individuals in terms of plural '≈'. Singular identity can be seen as just the special case of identity where only one thing is involved.[40])

However, even though a different number of names might appear on the two sides of a true '≈' claim, such identity claims always involve reference to the same individuals, and thus the same number of individuals, on both sides of the identity sign. Identity claims like 'Alice and Doris ≈ Alice' can be syntactically acceptable, but they are true only when the syntactic form is misleading about the number of individuals involved (as in the case of 'Alice and Doris', which refers to just one individual). There are several problems with the view that some things that are m in number are identical to some things that are n in number, where m and n are distinct numbers. In particular, there are problems in saying that some things that are more than one in number can be identical to some single thing.

Problem 1:

The first problem for the view that a mereological sum is identical to the things that compose it is a simple consideration based on Leibniz's Law. Alice, Bill and Carla are three in number and their mereological sum is one in number and not three in number, and so, by Leibniz's Law, the mereological sum of Alice, Bill and Carla is not identical to Alice, Bill and Carla.[41]

---

[40] Briefly, if we use 'XAY' for 'X are among Y', then that can be our primitive. '$X \approx Y$' is defined by 'XAY and YAX'. 'IX' is defined by '$[\forall Y : YAX] XAY$'. '$X = Y$' is defined by '$X \approx Y$ and IX'.

[41] Cf. Lewis 1991, 87.

This problem is exacerbated by the fact that, on the standard understanding of mereology, mereological sums have multiple decompositions. The mereological sum of Alice, Bill and Carla = the mereological sum of the molecules of Alice, Bill and Carla. Alice, Bill and Carla are three in number, but their molecules are not three in number. So again it seems that Alice, Bill and Carla cannot be identical to their mereological sum.

In the case of these numerical predications, there is a response that we should consider. One might argue that all counting is sortal-relative, so that there are no simple numerical predications of the sort employed here.[42] Alice, Bill and Carla are three people and millions of molecules (and many other numbers may apply, if other sortals apply to other decompositions of their sum). The millions of molecules are three people and millions of molecules. There is no problem in the identity claim, on this view.

We will consider the response in more detail after looking at a slightly different problem.

Problem 2:
Byeong-Uk Yi and Ted Sider[43] have called attention to another problem. Accepting the proposed identity claim will lead to a difficult conflict with some clear principles governing the 'is one of' relation. Consider distinct individuals Tom and Jerry, where Tom is a cat and Jerry is a mouse. Call their mereological sum 'Georgia'. According to the proposed view:

(30) Tom and Jerry $\approx$ Georgia

The following principles seem like good principles for 'is one of':

(31) x is one of y and z iff $x = y$ or $x = z$.
(32) x is one of y and z and w iff $x = y$, or $x = z$, or $x = w$. etc.

For example

(33) x is one of Tom and Jerry iff $x =$ Tom or $x =$ Jerry.

Now consider Georgia and Sylvester, where Sylvester is a cat and Sylvester $\neq$ Tom and Sylvester $\neq$ Jerry.

---

[42] Wallace, ms., pursues this position, and Link also endorses this position, Link 1998, 318ff and 337. Both cite Frege in support.

[43] Yi 1999a and Yi, forthcoming. Sider, ms. What follows is based mainly on Yi's presentation of the argument.

(34) x is one of Georgia and Sylvester iff $x =$ Georgia or $x =$ Sylvester

However, since, Georgia $\approx$ Tom and Jerry, we also would seem to have these:

(35) x is one of Georgia iff $x =$ Tom or $x =$ Jerry

(36) x is one of Georgia and Sylvester iff $x =$ Tom or $x =$ Jerry or $x =$ Sylvester.

But since Georgia $\neq$ Tom and Georgia $\neq$ Jerry (and none of them are identical to Sylvester), we have inconsistent identity claims (in (34) and (36)) when we consider what is one of Georgia and Sylvester.

One might try to use the sortal response in the following way:[44] 'is one of', like counting in general, is sortal relative (though identity needn't be). Then the 'one of' principle must be more complicated. One might first try to implement this idea with a minimal revision of the 'is one of' principles:

(37) x is one F of y and z iff x is F and $(x = y$ or $x = z)$

This gives us the result that Sylvester is one cat of Georgia and Sylvester. However, since Tom is also a cat, we can still get the result that Tom is one cat of Georgia and Sylvester and that he isn't one cat of Georgia and Sylvester.

(38) Tom is one cat of Georgia and Sylvester iff Tom is one cat of Tom and Jerry and Sylvester.

So Tom is one cat of Georgia and Sylvester.

(39) Tom is one cat of Georgia and Sylvester iff Tom is a cat and (Tom = Georgia or Tom = Sylvester).

But Tom $\neq$ Georgia, and Tom $\neq$ Sylvester, so Tom is not one cat of Georgia and Sylvester.

This can be saved, however, by a deeper revision of the 'is one of' principles as follows:

(40) x is one F of y and z iff x is one F of y or x is one F of z.

---

[44] Megan Wallace, ms., actually gives a slightly different response to this particular problem.

Let's also say that:

(41) If $x = y$ and x is F, then x is one F of y (i. e., if x is F, then x is one F of x).

(42) If x and $y \approx z$, and if x is F, then x is one F of z. etc.

Then we will have the result that Tom is one cat of Georgia and Sylvester but not the contradictory result that Tom is not one cat of Georgia and Sylvester. Although Tom is not identical to Georgia, Tom is one cat of Georgia.

This removes the clear contradiction, but if there is a common sortal for Tom and Georgia, then this still leads to odd results concerning counting. Let's suppose that 'thing' is the common sortal. Tom is one thing of Georgia and Georgia is also one thing of Georgia. That does not lead to contradiction based on the revised 'is one of' principle, but it does lead to a *prima facie* conflict with LL. The conflict with LL is again the simple one. If Georgia and Sylvester are two things and not three and Tom and Jerry and Sylvester are three things and not two, then Tom and Jerry are not identical to Georgia. If we make counting sortal relative, and if 'thing' is an acceptable counting sortal, then we still have this counting problem.

We could answer this in two ways.

Answer one: Georgia and Sylvester are both two things and three things. (Presumably at least one other number applies as well.) Saying that some things are two things does not conflict with saying that they are three things.

This makes counting difficult. I don't know of anyone who holds this view.[45]

Answer two: The predicate 'thing' is not an acceptable counting sortal.

This requires a theory of acceptability for sortals. Also, the efficacy of this response rests on a constraint that will probably be hard to live by: the constraint that no mereological sum decomposes in two different ways with respect to a single sortal and yields different "counts" as a result. There seem to be counter-examples to this claim. A region of

---

[45] Link 1998, 318ff. and 337 are unclear. He might be willing to endorse this view. Wallace's remarks also suggest that she might endorse it. (In discussing principles involving 'is one of', she says that allowing plural terms of the kind we are using "is going to give rise to all sorts of exceptions to standard inferences and intuitive principles.")

space, for example, decomposes in many ways into sub-regions, yielding many distinct counts. So unless we can give a theory of sortals that eliminates 'region' as an acceptable sortal, this will not prevent the conflict.

We should also note that it is not acceptable to reply that mereological sums of sub-regions are different sums (even when these mereological sums coincide). That would really give up the identity thesis, since it would correspond to saying that the sum of Georgia and Sylvester is distinct from the sum of Tom and Jerry and Sylvester (and thus that Georgia is not Tom and Jerry after all).

I leave it to the defenders of sortals to come up with something to deal with the metaphysical situation. I am not optimistic.[46]

When we come to the linguistic situation, it is clearer that there is nothing that the "sortalist" can do. That is, accepting SE sets some standards for what could be an acceptable sortal; since SE requires an account in terms of sums for all plurals, anything that can be pluralized must be acceptable. Some pluralizable terms allow for multiple decompositions of a mereological sum with respect to those terms, and yet the plurals are required for non-distributive predications involving those terms.

SE says that plurals are to be explicated as references to mereological sums. That will not work in these examples if one accepts CI.

Example 1:[47]

Some political jurisdictions I live in are nested. For example, Syracuse, Onondaga County and New York State are nested. (Each of the individuals x and y among them is such that either x is within y or y is within x.) Some political jurisdictions I live in are not nested. For example, the 25th US congressional district, the 49th New York State Senate district, Onondaga County, and New York State are not nested. But the mereological sum (New York State) is the same in these two cases. So when I use 'X are nested', I can't be predicating something of the sum when I predicate it (plurally) of these things.

---

[46] Cf. Hawthorne, 2003, 111–23, for a consideration of some problems for the related (but distinct) views of Geach on sortals and identity.

[47] David Lewis told me of an example of this kind in conversation (2001). The fact that (in Lewis 1991) he presented the idea of plural predication independently of his endorsement of mereology was no accident. He recognized that mereology, as he understood it, cannot be used for the account of plurals.

Example 2:
Similarly, if x and y overlap and the region of overlap is r, then x-r, y-r and r don't overlap, though the mereological sum is the same in the two cases. So 'overlap' applies to some things (x and y) but not to the mereological sum.

In short, the thesis that some things that are more than one in number can be identical to some single thing is metaphysically problematic. Even if the problems are solvable with an adequate theory of sortals (which seems unlikely), it cannot be combined with the semantic thesis that the semantics of plurals is to be explicated in terms of mereological sums.

COMPOSITION RELATIONS

This leaves us with a question, though. If a deck of cards is not identical to the 52 cards that compose it, then what is the relationship? The almost inevitable answer is that the 52 cards *compose* the deck without thereby being identical to it. The 52 cards, the four suits and the one deck are distinct things, though the 52 cards are the (for these purposes) independently existing individuals of which the others are composed. This may seem ontologically profligate; after all, are there really 57 (and more) things there? The answer that there are at least that many, though all but 52 are composite, seems adequate to me. Let's call this view "compositionalism" about decks of cards.[48]

In some cases we might prefer to take an antirealist position about alleged composite objects. For example, if I buy two dozen bagels (or two thousand paper clips), I might want to say that I have not bought just two of anything. Even though we say 'a dozen' (or 'a thousand') and 'two dozen' (or 'two thousand'), we are not counting one or two of anything. There is no single thing that is a dozen bagels, there are twelve things that are a dozen bagels. Such an anti-realist position is especially attractive when the phrase ('a dozen' or 'two dozen') is used in counting or measuring. The phrase 'a dozen' is only misleadingly singular.

We might wonder how far to extend such anti-realism. Perhaps someone would like to avoid ontological excess by taking an antirealist position about decks of cards and suits of cards. Others might extend this to flocks of birds and other groups of things (though this seems to have

---

[48] Cf. Uzquiano 2004 for some reflections on the composition of the Supreme Court.

the counter-intuitive result that a flock cannot survive a small change in membership). Still others (see van Inwagen 1990, for example) might extend this anti-realism to composites like tables and chairs (among other things).

I will not try to say exactly where the line should be drawn (though I will endorse the anti-realist idea that a dozen bagels is not any single thing). The key point is that anti-realism differs radically from the CI (Composition as Identity) view. The antirealist about decks of cards says that no single thing is a deck of cards – there are only the cards. (This leaves it to the antirealist to give an account of what I am doing when I buy three decks of cards, but perhaps that is not an insurmountable task.) It would seem that the antirealist can only be a strong ally against singularism in the semantics of plurals.

Consideration of one of Ted Sider's examples may be instructive. He points out that it is quite natural to say that the electrons (all the electrons there are) are the same things as the electron pairs (all the pairs of electrons there are). First, see that this can be regarded as true only if one takes an anti-realist position about the use of 'pair' here. Otherwise, the fact that the electrons are n in number and the pairs are $(n(n-1))/2$ in number, or the fact that the pairs overlap but the electrons do not, will show that the electrons are not the electron pairs. If we take the anti-realist position, we treat 'a pair' like 'a dozen' – it is misleadingly singular, it really refers to two things. On such a view, the identity of the electrons and the pairs can be expressed in a language with plurals. The anti-realism shows up in the fact that 'the pairs of electrons' is explicated as 'the electrons that are paired' ('in some pair', to put it in a misleadingly realist way).

[the X: [$\forall y$: Ey] $yAX \wedge$ [$\forall y$: yAX] Ey] [the Z: [$\forall V$: [$\forall y$: yAV] Ey $\wedge$ V are two in number] $VAZ \wedge$ [$\forall y$: yAZ] [$\exists V$: [$\forall y$: yAV] Ey $\wedge$ V are two in number] yAV] $X \approx Z$.

The use of grammatically singular subjects with plural verbs is akin to anti-realism, though it would be extreme to simply label it 'anti-realism'.

(43) Manchester have won the play-offs.
(44) The Parliament have acted.
(45) The graduating class have gone their separate ways.

These are ungrammatical in American English, but acceptable in some versions of English. The kinship to anti-realism lies in the fact that even though a grammatically singular term is used, we are to take that as a (non-distributive) plural reference. These seemingly singular terms make a plural reference to some people. One can use these terms in this way and be a realist or an anti-realist about teams, legislative bodies, or graduating classes. In any case, there seems to be no support here for singularism about the semantics of plural predication.

It might also be helpful to examine a more complex claim about composites, to see how the compositionalist and the antirealist might deal with it. Consider:[49]

(46) There are more straights than flushes in a deck of cards.

Since (46) involves a comparative count of straights and flushes, it is a *prima facie* problem for the antirealist (about straights and flushes). If straights, flushes and decks don't exist, then how do we count them? If there is not even one, then a cardinality comparison like (46) is incoherent, it would seem.

Let's consider the compositionalist position first. The compositionalist about straights, flushes and decks can start by saying that some cards from a deck compose a straight (or a flush). The straights and flushes exist, and there is no problem counting those and comparing the counts. If any paraphrase is required, it is just this:

(47) The cards from (i.e., among those that compose) a deck compose more straights than flushes.

Such an ontological view still allows one to condemn the idea that reference to composite individuals is needed for the semantics of plurals.[50] When I criticize singularism, I am criticizing the semantic position that the general understanding of plural sentences about cards requires such entities as decks or sets, i.e., that every plural sentence must be paraphrased by a singular sentence in order to provide an understanding of its semantics. I hope to have made at least part of the case that singularist semantics is not a good way

[49] This example comes from Harvey Friedman, who raises it as an objection to a certain attempted elimination of numbers. From the *fom* (Foundations of Mathematics) listserve, May 21, 2003: http://www.cs.nyu.edu/pipermail/fom/2003-May/006665.html.

[50] One version of this compositionalist view might be the view that flushes and straights are sets of cards and that some things compose a set when they are all and only its members. But I won't try to be so specific about the metaphysics of straights and flushes.

to understand plurals, and that some versions of it are not viable at all. But the weaker claim, that singularism is not necessary for semantics, is already enough to suggest that first-order logic deserves rethinking. In metaphysics, I can still be a compositionalist about various entities – decks, straights, flushes, perhaps even sets. That metaphysical question is distinct from the questions of what semantics requires or allows. As a metaphysical compositionalist, I can also hold the semantic position that endorsing plural sentences involving 'decks', 'straights' and 'flushes' will require the existence of decks, straights and flushes. That does not force me to endorse the view that the semantics of the plural 'cards' must involve some kind of collection of cards.

The antirealist will need to say a bit more in the face of complex sentences like (46). Since (according to such an anti-realist) there are no straights or flushes, we can't just count them. We might try something like the following:

(48) Among 52 deckwise cards, some cards can be arranged straightwise in more ways than some cards can be arranged flush-wise.

(Deckwise cards are 52 distinct cards that include an ace of spades, two of spades, ...) The statement involves comparing the counts of different ways of arranging cards, and no doubt many antirealists would not want to countenance such things as ways (or possible arrangements). I think that I will have to leave it to such antirealists (about flushes, straights, ways and possible arrangements) to say how they would paraphrase this acceptably. That is not a part of my project.

Besides compositionalism and anti-realism, there seems to be another position, the position that there is an important analogy between composition and identity that captures what was attractive in the idea that composition is identity. To pursue this is to say more about the special features of the composition relation; a composite object is in the same location as its parts, for example.[51] Since the composition relation plays no direct role in our semantics, however, such considerations are outside our scope. I believe that the formal logic of plurals can be neutral about whether there are any composite objects and about the nature of the composition relation, as long as composition is not thought to be literally the identity relation.

[51] Cf. Sider, ms.

THE PLURALLY PLURAL?

Sometimes people urge the adoption of a singularist account of plurals on the grounds that it is needed to account for the plurally plural or "perplural," as Allen Hazen calls it. I think that when we look at our ordinary language usage, it provides little comfort for the idea that there are perplurals or plurally plural constructions. Let's consider what is required for a language to have such a construction.[52]

One case for the plurally plural arises when we look for plurally plural predication.[53] I have argued that sentences like the following are best construed as having a monadic, non-distributive plural predicate, because such a predicate applies to any number of individuals (or at least to many different numbers of individuals):

> (49) Alice, Betty and Carol are competing for the cup.

However, if we are considering a team award, then it would seem that sentences like these would be possible:

> (50) The Yankees, the Red Sox and the Tigers are competing for first place.
>
> (51) These people, those people and those other people are competing.
>
> (52) As they spread out around the field, the Yankees thought about the fact that they were competing with the Red Sox and the Tigers for first place.

How can we construe these sentences if there are no such things as pluralities and so no such things as several pluralities?

If we were given only (50), we might simply regard the team names as names for individual teams. Then this sentence would follow the pattern of (49), but with different kinds of individuals (teams and not people) referred to in the subject position of the predication. That is ordinary plural predication; no special phenomenon of perplurals is evident when

---

[52] Allen Hazen 1997 has suggested that there might be one on Mars. Linnebo 2004 suggests that there are such languages on this planet. We will return to this issue in Ch. 6.

[53] This way of formulating the issue was developed in a conversation at Cornell University (April, 2004), and Harold Hodes and Mike Fara played the major role in getting me to see it. Communication being what it is, this is what I took away from the conversation and not necessarily what they brought into it.

we can understand such cases as plurals. As long as we recognize teams as entities, we can have plural predications that apply to them.

However, (51) brings out the problem more clearly, since it seems that the plural character of the individual pronouns or demonstratives should be preserved, but then, on the most salient reading, the pronoun must contribute one of three items towards the plural subject of the predication 'X are competing'.[54] Since our approach to plurals will not automatically introduce an object of which individuals are constituents when we have plural reference and predication, we do not automatically get, from the plurals, a single thing that might be several people and also one of three competitors. If we formed sets (or other composite objects) in the interpretation of all plurals, then we would have such an object immediately available and these would be straightforward plural constructions involving those objects and ordinary plurals; no perplurals needed. But since we do not automatically form sets in the interpretations of plurals, (51) seems to invite a special perplural interpretation, and we are left with a need to figure out how to understand such perplurals.

The resolution of this problem without perplurals lies in the identification of a special relationship that is contextually available. In these cases, we are talking about individuals who are the members of a team. We can refer to the team indirectly by referring to the individuals that constitute it, but the plural predication is a predication that applies to several teams. This view requires that (51) is understood in its context in something like the following way:

(51′) These people X are members of a team x, those people Y are members of a team y, and those other people Z are members of a team z such that x, y and z are competing.

This is very much like a singularist semantic analysis that requires that every plural is semantically associated with a single individual (set, mereological sum, plurality or whatever). However, we do not offer it

---

[54] Sentence (51) seems genuinely ambiguous, with three readings possible. Two readings do not raise the problem at issue here. On one reading, there is an individual award and many people (these, those and the others) are competing individually. Another unproblematic reading would refer indirectly to three competitions in which these people are competing (with each other), those people are competing (with each other), and the other people are competing (with each other). But (51) seems to have its problematic "perplural" reading also, perhaps a description of a board game or quiz game with three loosely organized teams, one of which will win.

as a general semantic analysis of plurals, because it is available only in special contexts where a suitable membership or constitution relation is available. It should not be a part of the general semantics of plurals because there are many different membership or constitution relations that would work in different cases. There is no single relationship (like set membership or mereological parthood) that works to singularize plurals in all cases without paradox.

We know that team names like 'The Yankees' don't just refer to some people; the membership in the team can change significantly, and it will be the same team even though it is not the same people. Teams are not sets. Even in a sentence like (51), the reading that has three groups competing will ordinarily allow a change in the membership of a group while still preserving the three competitors. That is, given the reading according to which there are three competing groups, competition can continue, with the same competitors, even if one person is replaced.[55] Our language of plurals does not need to make an accommodation in such cases, since this is then simply a plural predication applied to some objects (teams or groups) that have members. On this interpretation, sentences like (50)–(52) don't involve plural predication applied to some groups that are identified as a result of a fully general semantic process; they involve plural predication of groups (teams) that have pragmatically variable membership standards. I have no doubt that teams exist. They are not what we want for a general semantic account of plurals.[56]

I should provide a reasonable paraphrase of the difficult sentence (52), which seems to involve all sorts of predication of the Yankees and its members. The key idea here is that a felicitous use of (52) requires that the first clause of the following "paraphrase" is clear in the given context, though not overtly expressed.

(52′) Y are the (playing) members of the Yankees (y), and as Y spread around the field, each of Y thought about the fact that y was competing with the Red Sox and the Tigers for first place.

---

[55] On the reading of (51) that involves reference to many individual competitors, however, if one person (among these, those and the others) is replaced, then we no longer have the same competitors; a use of the sentence that preserves the reference to the original competitors will no longer be true.

(51″) X, Y and Z are competing.

[56] Cf. Uzquiano 2004.

Sentence (52) has a plural verb ('they were') where (52') has a singular verb ('*y* was'). However, reference to a team with a plural name requires agreement with a plural pronoun and verb, even when the team is not referred to indirectly by a reference to its members. (Compare to "New York is competing with Boston and Detroit for first place.")[57] This grammatical difference is superficial.

In any case, no general treatment of plurals as references to sets (sums, etc.) will account for uses such as the following:

> (53) One thing was certain about the Yankees; they had always been on top, even through many rapid and significant changes in membership.

> (54) As they spread out around the field, they thought about the fact that they had been on top for many decades.

These cannot just be perplural references to the individuals involved (the Yankees), since the individuals involved change over the time referred to. My account, which reifies the team in a topic-specific way, rather than as a product of a general semantic process of singularization, can account for these. We can refer to a team indirectly, by referring to its members, and we can then predicate a property of that team that is not at all a property of its individual members.

However, if we wish to resist even such topic-specific singularization in the analysis of (51), it seems that we can do so. First, we can consider what unites the people who are "competing together" as a team. Let's say that such people are maximally cooperative in the game:

> X are maximally cooperative iff (X are cooperative and $\forall Y$, if X are properly among Y, then Y are not cooperative).

X are people who are maximally cooperative in the game, as are Y and as are Z. (X, Y and Z are competing.) Identifying them as 'these people', 'those people' or 'those other people' depends on finding some such uniting characteristic (that they are maximally sitting together, that they are wearing shirts of the same color, or whatever) that separates them from the others. (We leave the full theory of plural demonstratives for other occasions.) Let's use 'maximally cooperative' to stand in for whatever characteristic might make the plural demonstratives work in a

---

[57] I continue to apply American grammatical standards here. I am not sure what variations are allowed in England and elsewhere.

case like the one under consideration. Then we could represent (51) in this way:

(51pl) [∀y: yAX] Py ∧ X are maximally cooperative ∧ [∀y: yAY] Py ∧ Y are maximally cooperative ∧¬Y ≈ X∧ [∀y: yAZ] Py ∧ Z are maximally cooperative ∧¬Z ≈ X ∧ ¬Z ≈ Y ∧ X, Y, and Z are competing

The last clause might seem wrong. If X are 4 people and Y are 4 people and Z are 4 people, then 'X, Y, and Z are competing' says that twelve people are competing. Maybe you wanted three competitors. We still have (51′) that gives us three competitors, but there are still two other ideas that can mitigate the sense that the account in terms of the twelve competitors X, Y, and Z is missing the mark.[58]

We might say that when some people compete, they compete in some groupings or other. Just as when I say that some money has been divided up, there is some particular way that that money has been divided up, a particular partition of it, when some people compete, they do so under some particular grouping or partition. In the example, there are twelve people competing, and the function of 'These people, those people and the other people' is to indicate how they are partitioned in the competition.

We also can accommodate the desire for a count of three, if there is some plural predication that unites each of the three "teams", some way of partitioning the competitors. Using 'XOY' for 'X overlap Y',[59] let's define:

$[\exists_n!X : FX]GX = df \exists X_1, \ldots, \exists X_n(FX_1 \wedge \ldots \wedge FX_n \wedge$

$(\neg X_1 \ O \ X_2 \wedge \ldots \wedge \neg X_1 \ O \ X_n \wedge \neg X_2 \ O \ X_3 \wedge \ldots \wedge \neg X_2 \ O$
$X_n \wedge \ldots \wedge \neg X_{n-1} \ O \ X_n) \wedge$

$[\forall Y: FY] \ (Y \approx X_1 \vee \ldots \vee Y \approx X_n) \wedge G \ (X_1, \ldots, X_n))$

Then we can say, for example:

$[\exists_3! \ X: [\forall y: yAX]$ Py ∧ X are maximally cooperative] X are competing

Three maximally cooperative "peoples" are competing. No special perplurals are evident in the analysis.

---

[58] Gabriel Uzquiano suggested both of these ideas for consideration.
[59] This is definable in terms of 'XAY' (X are among Y). XOY iff $\exists Z, ZAX \wedge ZAY$.

Singularization is not a semantic norm. When I say that some people are surrounding the building, that some students are shipmates, or that some doctors cooperate, I do not identify any single individual that is the agent of surrounding, shipmatehood or cooperation. In some special cases, such as the case of competition just considered, we have ways of indicating how individuals are grouped even without full singularization, and we also can singularize, speaking of teams or groups themselves, if we have reasons to do so. This introduction of groups is not, however, a part of the fundamental semantics of plurals.

MARTIAN PERPLURALS

But maybe teams are not the appropriate examples for making the case for perplurals just because they have these interesting identity conditions. Could we have a general process for perpluralization: when we have n Fs, we have $2^n - 1$ or $(2^n - 1) - n$ Fses (depending on whether we count a single F as one Fs)? When we have two teams with 9 players on each, we have 511 (or maybe 502) playerses.

Two of those playerses are more salient than any of the others, and so pragmatic processes might enable references to those two. If we spoke a language with perplurals, in actual usage we might typically ignore many (500 or so) of these playerses.[60] In talking about the two teams, we might speak as though there are just two playerses, because only two (of the more than 500) are the focus of conversation. This is a pragmatic phenomenon in such a language, not semantics.

To shift examples, if I command 30 soldiers, including 5 radio specialists, 5 drivers, 10 shooters and 10 support personnel, I might send out 5 soldierses (foursomes; 20 soldiers total), each with one radio specialist, two shooters and one driver. If someone asks me how many soldierses I sent out, I might say "three" (the radio specialists, shooters and drivers) or "five" (the foursomes) depending on the context. If a mathematician or philosopher asks, I might give the acontextual answer $2^{20} - 1$ (or $(2^{20} - 1) - 20$).

There is still the question of whether this is perpluralization or recognition of entities with members and then ordinary pluralization with respect to those (one soldiers, two soldierses, etc.). In other words,

---

[60] I am grateful to Allen Hazen for a tutorial on Martian pragmatics that indicated how such a language might work.

Martians might have a way of constructing general terms that apply to individuals that have members or constituents (catses, peoples, thingses, etc.), but then we still have ordinary pluralization with respect to the (complex) things so mentioned. What would make it perplural rather than just plural? Our actual usage in discussing groups of things favors the introduction of entities to which the basic individuals have a membership or constitution relation (and, except in the case of sets, one which does not obey a simple extensionality principle), rather than perpluralization. But perhaps a perplural language is possible, just not ours.

A perplural language will deal with our examples in the following ways:

> (51) These people, those people and those other people are competing.

This would be an unremarkable sentence in perplural. And we could go on to infer:

> (55) Three peoples are competing.

And for (52):

> (52) As they spread out around the field, the Yankees thought about the fact that they were competing with the Red Sox and the Tigers for first place.

One might take (52) as an unremarkable sentence also, where the Yankees are some players and one players, and the Yankees, Red Sox and Tigers are three playerses,[61] so that teams need not be separate entities – team names are just plural references to players. However, such a treatment would still run into difficulty with (53) and (54). There the team names cannot just be plural references to the players because they take in a history that involves a change in membership. And we have seen that there are ways of taking these as involving topic-specific singularization or pragmatically determined partitioning that would give us a representation of such sentences without special perplurals.

---

[61] They also include many other playerses, too. The pitchers, the fielders, the right-fielders, the Cubans, etc. But those might not be contextually relevant. That is where the Martian pragmatics comes in. Our own use of very general terms of collection involves similar pragmatic principles. If I say "Two groups of students are involved in planning the demonstration against the war," I recognize that the relevant students can be grouped in many other ways, but I refer to the two salient groupings.

In Chapter 6 we will return to perplurals to examine their status in light of a fuller account of the fundamental semantic relations *among* and *one-of*. So far, it has been hard to find anything in ordinary language that supports the existence of special perplurals. Some special understanding of a language with perplurals may be possible, but we need more clarity about our fundamental concepts before we can say more about how the understanding of plurals relates to the understanding of perplurals.

A LINGUISTIC ARGUMENT FOR SINGULARISM

Fred Landman's work provides some impressive reasons for considering groups to be a part of the necessary ontology for the semantics of plurals. (See Landman 2000, especially 152–64.) Some of these arguments are based closely on particular examples and some are based on more theoretical considerations. I will consider some of his examples in Chapters 3, 4 and 10, in the context of providing an alternative approach to the semantics of non-distributive plurals.

One important argument should be considered now, however. Landman points out that some verbs cannot apply to a single individual but can apply to groups or plurally to individuals.

> *John is gathering in the other room
> The boys are gathering in the other room.
> The committee is gathering in the other room.[62]

This fact, he argues, makes it clear that we should treat 'The boys' and 'The committee' in the same way, and thus that we should see 'The boys' as making a reference to a sum individual.

I would instead urge that the meaning of 'gather' prevents it from applying to a single ordinary individual. It can, however, apply to things that have members (composite individuals) and that can have a location – like committees. In general, many predicates that cannot apply to a single ordinary individual can apply either to some individuals or to a (single) group or composite. It will be instructive to return to our example of 'surround'. We can say

> The team surrounded the coach.
> The boys surrounded the coach.

[62] I guess that in British English one can also say "The committee are gathering in the other room."

We cannot ordinarily say:

?John surrounded the coach.

Ordinarily a single boy cannot surround the coach. But that is not because of a deep semantic division that puts plural predication and group predication on the same side and singular predication of individuals on the other side. A single rope or fence can surround the coach, and even John could do so if he were flexible enough. Gathering (in the relevant sense), on the other hand, is something that no ordinary single thing without members can do (no matter how flexible or talented it is). The fact that the boys and the committee can gather but John can't is an interesting fact about gathering, but it does not provide a reason to think that there is some single thing that the boys are or that non-distributive plural predication must really be singular predication.

THE PECULIARITY OF SINGULARISM

The semantic singularist must tell us some interesting things about the relationship of individuals to plural objects. Some of the most intuitive principles governing these objects cannot hold (on pain of paradox). Perhaps the singularist can tell us why these principles don't hold, and tell us what principles hold instead. But singularism is peculiar, not a simple development of natural ideas about plurality. We have learned to live with that strangeness because our logic has required it as the only way of representing non-distributive plurals, but I want to suggest that it is not a necessary part of logic or semantics at all. In fact, semantics can represent the meanings of sentences more simply and directly if we resist the idea that plurals are really singular.

3

Semantics

Here we will develop a systematic semantics for non-distributive predication with plural quantification that does not employ the resources of set theory or any other "singularization" of plural reference. This methodological constraint will have some value for philosophy (especially metaphysics), but it also has some value for linguistics and for the foundations of mathematics.

In linguistics and philosophy, the semantics developed for the formal language here might serve as a model that avoids artificially induced complexity that arises when semantics is based in set theory. For example, it is often necessary to "identify" singleton sets and their members, compound terms must be interpreted by singularizing objects such as sets, predicates must be shifted from non-distributive plural predicates of individuals in natural language (like 'they are arranged in a circle') to different predicates of sets (like 'set x represents a circle') in the formal semantics, and the representation of semantic roles (theta-roles) is correlatively distorted. Traditional semantics must always utilize a single subject of predication in the semantics, though some individuals are the joint subjects of non-distributive predication in the interpreted natural language.

In the foundations of mathematics, it would be worthwhile to explore how much of mathematics can be developed within a first-order plural formal language, to see where sets really become important in the expression of mathematical theories.[1]

Also, we must stay away from set-theoretic semantics because it is sure to get things wrong if we are giving a semantics for a very general language. If all sets are in the domain of interpretation, then some predicates ('$x = x$' and '$x \notin x$', for example) cannot be correctly interpreted by any set. Nevertheless, there are such things as what they are true of, even if there is no set of those things.

---

[1] There is further discussion of this issue in Ch. 6.

METALINGUISTIC RESOURCES

In the metalanguage we will make use of plural variables, which can look like set-theoretic talk. But the semantics does not require that we collect things into sets that are then treated as objects, and the plural variables are never treated as singular variables varying over collectible objects. Thus we will not use sets as semantic objects. Because of this, the semantics can ground the language in a way that accords with our methodological restriction against sets.

The function of variables in any metalanguage is to have many separate pronouns ('it1', 'it2', etc.) for clear cross-reference. When we want multiple cross-references, we need a large stock of pronouns for clarity. For example, in a purely singular case:

If i satisfies 'Bx', j satisfies 'Cx', and the relation represented by 'Rxy' relates i to j, then the relation represented by '(B x ∧ Cy) ∧ Rxy' relates i to j.

We will also want to use plural variables, upper-case letters, in both the formal language and the metalanguage. The plural metalinguistic variables relate to 'they' (and 'them') as singular metalinguistic variables relate to 'it'.[2]

If I ("these") satisfy 'BX', J ("those") satisfy 'CX', and the relation represented by 'RXY' relates I to J, then the relation represented by '(B X ∧ CY) ∧ RXY' relates I to J.[3]

We also need to employ the relation *among* as a fundamental relation in our semantic base. To make this clear, we provide examples to illustrate our use of 'among':

Chicago and Los Angeles are among Chicago, Los Angeles and Houston.

Houston is among Chicago, Los Angeles and Houston.

Chicago, Los Angeles and Houston are among Chicago, Los Angeles and Houston.

[2] Boolos introduces a similar use of variables (1985*b*, 165 in Boolos 1998).

[3] Others have used the notation '*xx*' or '*xs*' rather than '*X*' for a plural variable. These have the advantage of emphasizing the first-order character of plurals, but we will not follow that practice here. Another notation, "the *x*'s" is very misleading, since it treats '*x*' as though it were some sort of general term (and it introduces whatever complexities might be associated with plural definite descriptions).

This is a reflexive, transitive relation. Also, if I are among J and J are among I, then I are J. In the case of an individual i, we can say either that i is among J or that i is one of J.[4] The *among* relation is distributive in its first argument place and non-distributive in its second argument place.

Since we are employing capital letters for plural variables (in the object language and the metalanguage), some might be tempted to think that there is something second-order about what we are doing. There isn't. We are quantifying into argument positions, not into predicative positions. Quantifiers, whether singular or plural, quantify with respect to the individuals in the domain (some, three, many, etc.), not in any other way. We are using our understanding of non-distributive plural predication and our understanding of plural pronouns as a base for understanding the formal apparatus of predication and quantification. The connection that exists between plurals and monadic second-order logic will be discussed in Chapter 6.

TERMS

In the formal language, we need a way to represent compound terms that may be used with non-distributive predicates.

(1) Alicia, Betty and Carla are meeting together.

We will treat a non-distributive predicate like "X are meeting together" or "X are shipmates" as a monadic predicate (a predicate with one argument place) that can be satisfied by several individuals together. Each of these two predicates of English ("X are meeting together" and "X are shipmates") lexically requires at least two individuals. A predicate like "X lifted the table" allows reference to several individuals or to a single individual in its argument place. (Our formal language will not incorporate any syntactic restrictions that correspond to such lexical restrictions.)

With several separately named individuals, we need to introduce a notation to indicate that the names are all within a single argument place. We could, for example, just put them in a column:

---

[4] Some others who have discussed plurals have highlighted the relation 'x is one of Y' rather than 'X are among Y'. (For example, Yi and Rayo.) The *among* relation allows both plural and singular terms in either place, and so 'x is one of Y' is just the case in which the first term in the *among* relation is singular (x is among Y). In comparing *among* theory to set theory, the *among* relation would be the analogue of both the *membership* and *subset* relations. In Ch. 6 there is a general account of *among* and a discussion of two ways of interpreting *is one of*.

(1)   Alicia, Betty and Carla are meeting together.

(1′) S a
     b
     c

indicating that all are associated with the one argument place in the sentence (the one they are lined up with vertically).

(2)   John Wayne circled wagons 1–7 around a campfire.

(2′) Cjw1
     w2
     w3
     w4
     w5
     w6
     w7

But this is awkward. Our typography thrives on horizontal linearization, so we will introduce things like

⌊a, b, c⌉

which go into a single argument position – in effect, '⌊a, b, c⌉' is a single compound phrase, like 'Alicia, Betty and Carla' in English.

(1″) M⌊a, b, c⌉

(2″) Cj⌊w1, w2, w3, w4, w5, w6, w7⌉

QUANTIFIERS

Use of a plural variable indicates the possibility of non-distributive satisfaction relative to the argument position of the variable; a singular variable always indicates individual satisfaction of a predicate. For example, consider a predicate like "α lifted β", in which either several individuals or just one can be the satisfiers with respect to either argument place ("Several students (together) lifted Bernie" or "Alice lifted three tables", for example). We will have multiple representations of an ambiguous sentence like:

Some students lifted Bernie

The following representations should be equivalent:

(3)   At least one student (some students distributively) lifted Bernie

(3′) [∃x: Sx] Lxb

(3″) [∃X: [∀y: yAX] Sy] [∀y: yAX] Lyb

We will also have a related non-distributive sentence:

(4) [∃X: [∀y: yAX] Sy] LXb

which will not be equivalent to the others. According to our semantics, (3′) (or (3″)) will entail (4), however. If some one student lifted Bernie, then we will regard (4) as true. A plural is pragmatically inappropriate when the speaker knows that only one individual satisfies a predicate. But, as usual in logic, we will take it that a plural existential is true in such a case, even if the speaker's knowledge makes it pragmatically inappropriate. Then a universal quantifier ∀ can still be defined in the usual way, as the dual of the existential.

(5) No one lifted Bernie.

(5a) ¬[∃X: SX] LXb

(5b) [∀X: SX] ¬LXb

(5c) ¬[∃x: Sx] Lxb

(5d) [∀x: Sx] ¬Lxb

We want (5a) and (5b) to be equivalent, and they indicate that Bernie was not lifted by students (whether individually or in a group). We want (5c) and (5d) to be equivalent, and they will indicate that no student lifted Bernie on his own (though some students may have done so in a joint effort). Either of (5a) or (5b) will entail (5c) (and (5d)), but not vice versa.[5]

THE FORMAL LANGUAGE

Syntax

Basic elements[6]

Relation (including predicate) symbols: B^n, $B_1{}^n$, $B_2{}^n$, ..., C^n ..., for each $n \leq 1$. 'A' will be reserved for a designated logical relation (*among*).

---

[5] In Ch. 6 we will fully eliminate the singular variables, treating them as a special case of the general, plural variables.

[6] I have not included plural constants in the inventory of basic elements. Perhaps this is an American bias. In some parts of the world where English is spoken these seem to play a more significant role. If *The Storm* is the name of a team, then *The Storm have won* is acceptable in many versions of English (I am told), as is *Manchester are taking the field*. And I guess that even *The Parliament have acted* and *The committee are gathering* are acceptable in these dialects. These seem to be cases of using a name or a syntactically

Individual constants: a, b, c, . . .
Singular variables: x, y, z, . . .
Plural variables: X, Y, Z, X_1, X_2, . . .
Unary sentential operator: $\neg$
Binary sentential connective: $\wedge$
Basic quantifiers: $\exists$, κ, σ, $\Lambda^{\exists}$, μ, 1, 2, 3, . . . etc.

Terms
Individual constants are terms.
Variables are terms.
If T_1, . . . , T_n are terms, then $\lfloor T_1, \ldots, T_n \rceil$ is a term.

Clauses
$B^n T_1 \ldots T_n$ is a clause (where B^n is an n-place relation symbol, and T_1, . . . , T_n are n terms).
$T_1 A T_2$ is a clause.
If G is a clause, then $\neg$G is a clause.
If G and H are clauses, then $G \wedge H$ is a clause.
If Q is a quantifier, ν is a variable, and G and H are clauses, then $[Q\nu: G]$ H is a clause.
A sentence is a clause with no free variables.

Additional connectives can be defined in terms of negation and conjunction, and additional quantifiers can be defined in terms of the basic ones (in ways to be discussed).

SEMANTICS

Our semantics will allow for non-distributive and non-cumulative predication, for conjoined plural terms (functioning like 'Alice and Bill'), and for a wide range of plural quantifiers (besides *all* and *some*, we will have *several*, *a few*, *nine*, *most*, etc.).

---

singular definite description to refer to many things – a non-distributive, plural name or description.

I also have not included definite descriptions as basic elements. With restricted quantifiers, 'the' is syntactically just another quantifier (determiner), used in creating noun phrases (determiner phrases, quantifier phrases) such as 'the doctor', 'the students' and 'the students who are surrounding the building'. However, I am leaving the full consideration of definite descriptions, plural and singular, for discussion in Chs. 7 and 8. There are some interesting issues and some surprises when we consider plural definite descriptions.

Proportional and Non-proportional Quantifiers

One factor that any theory of plurals and quantifiers must confront is the distinction between proportional and non-proportional quantifiers. If I use a non-proportional quantifier:[7]

(6) Seven (many, several) dogs are making a racket in the yard.

(7) $[7X: DX] MX$

I can paraphrase (6) as

(8) Some dogs that are seven (many, several) in number are making a racket in the yard.

That paraphrase can be the basis for the semantics for the quantifier in (7). But when we have a proportional quantifier such as 'most', no such paraphrase is available.

(9) Most (all, half the) students are now gathering together on the lawn.

(10) $[\mu X: SX] GX$

(11) *Some students who are most (all, half) in number are gathering together on the lawn.

For proportional quantifiers, our semantics can be based on a different paraphrase, however, one that involves a plural definite description.

(12) The students are such that most (all, half) of them are gathering on the lawn.

This kind of paraphrase would also work for non-proportional quantifiers in this example:

(13) The dogs are such that seven (many, several) of them are making a racket in the yard.

However, a paraphrase on the model of (12) introduces the possibility of semantic anomaly that is not really present for non-proportional quantifiers, so it is best to use our first paraphrase (8) as the basis for the semantics of non-proportional quantifiers.

---

[7] There may also be proportional variants of 'many'; perhaps we could have many jazz superstars at a party without having many people there. Such uses would require a different semantics, to be indicated presently.

Semantic anomaly is possible in sentences built on the model of (12) whenever the place of 'students' in such a sentence is taken by a non-cumulative predicate. If a predicate F is non-cumulative, then there may be no such thing as *the* F*s*, even when some things are F. For example, if there are several separate student groups meeting in different places in the library, then the sentence

> (14) ?All (most) students meeting together in the library are wearing shorts.

is semantically anomalous because there are no such things as "All (most) students meeting together in the library." In such situations, no matter how you pick some students I who are meeting together, there are others J who are meeting together as well (and who are not meeting with I). You cannot simply consider I and J together, since then you are no longer considering students who are meeting together. The plural description "The students who are meeting together" is improper. This is possible whenever a predicate is non-cumulative.[8]

Modeling the semantics for (14) on (12) appropriately accounts for the semantic anomaly in (14), because the semantics for (14) will involve an improper plural definite description. However, if we were to model our semantics for non-proportional quantifiers on (12) and (13), we would introduce a source of anomaly into the semantics for non-proportional quantifiers, even though no such anomalies exist for non-proportional quantifiers. That would be a mistake.

> (15) Seven (many, several) students meeting together in the library are wearing shorts.

(15) is perfectly acceptable even if there are several meetings going on in the library, as long the participants in one of the meetings make it true.

Generally, we must require that when Q is a proportional quantifier, then $[QX: AX]$ has an interpretation only when some things are identifiable as "the A*s*."[9] This happens when A is cumulative (and there

---

[8] A description 'the F' (singular or plural) can also be improper because there are no F*s*. But that would pose no problem in the case of existence-entailing quantifiers, because we can make all such sentences false in that case. Quantifiers that are not existence-entailing will be considered later in this chapter.

[9] This may connect with a certain fact about English usage. Consider these two sentences:

> Most students who are surrounding the building are vegetarians.
> Most of the students who are surrounding the building are vegetarians.

are some As), but it may also happen for purely contingent reasons. For example, the sentence

(16) All (most) students meeting together in the next room are wearing shorts.

is acceptable when there is only one meeting in the next room, even though it would not be acceptable if there were several separate meetings. We will parallel natural language here, allow for the syntactic acceptability of such sentences, and provide for cases in which sentences with proportional quantifiers are semantically anomalous.[10]

Since such anomalies exist for proportional quantifiers (as in (14)), a semantics based on a paraphrase like (12) is completely appropriate for those. Since they do not exist for non-proportional quantifiers, we need to retain the semantics that does not employ the plural definite description. So our semantics will treat the two classes of quantifiers differently. One could distinguish them syntactically as well, though I have not done so.[11]

Interpreting Plurals

Ordinarily a model **M** associates a semantic value with each basic item of a formal language. On a formal account, a model is an ordered n-tuple of sets and functions. Since we will not just help ourselves to general set theory, we will specify the interpretation of our language somewhat differently.

An interpretation of a language is based on some individuals **D** that are the things the language talks about. In interpreting the language, we

---

Many of us find the second of these to be much more natural than the first. (Helen Cartwright goes as far as to call sentences of the first type ungrammatical. Cartwright 2000, 241–2. I would not go so far.) This may be because a proportional quantifier like 'most' requires some definite things, "the students who are surrounding the building," that it takes a proportion of. The use of the definite description in the second sentence clearly indicates that there are some such antecedently identifiable individuals (most of whom are vegetarians).

[10] Alternatively, one could simply judge that when the uniqueness condition is not met, i.e., when there are no things with a unique claim to being *the As*, then all sentences with proportional quantifiers [QX: AX] are false. However, I have not been able to develop any satisfying semantics based on that approach.

[11] Rayo (2002) uses definite descriptions in the account of generalized quantifiers, and so his approach suffers from the inadequacies just mentioned in the account of non-proportional quantifiers. It would introduce the possibility of semantic anomaly where such a possibility does not exist in natural language.

will talk about ordered n-tuples involving elements of the language and
such individuals. Although ordered n-tuples are ordinarily modeled by
sets (when the general resources of set theory are available), we can take
them as objects themselves. Our reference to them does not compromise
our goals of avoiding set-theoretic paradoxes and maintaining plural
subjects of predication. For example, instead of saying that there is
a function that assigns an individual to each individual constant,
we will say that there are some ordered pairs **C** that fulfill certain
conditions:

> **C** are functional: if $\langle n, m \rangle$ and $\langle n, k \rangle$ are among **C**, then m = k.
>
> If $\langle n, m \rangle$ is among **C**, then n is an individual constant of the
> language and m is among **D**.
>
> For each individual constant n, some ordered pair $\langle n, m \rangle$ is
> among **C**.

To interpret names, we must associate each name with a referent.[12]
The ordered pairs model that process of association. Similarly, we must
associate each plural variable with some things in **D** and each singular
variable with one thing in **D**. So let's identify some ordered pairs **R**
fulfilling these conditions:[13]

> If $\langle n, m \rangle$ is among **R**, then n is a variable of the language and m is
> among **D**.
>
> For each variable n, at least one ordered pair $\langle n, m \rangle$ is among **R**.
>
> If n is an individual (singular) variable, then if $\langle n, m \rangle$ and $\langle n, k \rangle$
> are among **R**, then m = k.

Interpreting relational expressions

For the semantics of predicates and relations, it seems that we must
associate each n-place predicate ($n \geq 1$) with an n-place relation. This
will make some philosophers unhappy. We avoid sets only to introduce
n-place relations as elements of our semantics. My primary goal,
however, is not ontological reduction. My goal is to give a semantics

---

[12] We are not making a place for empty names, names that lack reference. Making a
place for them would raise several interesting issues, but these issues do not relate directly
to questions about plurals or non-distributive predication and so would distract us from
our main concern.

[13] See Boolos 1985, 81 in Boolos 1998.

that avoids the singularizing effects of set theory (like paradoxes and incorrect theta-role assignments). Referring to ordered pairs in which the first item is an expression of the formal language and the second is an individual from among those interpreting the language will not introduce those singularizing effects.

For distributive predicates, we could use methods like those employed for variables and individual constants, and avoid the direct introduction of n-place relations in the ontology of the meta-language. For example, a monadic distributive predicate P can be interpreted by some ordered pairs **N** fulfilling the following conditions:

If $\langle P, m \rangle$ is among **N**, then m is among **D**.

And this could readily be extended to n-place predicates that are distributive in every argument place, using ordered $n + 1$-tuples. (If a monadic predicate P is such that no ordered pair $\langle P, m \rangle$ is among **N**, then that predicate is not satisfied by anything in the model.)

However, when we consider non-distributive plural satisfaction of predicates (think of 'X are meeting together'), nothing that simple will work, since we will not take some things to be a single object (that can be the second element of an ordered pair). If we associate a property with a predicate P^1, then we can say that P^1 is true of some things whenever those things have the property associated with that predicate.[14] So for predicates and relations (for $n \geq 1$), **P** are some ordered pairs $\langle P^n, m \rangle$ such that:

If $\langle P^n, m \rangle$ is among **P**, then P^n is an n-place predicate and m is an n-place relation.

If P^n is an n-place predicate of our language, then exactly one ordered pair $\langle P^n, m \rangle$ is among **P**.

Instead of talking about interpreting our language in a model **M**, our discussion should be thought of as indicating what the semantic value is "according to **C**, **R** and **P**".[15] For convenience, we can use subscripts in indicating semantic values of expressions.

---

[14] An interpretation of the metalanguage would need to treat those properties as objects and so introduce appropriate resources for avoiding paradoxes, perhaps analogous to those that exist for set theory.

[15] One might argue that with **C**, **R** and **P** indicating "according to **C**, **R** and **P** ", they are really used within an adverbial phrase and should be associated with the verb in sentences. So we should really have this:

If c is an individual constant, then c is$_C$ an individual.

If c is an individual constant, then c_C is an individual.

If v is a variable, then v_R are some individuals.

If P^n is an n-place predicate ($n \geq 1$), then $P^n{}_P$ is an n-place relation.

A relational symbol C^3 (for example) might be interpreted by a relation allowing plurality in one or more of its argument places; for example, *X circled Y around Z*, which relates (say) Gabby, Buster and Jed to wagons 1–9 and to Carla and Kate. This is a fundamental difference from singularist approaches, which must always identify a single individual for each argument place. For example, in a traditional, singularist treatment, the sentence:

(17) Gabby, Buster and Jed circled wagons 1–9 around Carla and Kate.

would need to be transformed into something that is about three sets (or other non-atomic entities), {Gabby, Buster, Jed}, the set with wagons 1–9 as its only members, and {Carla, Kate}. Also, since sets aren't agents of action and are neither encirclers nor things encircled, one must really change the predicate as well as the subject, on such a singularist approach.[16] Because the semantics here will not employ such singularizing entities, we will think of a plural variable as being related (non-distributively) to one or more things, the things that **R** associates it with.

Spelling out the approach in the way we just did assumes that properties and relations exist. If we simply add relations naively to the domain of the object language, then we are back in paradox country. Think of the property of *not applying to itself*. One might have a theory of relations that avoids this, analogous to standard set theory. Or one might hold that a metalanguage must always have an ontology that includes relations that are not in the object language (associating an escalation of ontology with an ascent through a metalinguistic hierarchy).

There are two other approaches that might avoid direct talk of relations. The first involves some additional use of ordered pairs in

---

If v is a variable, then v are$_R$ some individuals.

If P^n is an n-place predicate, then P^n is$_P$ an n-place relation.

That is probably right. But adhering to this would produce unnecessary wordiness in some cases – we would have to introduce a verb for the **C**, **R** and **P** to attach to when otherwise there would be a more succinct presentation.

[16] Cf. Oliver and Smiley 2001. Also, Chs. 2 and 5 discuss related issues about the status of semantics and semantic objects.

interpreting even non-distributive predicates.[17] For example, we might take a non-distributive 'are classmates' (M) and have the following ordered pairs interpret it (in a domain containing Al, Betty, Carla and Dave):

$\langle M, \langle 1, \text{Al} \rangle \rangle$
$\langle M, \langle 1, \text{Betty} \rangle \rangle$
$\langle M, \langle 2, \text{Carla} \rangle \rangle$
$\langle M, \langle 2, \text{Dave} \rangle \rangle$

These indicate that Al and Betty are classmates and that Carla and Dave are classmates (if that is how M is being interpreted in this model). But this method has a limitation, since it uses the natural numbers as indexes. If the natural numbers are in our domain, and we consider a predicate like 'scattered' ("The primes are scattered among the natural numbers"), there are more ways for natural numbers to scatter than there are natural numbers. So we would need some other things to serve as indexes. But then it seems inevitable that whatever we use for indexes will run out, for similar reasons, if the indexes themselves are in the domain of the object language.

Another way to avoid adding relations is to interpret our object language by indicating how to *translate* each formula of the object language into a corresponding statement in the meta-language. So for example,

(18) $C^3 \lfloor g, b, j \rfloor, \lfloor w1, w2, w3, w4, w5, w6, w7, w8, w9 \rfloor, \lfloor c, k \rfloor$

in the object language might be translated by (17). We then determine how it is with those things (Gabby, Buster and Jed, the nine wagons, and Carla and Kate) in an intended model in order to determine whether the sentence is true or false in that model. Through such a translation procedure, we could eliminate the need for reference to relations in the semantics.[18] A translation scheme then replaces (or should we say "determines"?) **P** in our semantics.

We might take a slightly different view of the role of translation, also. We might view the formal language as a "regimentation" of a portion natural language,[19] with the semantics indicating how the meanings of

---

[17] Gabriel Uzquiano suggested this, and he cites Shapiro 1991, 103–4 as a source for the method.

[18] Boolos 1984 (in Boolos 1998, 67–8), Rayo 2002, and Linnebo 2004, present such translation procedures in detail.

[19] This would be a portion of the natural language that has been supplemented with an infinite stock of singular and plural pronouns for cross-reference.

the elements of the language are related. The translation indicates what portion of the natural language is being regimented and how we are to connect particular elements of the formal language (particular constants and predicates) with the natural language and, through it, with the world.

Translation also has limitations. In discussing logical truth, we must discuss all ways of interpreting a predicate. This would mean considering all possible translations of it, and it is difficult to see how to specify those.

So we will assume that some suitable theory of relations exists, rather than trying to avail ourselves of either the ordered-pairs reduction of non-distributive predications or the translation method of interpretation. Our main interest is in preserving the non-distributive plural reference of plural variables and avoiding the introduction of singular surrogates, and we do not need to develop the theory of relations to do that.[20]

Terms

When an expression has variables, the ordered pairs R are involved in modelling the interpretation of the expression. For any variable v, R have the effect of relating v to some (one or more) individuals. If v is a singular variable, then R relate v to just one individual. Otherwise, R relate v to one or more individuals. For any term T, C and R together relate T to some (one or more) individuals $T_{C,R}$.

For an individual constant c, if c_C is d, then $c_{C,R}$ is d.

If v is a variable, then $v_{C,R}$ are the individuals that R relates v to.

For a compound term $\lfloor T_1, \ldots, T_n \rfloor$, $\lfloor T_1, \ldots, T_n \rfloor_{C,R}$ are the individuals $T_{1C,R}, \ldots, T_{nC,R}$.[21]

(There may be redundancies in the list $T_{1C,R}, \ldots, T_{nC,R}$. That is not important. The list 'John, Mary, John, Alice' has the same semantic value as the list 'John, Mary, Alice'. Each list refers non-distributively to them, John, Mary and Alice.)

---

[20] There is some further discussion of the use of properties in the semantics in Ch. 5, where we develop and assess a set-theoretic semantics.

[21] Some readers have expressed some discomfort about this clause. If we read '$\lfloor T_1, \ldots, T_n \rfloor_{C,R}$' as 'the interpretation of "$\lfloor T_1, \ldots, T_n \rfloor$" according to C and R' it might seem that a singular verb is required. That, however, is a mistake. Since we now allow that some things may (non-distributively) interpret an expression, it is better to read the expression 'the interpreter(s) of "$\lfloor T_1, \ldots, T_n \rfloor$"' according to C and R'. For English, we would say that John, Mary and Alice are (jointly) the interpreters of 'John, Mary and Alice'.

Clauses

A clause that is not semantically anomalous is assigned a truth-value according to **C**, **P** and **R**, depending on the properties of the individuals in **D**. We can write '**C**, **P**, **R** $|= S$' for 'S is true according to **C**, **P** and **R**' (or for '**C**, **P** and **R** verify S'). Our semantics will allow that some clauses are semantically anomalous (so that for some sentences S neither **C**, **P**, **R** $|= S$ nor **C**, **P**, **R** $|= \neg S$).

Instead of talking about a set that is the extension of a predicate or open sentence, we must be able to talk (plurally) about the satisfiers of a monadic, distributive predicate or of an open sentence relative to a variable v. If **R** relate each variable to some things, then **R**v/I are some ordered pairs just like **R** except that **R**v/I relate v to I (i.e., for each d among **D**, $\langle v, d \rangle$ is among **R**v/I iff d is among I).

> If v is a singular variable, then a clause G may have some v-satisfiers$_{C,P,R}$. An individual i is a v-satisfier$_{C,P,R}$ of G iff **C**,**P**,**R**v/i $|= $G. For singular variable v, some things I are *the* v-satisfiers$_{C,P,R}$ of G iff every v-satisfier$_{C,P,R}$ of G is among I, and every individual i among I is a v-satisfier$_{C,P,R}$ of G.

> If v is a plural variable, then a clause G may have some v-satisfiers$_{C,P,R}$. Some things I are v-satisfiers$_{C,P,R}$ of G iff **C**, **P**, **R**v/I $|= $G. Sometimes we can speak of *the* v-satisfiers$_{C,P,R}$ of G. For a plural variable v, some things I are *the* v-satisfiers$_{C,P,R}$ of G iff I are v-satisfiers$_{C,P,R}$ of G, and whenever some things J are v-satisfiers$_{C,P,R}$ of G, J are among I.

Atomic relational clause: **C**, **P**, **R** $|= B^n T_1 T_2 \ldots T_n$ iff B^np relates $T_{1C,R}$ to $T_{2C,R} \ldots$ to $T_{nC,R}$.[22] Special case: **C**, **P**, **R** $|= T_1$ A T_2 iff $T_{1C,R}$ are among $T_{2C,R}$.[23]

$\neg$: If G is not semantically anomalous, then **C**, **P**, **R** $|= \neg$G iff it is not the case that **C**, **P**, **R** $|= $G. If G is semantically anomalous, then $\neg$G is semantically anomalous.

---

[22] Here I adopt a slightly odd way of speaking in order to get a general way of talking about relations. For example, here we might say C^3p relates John and Buddy to w1–w9 [wagons] to c [campfire]. Using the word 'to' here separates the references to things associated with each argument place. Otherwise, 'relates John and Buddy, w1–w9 and c' might be read as involving a single plural term, or the division into separate plural arguments might not be clear.

[23] Identity can be defined in terms of the A (*among*) relation. This is spelled out in Ch. 6.

∧: If G and H are not semantically anomalous, then C, P, R |= (G ∧ H) iff C, P, R |= G and C, P, R |= H. If either G or H is semantically anomalous, then (G ∧ H) is semantically anomalous.

Singular quantification: If either G or H is semantically anomalous, then [Qν: H] G is semantically anomalous. Otherwise, C, P, R |= [Qν: H] G iff some things J are the ν-satisfiers$_{C,P,R}$ of H, and some things I are ν-satisfiers$_{C,P,R}$ of G such that I are Q of J.

Plural, non-proportional quantification: For a plural variable ν, and a non-proportional quantifier Q, if H and G are not semantically anomalous, then C, P, R |= [Qν: H] G iff some things I are such that C, P, Rν/I |= G, and C, P, Rν/I |= H, and I are Q in number. If either G or H is semantically anomalous, then [Qν: H] G is semantically anomalous.

Plural, proportional quantification: If Q is a proportional quantifier and it is not the case that some individuals J are the ν-satisfiers$_{C,P,R}$ of H, then [Qν: H] G is semantically anomalous. Also, if either G or H is semantically anomalous, then [Qν: H] G is semantically anomalous. Otherwise, C, P, R |= [Qν: H] G iff some things J are the ν-satisfiers$_{C,P,R}$ of H, and some things I are such that C, P, Rν/I |= G and I are Q of J.

Closed sentence S: C, P |= S iff C, P, R |= S for some pairs R.

Logical truth: A closed sentence S is a logical truth iff whenever C′ interpret the individual constants of S and P′ interpret the variables of S, C′, P′ |= S.

SPECIFIC QUANTIFIERS

The use of the bold-face Q in the semantics is schematic. For each quantifier, we can put in place of Q the account (or the meta-linguistic "translation") of that quantifier. The semantic stipulations for quantifiers can then be specified individually. For example, assume in each off the following that H and G are not semantically anomalous.

Some non-proportional plural quantifiers:

C, P, R |= [∃ν: H] G iff some things I are such that C, P, Rν/I |= G and C, P, Rν/I |= H (and I are some things).

C, P, R |= [κν: H] G iff some things I are such that C, P, Rν/I |= G, C, P, Rν/I |= H, and I are many things.

C, P, R $|=$ [σv: H] G iff some things I are such that C, P, Rv/I $|=$ G,C, P, Rv/I $|=$ H, and I are several things.

C, P, R $|=$ [7v: H] G iff some things I are such that C, P, Rv/I $|=$ G,C, P, Rv/I $|=$ H, and I are 7 things.

Some proportional plural quantifiers:

If some individuals J are the v-satisfiers$_{M,R}$ of H, then C, P, R $|=$ [Λ^3v: H] G iff some things I are such that C, P, Rv/I $|=$ G, some things J are the v-satisfiers$_{C,P,R}$ of H, and I are all of J. [24]

If some individuals J are the v-satisfiers$_{C,P,R}$ of H, then C, P, R $|=$ [μv: H] G iff some things I are such that C, P, Rv/I $|=$ G, some things J are the v-satisfiers$_{C,P,R}$ of H, and I are most of J.

If some individuals J are the v-satisfiers$_{C,P,R}$ of H, then C, P, R $|=$ [1/3v: H] G iff some things I are such that C, P, Rv/I $|=$ G, some things J are the v-satisfiers$_{C,P,R}$ of H, and I are 1/3 of J.

We can think of this as taking the existential quantifier as basic and then defining the other quantifiers in terms of the existential and two distinct kinds of quantitative (non-distributive, plural) properties, the non-proportional

I are Q "in number" (I are Q things)

and the proportional

I are Q of J.

This does not get us the full set of standard singular quantifiers. For example, it provides only for quantifiers that entail existence, i.e., [Qv: H] G entails [∃v: H] G. However, specifying these quantifiers directly provides us with resources to define others.[25]

EXISTENCE ENTAILMENTS

If a quantifier clause [Qv: H] G is interpreted directly by this semantics, then its truth requires the existence of something satisfying the conjunction of the predicates H and G. Because of this requirement, this

---

[24] The symbol 'Λ^3' is for a universal quantifier that entails existence. We will discuss the existence entailment and alternative universal concepts in this chapter.

[25] These are issues that one must face whether or not one gives a non-singularist semantics.

semantic clause cannot directly interpret quantifiers like 'no', 'fewer than *n*', 'few'. We also get non-standard accounts of proportional quantifiers like 'all' and 'most', because on our semantics, sentences of the form [Q*v*: H] G come out false when there are no H.

We can define the missing quantifiers. For example, we can define quantifiers that lack existence entailments:

> M, R $\models$ [Λ*v*: H] G iff M, R $\models$ [Λ$^\exists$*v*: H] G is T$_{M,R}$ or there are no *v*-satisfiers$_{M,R}$ for H.
>
> M, R $\models$ [0*v*: H] G iff M, R $\models$ ¬[∃*v*: H] G. ("No H are G.")

Although these definitions are stated in a fully general way, perhaps we should really restrict this use of the defined universal to the representation of natural language cases without non-distributive predicates. Consider a situation in which there are no students from Croatia. Should we automatically say that each of these is true?

> (19) All students from Croatia are surrounding the building.
> (20) All students from Croatia are shipmates.

Sentences (19) and (20) seem false to me (in the imagined circumstances), so I am not inclined to see plural quantifiers that do not entail existence as useful for representing semantic features of these examples from natural language.

There are compelling reasons for taking universal quantifications with distributive predications as not entailing existence in ordinary English. The inference from (21) to (22) is valid:

> (21) All students in my class are chemistry majors.
> (22) All students in my class who are Italian are chemistry majors.

Since there might be no Italians in the class, even though (21) is true and the inference is valid, we must allow that in sentences without non-distributive predication, 'all' does not entail existence.

The corresponding argument does not go smoothly with plurals and non-distributive predications.

> (23) All students in my class are surrounding the building.
> (24) All students in my class who are Italian are surrounding the building.

I think that (24) can be false, even though (23) is true and there are Italian students in my class. (24) will be false if the 37 students in my class are surrounding the building and some of them are Italian, but the Italians are all on one side of the building. The inference from (23) to (24) is just not valid. So even though there is a compelling argument for taking the universal with a singular variable, and thus with distributive predicates, as not entailing existence, that argument does not carry over to the general case of plural quantification, which allows non-distributive predication.[26]

If the conclusion explicitly refers to the students who are Italian, then it is even clearer that it does not follow from (23).

(25) All of the students who are Italian are surrounding the building.

(25) implies that some students are Italian – by referring to *the students who are Italian*, and says that all of them are surrounding the building. Since (23) does not say that there are any students who are Italian, (25) cannot follow. As we have indicated, (25) is the semantic value of (24).

We should take care to distinguish (24) from (26).

(26) All students who are Italian are <u>involved in</u> surrounding the building.

(26) adds *involved in*,[27] which is a way of making a distributive predicate from a non-distributive predicate. Although it is not true that all Italian students are surrounding the building, it is true that every Italian student is involved in surrounding the building. (26) will follow from

(23′) All students in my class are involved in surrounding the building.

because that change returns us to the situation we had with quantification with purely distributive predicates. And the meaning of *involved in* guarantees that if (23) is true, so is (23′), so (26) will follow from (23). (26) is very different from (24).

Proportional quantification, including universal quantification, with non-distributive predicates seems to entail existence. That is the assumption that I will make about the representation of English. In any case, formal-language quantifiers that do not entail existence are definable.

---

[26] Hanoch Ben-Yami points out (personal communication) that one could regard all universals as carrying existential assumptions, regard (22) as truth-valueless rather than false, and still accept the general form of argument from (21) to (22) as valid because it never goes from a true premise to a false conclusion. Such an approach would be consistent with my approach to plural quantification, but it is not required by it.

[27] See Ch. 4, 78–9, for a fuller discussion of *involved in*.

DUAL QUANTIFIERS

It is also important to see that we really need two very different universal quantifiers with plurals, $\Lambda^{\exists}$ and $\forall$.[28] The universal $\Lambda^{\exists}$ (or even Λ) is not a dual of $\exists$. That is, we cannot define $\Lambda^{\exists}$ (or Λ) as $\neg\exists\neg$, as is usual for the universal. The reason is simple. The following may be true together:

> (27) All (of the) students are surrounding the building.
> [$\Lambda^{\exists}X$: X are students] X are surrounding the building
> (28) Some students are not surrounding the building.
> [$\exists X$: X are students] X are not surrounding the building

If three hundred students surround the building, and they are all of the relevant students, then (27) is true. But if we consider two students among them who are standing together, they do not surround the building.[29] So (28) is also true. Thus the sentence:

> (29) It is not the case that: some students are not surrounding the building.

is false. But a representation of (29) with Λ or $\Lambda^{\exists}$ would need to be true if Λ or $\Lambda^{\exists}$ were simply equivalent to $\neg\exists\neg$.

The standard universal quantifier symbol, $\forall$, will be defined as the dual of $\exists$.

> A sentence of the form [$\forall\nu$: G] H is true iff the corresponding sentence of the form $\neg$[$\exists\nu$: G] $\neg$H is true.

As it turns out, both universals are needed if we wish to represent English smoothly. We seem to have two distinct ways of using universal words in conjunction with non-distributive plurals, corresponding to the two different universals that we have introduced. The first kind of universal sentence, corresponding to $\Lambda^{\exists}$, includes sentences like:

> (27) All (of the) students are surrounding the building.
> (30) All (of the) students in my class are shipmates.

---

[28] This is another issue that one must face whether or not one's semantics is non-singularist.

[29] They are involved in surrounding the building, but that distributive predicate is not what we are interested in here.

However, we must recognize another use of 'all' with plurals.

(31) All companies that compete share common interests.[30]

I take (31) to be saying of companies that compete with each other, that they share common interests. For example, (31) says that Toyota and GM share common interests, and that Calvin Klein and Versace share common interests, etc., but not that Toyota and Versace share common interests. As we defined Λ^3, it would not give us the result we want. The quantifier phrase '$\Lambda^3 X$: X are companies that compete' will be anomalous when there are no companies that compete (with each other) such that all companies that compete (with each other) are among them. That is the actual situation. Toyota and GM compete, and Calvin Klein and Versace compete, but it is not true that Toyota, GM, Calvin Klein and Versace compete. In other words, the predicate is non-cumulative, so proportional quantification is semantically anomalous. So in the actual world, the sentence would be anomalous with Λ^3, and so the quantifier Λ^3 is unsuitable for representing this sentence. The universal quantifier $\forall$, though, is what we want.

(31a) [$\forall X$: X are companies that compete] X share common interests

(31b) $\neg$[$\exists X$: X are companies that compete] $\neg X$ share common interests

These represent the English sentence appropriately. Although the semantics for $\forall$ cannot be made to fit the basic semantic clauses for quantifiers, we can introduce it definitionally in this way, and so no revision is required for the basic semantics.

With singular variables, the difference between Λ and $\forall$ disappears.[31] These are equivalent if G and H are distributive and cumulative:

[$\forall x$: G] H
[Λx: G] H

---

[30] This example is Link's (1998, 98). Link also discusses some variants of this that are of questionable interpretability. (For example, "Most companies that compete share common interests.")

[31] When all variables are singular, the semantics is a simple adaptation of the semantics of Brown 1984. He shows there that a wide range of quantifiers are interpretable. (However, 'only' cannot be treated as a quantifier word on this approach.)

The distinction between two distinct plural universals also enables us to note an interesting relationship. The following is true whenever it is not anomalous:

(32) $[\Lambda^{\exists}X\colon GX]\ [\forall Y\colon GY]\ YAX$

(The students that are "all students" are students X such that, no matter what students Y you pick, Y are among X.) (33), however, is not in general true:

(33) $[\forall X\colon GX]\ [\Lambda^{\exists}Y\colon GY]\ YAX$

(It is not generally true that, no matter what students you pick, all students are among them.)[32] This is to be expected, since the first argument place of *among* is (strongly) distributive but the second is not.

The kind of definition just given for $\forall$ can serve as a more general source for quantifier expressions, the duals of the quantifier expressions that we introduce directly. This enables us to add quantifiers with properties that the basic quantifiers do not have.[33] The extent to which other duals of our basic quantifiers play a role in natural language sentences with non-distributive plurals remains to be explored.[34] For example, one other quantifier that might be defined is 'few'. There seem to be at least two different semantically basic concepts, *almost all* (proportional)

---

[32] We can also note that the following is always true:

$[\Lambda X\colon GX]\ [\Lambda Y\colon GY]\ YAX.$

But the following is not, in general, true:

$[\forall X\colon GX]\ [\forall Y\colon GY]\ YAX.$

[33] We will explore some examples in Ch. 4.

[34] I believe that in Lewis 1991, $\exists$ and $\forall$ are the only plural quantifiers explicitly employed in the discussion. However, this is largely because Lewis sticks to a more narrowly regimented version of English, something like the language used in giving our semantics. So instead of having sentences like

(i) Seven students are surrounding the building.

in Lewis's usage we would say

(ii) Some students are surrounding the building, and they are seven in number.

This is unobjectionable. Indeed, (ii) is our semantic account of (i), and so we could limit ourselves to this more austere language (with an existential quantifier and with non-proportional and proportional numerical predicates and relations) and say the same things as with the full range of quantifiers. I choose to develop a formal language that includes more quantifiers and so models more of what is available in ordinary English in a direct way. (I profited from a conversation with David Lewis on these matters.)

and *more than a few* (non-proportional) that could be used to define different concepts of *few*. 'Few G are H':

> Almost all G are non-H.
> It is not the case that more than a few G are H.

'Almost all' is a directly specifiable proportional quantifier. The quantifier 'more than a few' is directly specifiable within the context of our semantics, as a non-proportional quantifier, given that we can specify (in any particular context for a semantics) how many are more than a few. (Note also that the quantifier 'a few', with the meaning *at least a few*, is already directly interpretable as a non-proportional quantifier.)

Some other defined quantifiers will arise in the context of further discussion of natural language examples, and the formal language will provide us with ways of representing the propositional content of the natural language examples. Obviously more would need to be said to get a fully integrated theory of how these propositions relate to English syntax. In Chapter 4 we explore a number of issues, indicating in more detail how we interpret quantifiers, how we deal with distributive predication, and how our semantics relates to some particular issues in the interpretation of natural language. We will not provide a fully integrated theory of natural language plurals and quantifier words. Rather, we use natural language examples to illustrate the expressive resources of this plural first-order language.

4

Natural Language Issues

When a stone rolls down a bumpy hill, the laws of physics apply and determine its precise trajectory, but it is not always easy for us to apply them. But we can learn from the effort. Our formal semantics tells us how to interpret sentences with non-distributive predications, but we understand it better when we see how to represent more examples in ordinary language, where many special considerations make interpretation difficult.

DISTRIBUTIVE CORRELATES

Non-distributive predicates often have distributive correlates. We can express this most clearly by adding something like 'involved in' in English. Thirty students (including John) surrounded the building; John did not surround the building, of course; but John was involved in surrounding the building. The predicate 'X were involved in surrounding the building' is distributive but 'X surrounded the building' is not. Three people lifted the piano together. Did Alice lift the piano? Well, she was involved in lifting the piano, but she didn't lift it by herself.

One thing that confounds our intuitions in the exploration of plural predication is the fact that we can often shift from a non-distributive interpretation of a predicate to a distributive one without an explicit lexical signal like 'involved in'.

> (1) Four students are meeting in the library and discussing a physics project, and five students are meeting in the library and planning a demonstration. At least seven students who are meeting in the library are women.

In the last sentence of (1), we need to take 'are meeting' in a distributive way, even though it is not distributive in the first sentence. It is not true that seven students are meeting (*non-distributive*, i.e., *together*) in the library. The largest meeting mentioned involves five people. But there may be seven students involved in meeting there, since there is more than one meeting.

It may be useful to indicate that a predicate and its distributive correlate are related. To do so we can mark the distributive correlate with a superscripted 'd'.

(2) Four students are meeting in the library, discussing a physics project.

(3) Seven students meeting^d in the library are women.

(2a) $[4X: SX]$ $(MX \wedge X$ are discussing a physics project).

(3a) $[7X: SX \wedge M^d X]$ WX

The non-distributive predicate and its distributive correlate are semantically related but distinct predicates. (Some individuals J are discussing a physics project only if each of J is discussing^d, i.e., is involved in discussing, a physics project. For any predicate P, $P^d y$ iff $[\exists X: yAX]$ PX.)

'AT LEAST', 'AT MOST', AND 'EXACTLY'

The approach we have developed provides a satisfying account of numerical statements. Consider:

(4) Five classmates moved a piano together.

A *bare numerical* statement like that allows the possibility that either of these is also true:

(5) Three classmates moved a piano together.
(6) Seven classmates moved a piano together.

(4) does not imply either of these statements or their negations, because the numerical element of the claim is governed by an existential in the semantics. We have a semantics that indicates that (4) could be paraphrased in the following equivalent ways:

(4a) $[5X: CX]$ MX
(4b) $[\exists X: X$ are 5 in number and $CX]$ MX

When we turn to sentences with 'at least n', however, it is less clear how we should take the English sentences.

(7) At least five classmates moved a piano.

(8) At least five students moved a piano.

(9) At least five people who moved a piano are women.

I find that my first instinct is to seek a distributive reading relative to the predicate '... moved a piano'. There are two distributive readings available:

(7a) At least five classmates are such that each of them moved a piano.

(7a1) $[5X: X \text{ are classmates}] [\forall y: yAX]$ y moved a piano

(7a2) $[\exists X: X \text{ are classmates and } X \text{ are at least 5 in number}]$ $[\forall y: yAX]$ y moved a piano

(7b) At least five classmates are such that each of them was involved in moving a piano.

(7b1) $[5X: X \text{ are classmates}] [\forall y: yAX]$ $(y \text{ moved a piano})^d$

(7b2) $[\exists X: X \text{ are classmates and } X \text{ are at least 5 in number}]$ $[\forall y: yAX]$ $(y \text{ moved a piano})^d$

(7a) is the ordinary distributive reading, and (7b) substitutes the distributive correlate for the main predicate of the sentence. Our semantics provides a non-distributive reading as well, which we could paraphrase as follows:

(7c) $[\exists X: X \text{ are at least 5 in number and } CX]$ X moved a piano

This seems to be a third possible reading for (7). Note that this non-distributive reading (7c) still allows the possibility that two classmates moved a piano (together). That seems possible, since there can be more than one moving that takes place.[1]

English sentences with *at most n* seem to have a more global implication, however.

(10) At most five classmates moved a piano.

As with (7), two distributive readings (of 'moved a piano') are available, and those have the usual implications: *at most 5* implies *at most 7*, it is consistent with *at most 3* but does not imply it. However, as I understand

---

[1] Schein has argued that we need quantification over events in dealing with plurals. Perhaps that would solve the problem by differentiating events of piano-moving, but I would like to solve it without introducing an event parameter, in so far as possible. I think that the central phenomena of plurality are independent of the issues that arise in the introduction of an event parameter (cf. Ch. 10).

it, the non-distributive version of (10) has an implication that does not correspond to any implication of (7). With a non-distributive reading of the argument place in *X moved a piano*, (10) implies that it is not the case that seven classmates moved a piano (together). It says something about all other moving that went on. This is reflected in our treatment of this quantifier. It must be defined in terms of *greater than 5*.

(10a) ¬[>5 *X*: C*X*] M*X*
(10b) ¬[∃*X*: *X* are greater than 5 in number and C*X*] M*X*

Either (10a) or (10b) will have the right implications. A direct definition of *at most 5* as in (10*c*) does not work, because it does not have this stronger implication.

(10c) [∃*X*: *X* are at most 5 in number and C*X*] M*X*

What about the following then?

(11) Exactly five classmates moved a piano together.

As with (7) and (10), distributive readings are available. There may also be two non-distributive readings. The first is (4a), the non-distributive version of the bare numerical. This allows that maybe two classmates also moved a piano together and that maybe seven classmates also moved a piano together. There may also be a non-distributive reading that is the conjunction of (7*c*) and (10b).

(11a) [∃*X*: *X* are at least 5 in number and C*X*] M*X* ∧ ¬[∃*X*: *X* are more than 5 in number and C*X*] M*X*

This still allows the possibility that three classmates moved a piano together, but it rules out the possibility that seven classmates moved a piano together. I doubt that there is such a reading of that English sentence, however.

MARKING DISTRIBUTIVE PREDICATION

It is useful to have a way to readily distinguish non-distributive predication from distributive predications. For example, we need a way to mark the ambiguity in sentences like:

(12) Alice, Bob and Carla lifted the table.

(12) can be true in virtue of either a non-distributive or a distributive satisfaction of the predicate. We can distinguish these by saying, for example:

> (13) They lifted the table collectively (together) and did not lift the table distributively (individually).

> (14) They lifted the table distributively (individually) and lifted the table collectively (together).

> (15) They lifted the table distributively (individually) and did not lift the table collectively (together).

Some have introduced ways of marking each argument place with 'C' or 'D' to indicate whether the argument place is to be taken non-distributively or distributively with respect to that use of the predicate.[2]

> (16) $L\lfloor a,b,c\rceil_C \wedge \neg L\lfloor a,b,c\rceil_D$

Using the predicate 'x is among Y' (or 'x is one of Y'), we can also say:

> (17) They lifted the table, but no one person among them lifted it.

> (18) $L\lfloor a,b,c\rceil_C \wedge [\forall x: x$ is a person among $\lfloor a,b,c\rceil_C]\neg Lx$

Even in the case in which they lift the table individually and collectively, we can distinguish those.

> (19) They lifted the table collectively and they lifted the table distributively.

> (20) $L\lfloor a, b, c\rceil_C \wedge L\lfloor a, b, c\rceil_D$

The subscript here indicates how the term is related to the predicate (non-distributively (C) or distributively (D)), it does not create a new term. It should be thought of as a marker on the argument place rather than the term.

With C and D subscripts, we would distinguish two types of relationship that a plural term can have to a predicate.

> '$F\lfloor a, b, c\rceil_C$' will be true iff F applies (non-distributively) to a, b, and c.

> '$F\lfloor a, b, c\rceil_D$' will be true iff F applies to a, F applies to b, and F applies to c.

---

[2] Link 1998, 109ff; Craige Roberts 1990, see 159–62, 215–34 and Roger Schwarzschild 1996, 61–2 introduce such operators on predicates or on argument places.

When we distinguish collective and distributive satisfaction of predicates, this enables us to see how a single term can be the subject of two predicates, one collective and one distributive.

(21) Alice, Bob and Carla are students (D) from different countries (C) who put on gloves (D) and lifted the table (C).

(22) $\lfloor a, b, c \rfloor_D$ are students $\wedge \lfloor a, b, c \rfloor_C$ are from different countries $\wedge \lfloor a, b, c \rfloor_D$ put on gloves $\wedge \lfloor a, b, c \rfloor_C$ lifted the table

Examples of this kind make it clear why we must be able to regard differently subscripted terms as a single term, but with an indication of the distinct relationships to the various predicates. The subscripts must be thought of as attaching to the argument places, not to the terms.

However, we actually have the resources for making this distinction in a better way, without any special operators.

DISTRIBUTION: A BETTER APPROACH

What we have said so far about the difference between D and C readings of predications would lead to the following representations of the quantified sentence:

(23) Some students lifted a table.
Non-distributive reading: (23a) $[\exists X: SX_D]\ [\exists y: Ty]\ LX_C y$
Distributive reading: (23b) $[\exists X: SX_D]\ [\exists y: Ty]\ LX_D y$

But the distributive reading might be thought to represent something with an underlying universal quantifier. Using 'ZAX' for 'Z are among X' (or say 'z is one of X', when z is singular), we can represent the distributive reading without subscripts, in the following way:

(23c) $[\exists X: [\forall z: zAX]\ Sz]\ [\forall z: zAX]\ [\exists y: Ty]\ Lzy$

With such a translation of the distributive subscripts, it would appear that

(24) .... X_D ...

could always be paraphrased as

(25) $[\forall z: zAX]$ .... z ...[3]

---

[3] As long as .... X_D ... is free for 'z'.

thus eliminating the need for the subscripting. Plural quantifiers and variables would always be non-distributive, and singular quantifiers would always indicate distribution. A sentence with a preliminary representation that has a variable occurring in both distributive and non-distributive positions, would be replaced by a sentence that has variables that are linked by the *among* relation.[4]

(26) Some students wore hats and lifted a table.
(26a) $[\exists X: SX_D]\ (HX_D \wedge [\exists y: Ty]\ LX_Cy)$
(26b) $[\exists X: [\forall z: zAX]\ Sz]\ ([\forall z: zAX]\ Hz \wedge [\exists y: Ty]\ LXy)$

On the reading where the lifting is non-distributive (but the wearing of hats is, as usual, distributive), either (26a) or (26b) will adequately represent (26).

When we have two quantifier phrases related in the indicated way, where one is a plural quantifier in a clause $[QX: G]\ H$ and the other is a universal quantifier $[\forall z: zAX]$, and where $[\forall z: zAX]$ is within the scope of the quantifier QX as a part of G or a part of H, let us say that $[\forall z: zAX]$ *distributes* X. We can take a distributing universal quantifier phrase to be an implicit element in an English sentence that includes a quantified distributive predication.

There is an advantage to this approach. If we assume that there is an underlying distributing universal in distributive plurals, we can make a distinction that reflects an ambiguity in the distributive reading of (23).[5] Even when understood distributively, sentence (23) seems to have two readings, depending on the relative scope of the quantifiers. The sentence could say that the students lifted the same table, or it could be uncommitted about whether they lifted the same table. But if we look at (23*b*) only, it will be very difficult to explain this ambiguity. Varying the order of two existential quantifiers ordinarily produces an equivalent sentence. If we look at (23c), though, it is evident what is happening.

(23d) $[\exists X: [\forall z: zAX]\ SX]\ [\exists y: Ty]\ [\forall z: zAX]\ Lzy$

Sentence (23d) is not equivalent to (23c). Changing the relative scope of the quantifier phrases '$[\exists y: Ty]$' and '$[\forall z: zAX]$' will produce the non-equivalent distributive readings of sentence (23).[6]

---

[4] This is the situation when we have separate singular and plural variables. The situation is slightly different in Ch. 6.
[5] Roger Schwarzschild also takes note of a similar ambiguity, Schwarzschild 1996, 61–2, and he notes the key advantages of this approach.
[6] It would amount to the same thing to think of this as shifting the relative scopes of the quantifier complex '$[\exists X: [\forall z: zA\bar{X}]\ SX]\ [\forall z: zAX]$' and the existential quantifier

Our recognition of two distributive readings for (23) also indicates that the subscript notation is not adequate as it stands. We must indicate what the scope of the subscript is, since (23c) and (23d) are not equivalent. Without a scope indication, either of these might correspond to (23b). However, rather than elaborating the subscripting apparatus, it seems that the best approach is to employ it only as a semi-formal intermediate between English and our formal language. When the D subscript occurs in such a semi-formal intermediate, it will indicate that a distributing universal is needed in the formal representation, but will not indicate the scope of that universal. Thus the subscript notation will retain some of the ambiguities that exist in English sentences. I will not make it a part of our formal language.[7] The full formal-language representation of distributive predication will need a distributing universal quantifier.

Since the same kind of ambiguity arises in unquantified cases, we can use a distributing universal there, too.

(27) Alice, Betty and Carlos lifted a table.

(27a) $[\exists y: Ty] \, L\lfloor a, b, c \rceil_C y$

(27b) $[\exists y: Ty] \, L\lfloor a, b, c \rceil_D y$

We can think of (27b) as introducing a distributing universal, in this case $[\forall x: xA\lfloor a, b, c\rceil\,]$, and we have the same ambiguity we had in the quantified case. The two distributive readings would be these:

(27c) $[\forall x: xA\lfloor a, b, c\rceil] \, [\exists y:Ty] \, Lxy$

(27d) $[\exists y:Ty] \, [\forall x: xA\lfloor a, b, c\rceil] \, Lxy$

We can see this as scope variation only by introducing the implicit distributing universal.

Taking this approach, we do not locate the ambiguity in (12) in either the subject term or the predicate. The ambiguity is instead due to whether or not there is a distributing universal quantifier binding an argument position. One lexical feature of a predicate or relation is that certain kinds of argument positions are available to it, i.e., distributing universals may be required, allowed or forbidden.

'$[\exists y: Ty]$' from (23c). This would produce '$[\exists y: Ty] \, [\exists X: [\forall z: zAX] \, SX] \, [\forall z: zAX] \, Lzy$' which is equivalent to (23d).

[7] This approach is like Rayo's (2002) in introducing 'D' to mark distributive cases, but not in the ultimate formal language. Rayo, however, does not discuss the need to associate 'D' with particular argument places, and, more importantly, he does not note the fact that the scope of the distribution will be unclear, thereby producing ambiguities.

X are numerous	The position for *X* must be non-distributive.
X lifted Y	The positions for *X* and for *Y* can be distributive or non-distributive.
X are feline	The position for *X* must be distributive. (*X* are feline iff each of *X* is feline.)

In any particular claim, every argument position (token) is either distributive or non-distributive. A sentence like 'Alice, Bob and Carlos lifted the table' has two different readings, and any use of it involves one meaning or the other. There is no such thing as a neutral use of that sentence, one that is not intended to say whether they lifted the table individually or together, just as there is no neutral use of 'The banks are failing,' that is not intended to make a commitment about whether it is river banks or financial institutions that are under discussion. Since natural language sentences do not carry overt markers of distribution (even when the predicate may be either distributive or not), perhaps it would be formally viable to allow for unmarked, neutral interpretations. The claims made would be true if either the distributive or non-distributive interpretation for the argument position yields a true sentence. It seems to me, however, that this is a genuine ambiguity with no neutral interpretation possible in ordinary language, and the formal system will accord with that. Someone who uses 'Alice, Bob and Carla lifted the table' to make an assertion intends one interpretation, distributive or non-distributive. (This is at variance with Scha 1981 and others who have suggested that we should account for such neutral interpretations.)[8]

Marking distributive readings with a distributing universal has a consequence. When we represent distributive predications, we will write sentences in our formal language that are not very much like the sentences of English that they would correspond to. The formal sentences will explicitly contain distributing universals that are implicit in the English.

(28) Some students are tall.

(28a) $[\exists X: [\forall y: y \mathrel{A} X] \mathrel{S} X] \, [\forall y: y \mathrel{A} X] \mathrel{T} X$

The situation here, though, is not much worse than the situation with ordinary quantification. An ambiguous English sentence like

(29) Many doctors treat some patients

---

[8] See Scha 1981, Link 1998, 54–9, and van der Does, 1993, for discussions of this. I take the same ultimate position as Link, but my reasons are somewhat different.

fails to explicitly represent the scope relations of the two quantifier phrases, and so our formal representation must have some features that are different from the English. In particular, in our formal representation, we put the quantifiers in front of the predicates and relations (and more complex compounds) where we can indicate their scope relations independently of indicating their thematic roles (subject, object, etc.) within the sentence.

(29a) [Many x: Dx] [∃y: Py] x treats y
(29b) [∃y: Py] [Many x: Dx] x treats y

In this way, our formalization differs from the way quantifier phrases appear in simple English sentences, where position ordinarily indicates thematic role, but where quantifier subordination relations are often not clearly indicated by the syntax.

When we make non-distributive plural predication the "unmarked" case, we must recognize implicit distributing universals in what we have previously seen as ordinary, quantification with distributive predicates.[9] But there seems to be no sound, non-singularist way of developing an adequate representation of plurals and non-distributive predication if we start with distributive predication only.

This approach to distribution also avoids Landman's objection to accounts of plurals that employ the same subject in both distributive and non-distributive predications.[10] He considers views that assign a composite object to plural subjects, and then points out that such views must then introduce a special meaning postulate to derive the distributive reading of a predication. If we consider a sentence like 'Alice, Betty and Carla are singing', then the distributive reading requires the additional postulate that on one of its meanings, 'X are singing' is equivalent to 'each [individual] part [or element] of X is singing'. This, he points out, means that there is a mismatch between the syntactic subject of predication (the composite individual) and the actual agents of the action (the parts or elements). He concludes that then "**there cannot be any semantic content to the notion of agent at all**" (bold-face is Landman's emphasis), if one takes this approach.

Our approach has no such liability. Even if a sentence like 'X are singing' or 'X moved the table' has multiple interpretations, both interpretations still have the right subjects for the predication, some things

---

[9] Tense and aspect are also often thought to be properly represented by implicit quantifiers.

[10] Landman 2000, 167–8.

(together) in the non-distributive case and the individuals (separately) in the distributive case.

⌊a, b, c⌋ are singing (in three-part harmony)

[∀x: x is among ⌊a, b, c⌋] x is singing (in the shower)

No special semantic postulates are needed, and the "correct" individuals are semantically associated with the satisfaction of the predicate. In addition, we can represent sentences in which a plural subject term figures in both distributive and non-distributive predication:

Alice, Betty and Carla are children and are singing in three-part harmony.

[∀x: x is among ⌊a, b, c⌋] Cx ∧ S⌊a, b, c⌋

INTERMEDIATE DISTRIBUTIONS AND COLLECTIVE OBJECTS?

Our approach allows for non-distributive cases and cases in which a property is distributed over the individuals who are said to (plurally) have that property. Some people have suggested that there are intermediate distributions, but many of the examples offered simply seem implausible. We cannot use "Seven students moved a table" to describe a situation in which several overlapping groups of students moved a table (groups of three, four and five, say) and the total number of students involved in the various table-movings is seven. At least we cannot do it without very special context. Any such special context is better seen as a context that leads us to understand 'moved' as a distributive correlate 'were at some time involved in moving'. Then the distribution is to the individuals, not some intermediate groups.

Roger Schwarzschild, however, has a more plausible example (Schwarzschild 1996, 67–8). Consider a situation in which a produce seller has only two scales, one gray and one black. The gray one is very refined and will weigh only small amounts – individual spears of asparagus, but not ordinary bunches. The black one is suitable for weighing large crates of vegetables that wholesalers bring in, but not smaller amounts. When considering the prospect of making retail sales, we might say:

(30) The vegetables are too heavy for the gray scale and too light for the black one.

In this case, however, I would argue that the sentence is not literally true. The gray scale is fine for weighing a vegetable; the black scale is fine for weighing (larger crates of) the vegetables. (30) will be correct only if we understand "The vegetables" as standing for "The retail portions of vegetables." With that understanding, the retail portions of vegetables are the individuals under discussion, and the sentence will have an ordinary interpretation.

(30a) [The X: VX_D][$\forall y$: y is among X] (y is too heavy for the gray scale and y is too light for the black scale)[11]

The predicate 'VX_D' can be interpreted as "each of X is an ordinary retail portion of vegetables." If this is a plausible interpretation, then this example does not show a need to make a place for intermediate distributions.

One might worry that allowing for this kind of group formation (retail portions) opens the door to the singularism that we are trying to avoid. That would be a mistake. I do not wish to deny that committees, flocks of geese, decks of cards, and retail portions of vegetables exist. The view being developed here is that when we predicate something non-distributively of some Fs, the semantics for such a predication does not in general require that there is some single thing to which all the Fs are related (a group, collection, set or sum) that is the true subject of predication. We can allow that committees, flocks, decks and retail portions are all individuals that are fit subjects of predication without any way compromising that semantic claim. Sentence (30a) predicates a property of some individuals – ordinary retail portions of vegetables – that have parts or elements. To challenge my semantic view, we would need arguments that show that non-distributive plural predications must be understood systematically as predications involving sets or other generally available, topic-neutral collections. If (30) were illustrative of a general need for collecting, rather than a particular case

---

[11] There are other possible interpretations that might be represented in one of these ways:

[The X: VX_D][Qy: y is among X] (y is too heavy for the gray scale and y is too light for the black scale)

[The X: VX_D] ([Qy: y is among X] y is too heavy for the gray scale and [Qy: y is among X] y is too light for the black scale)

Where Q is replaced by a quantifier representing *some*, *many*, or *most*.

of lexical shorthand ('vegetables' for 'retail portions of vegetables'), it would pose a challenge.[12]

Another approach to this example is also available within the general framework that we are developing. Rather than using a distributive predicate 'VX_D' that means that each of X is a retail portion of vegetables, we could employ a non-distributive predicate 'PX' that means "X are retailable". If the context clearly indicates that we are talking about vegetables that are retailable, then we can represent (30) in the following way:

(30b) [$\forall X$: PX] (X are too heavy for the gray scale and X are too light for the black scale).

This approach is like Schwarzschild's, except that his focus on examples involving definite descriptions has led him to require that 'P' represents a property that partitions or "covers" X.[13] There is no need for that. As long as context indicates that vegetables X satisfying 'PX' are the focus, there is no reason why we couldn't similarly say:

(31) Some vegetables are too heavy for the gray scale and too light for the black one.

and mean

(31a) [$\exists X$: PX] (X are too heavy for the gray scale and X are too light for the black scale)

Such a claim would not suggest (and certainly not require) that 'P' partitions or covers the vegetables.

Another example, discussed in Landman 2000, 160ff, is worth considering in this regard. He says that it "may seem that we want to distribute in these cases, but not all the way down to the individuals."[14] Suppose that, speaking of a deck of cards, we say:

(32) The cards below seven and the cards from seven up are separated.

---

[12] Cf. Ch. 2, 42–5.

[13] P covers X iff for each thing y among X, there are some things Z such that y is among Z and 'PZ' is true. P partitions X iff P covers X and for any Y and Z among X, if 'PY' and 'PZ' are true, then Y are among Z, Z are among Y, or Y and Z are disjoint.

[14] Landman 2000, 160. Landman also considers this example in Landman 1989, but with some other goals in mind there.

Clearly we cannot simply take that to be the following monadic, plural predication:

(32a) Separated ⌊the cards below 7, the cards from 7 up⌉

since ⌊the cards below 7, the cards from 7 up⌉ are the same cards as ⌊the cards below 10, the cards from 10 up⌉, but we do not want to say that the cards below ten and the cards from ten up are separated. There are several ways to interpret (32), all needing to consider the fact that 'separated' is not simply a monadic predicate of some things. To say

(33) They are separated

of several individuals, without further context, is very odd. The only way to interpret it without context would be to understand (33) to be saying that each of them is separated from each other of them. But that interpretation is not relevant to the example at hand (at least not directly).

One might understand (32) as the predication of a plural dyadic relation, with *the cards below 7* as one term and *the cards from 7 up* as another term. This invites no confusion with *the cards below 10* and *the cards from 10 up*, since those would just be entirely different terms in a dyadic relation in the sentence

(34) The cards below ten and the cards from ten up are separated.

So that analysis would not raise the concerns indicated here.[15]

Landman's concerns here apply only if we treat '*X* are separated' as a monadic predication of some things. However, for us to do that, there must be something in the context that indicates *how* the things are separated (if the separation is not to be understood as a pairwise complete separation relative to the individuals in the group). '*X* are separated' is not a complete monadic predicate. In (32), the phrase 'The cards below seven and the cards from seven up' indicates what kind of separation the cards have undergone, not merely what has been separated. It is still the cards that are so separated.[16] Thus this example does not contribute to a compelling case for the existence of intermediate, group distribution.

---

[15] Without further account, this analysis might raise other concerns, like those posed for the dyadic analysis of plurals considered early in Ch. 2.

[16] Essentially this answer is embedded in the fuller discussion of "reciprocal" predicates (like 'separated') in Schwarzschild 1992.

It is a more complicated predication of the cards; they are separated so that those below 7 are separated from those from 7 up.

Finally, one might take 'separated' as a dyadic relation of individuals, with the seemingly monadic predication of pluralities defined in terms of that.

(35) The cards X that are below 7 and the cards Y from seven up are such that each of X is separated from each of Y.

(36) $[\imath X: CX_D \wedge <7 X_D] [\imath Y:CY_D \wedge \geq 7 Y_D] [\forall x: xAX]$
$[\forall y: yAY]\, Sxy$[17]

This predicates the following (non-distributive) relation between the cards X below seven and the cards Y from seven up: $[\forall x: xAX] [\forall y: yAY]\, Sxy$.[18] No similar relation needs to hold between the cards below ten and the cards from ten up for (35) to be true.

We have adequate resources for dealing with this example while still treating this as a sentence about cards rather than about groups.

MULTIPLE QUANTIFICATION

As we noted earlier, we will also want to be able to write and interpret sentences involving multiple quantification. We have already looked at some examples, but it is worth seeing some of the other cases that can arise.

(37) Two cowboys (together) circled some wagons around a campfire.

(37a) $[2X: CX_D][\exists Y: WY_D] [\exists z: Fz]\, EXYz$

(37b) $[2X: [\forall y: yAX]\, Cy][\exists Y: [\forall z: zAY]\, Wz] [\exists z: Fz]\, EXYz$

(We use (37a) as an intermediate step to (37b), our ultimate representation of the (37).)

---

[17] The '$\imath$', the definite description quantifier, will be discussed in detail in Chs. 7 and 8.

[18] One might suspect that this dyadic analysis is subject to the problems discussed in connection with the dyadic analysis of 'meeting together' early in Ch. 2. However, 'are separated' and 'are meeting together', as dyadic predicates of individuals, have different logical properties that are relevant. We do not have an analysis analogous to (36) for "The boys and the girls were meeting together," for example. We need the monadic plural predicate in the case of meeting.

(38) Two cowboys (each) circled some wagons around a campfire.

(38a) $[2X: CX_D][\exists Y: WY_D]\ [\exists z: Fz]\ EX_D Yz$

(38b) $[2X: [\forall y: yAX]\ Cy]\ [\forall w: wAX]\ [\exists Y: [\forall z: zAY]\ Wz]\ [\exists z: Fz]\ EwYz$[19]

Because of the kind of compound terms we have introduced, we can have multiple quantification even in the case in which the main predicate of a sentence is monadic. Two variables can occur in a single compound term.

(39) Three boys and four girls are meeting together.

(39a) $[3X: BX_D][4Y: GY_D]\ M\lfloor X,\ Y\rceil$

(39b) $[3X: [\forall z: zAX]\ Bz][4Y: [\forall z: zAY]\ GY]\ M\lfloor X,\ Y\rceil$

(This interprets (39) as saying that there was a single meeting involving three boys and four girls. Sentence (39) might also have this interpretation:

(39d) $[3X: BX_D]\ MX \wedge [4Y: GY_D]\ MY$

(39e) $[3X: [\forall z: zAX]\ Bz]\ MX \wedge [4Y: [\forall z: zAY]\ GY]\ MY$

where there are two separate, gender-uniform meetings.) A corollary of this is that a distributing universal may be connected with more than one quantifier, if two quantifiers bind variables within a conjunctive term.

(40) Most (of the) men and several women tasted tequila.

(40a) $[\mu X: [\forall y: y\ A\ X]\ My]\ [\sigma Z: [\forall y: yAZ]\ Wy]\ [\forall y: yA \lfloor X,\ Y\rceil]Ty$

Compare this with the case in which the main verb is non-distributive.

(41) Most (of the) men and several women gathered around the bar.

(41a) $[\mu X: [\forall y: y\ A\ X]\ My]\ [\sigma Z: [\forall y: yAZ]\ Wy]\ G\lfloor X,\ Y\rceil$

CUMULATIVE READINGS OF MULTIPLE QUANTIFICATION

Ordinarily our interpretations of multiply quantified sentences can be understood as scoped readings – quantifiers have scope relations.

[19] If we give the universal quantifier smaller scope, then other readings are possible, but those are not plausible in this case.

(42) Many doctors treat some patients.

In order to interpret this, we must determine the relative scopes of the quantifiers.

(42a) [Many x: Dx] [$\exists y$: Py] Txy
(42b) [$\exists y$: Py] [Many x: Dx] Txy

The sentence is ambiguous, with either scope relationship a possibility. Sometimes the scope relations are not semantically significant because varying the scope simply produces logically equivalent sentences (as when we have two existential quantifiers).

However, some multiply quantified sentences, especially some involving two numerical quantifiers, have a reading that seems to require that the quantifiers have independent scope.

(43) Three doctors treated seven patients.

(43) actually has many scoped interpretations (eight, two of which are equivalent) depending on whether we take the argument places in 'X treated Y' distributively or non-distributively, and depending on how we vary the scope of quantifiers. But even with all that, there is an additional natural reading – that (in the situation under discussion) the total number of doctors treating patients is three and the total number of patients treated is seven.

(43a) [3 X: DX_D] [$\exists Y$: PY_D] TXY $\wedge$ [7Y: PY_D] [$\exists X$: DX_D] TXY

Taking the argument places in TXY non-distributively, (43a) is equivalent to the straight non-distributive quantification, no matter what the scope of the numerical quantifiers is.

(43b) [3 X: DX_D] [7Y: PY_D] TXY
(43c) [7Y: PY_D] [3 X: DX_D] TXY

The following are equivalent for the quantifiers that our semantics interprets directly:

(44) [QX: DX] [$\exists Y$: PY] TXY $\wedge$ [Q'Y: PY] [$\exists X$: DX] TXY
(45) [QX: DX] [Q'Y: PY] TXY
(46) [Q'Y: PY] [QX: DX] TXY

Thus it might seem that we have no need to make a special accommodation for these cumulative readings. If we understand the *treatment* relation as one that is being said to hold between three doctors and seven patients, then we do not need any special handling for the quantifiers, as long as we stick to our fundamental quantifiers. However, there are two complications, one involving the understanding of the *treatment* relation, and the other involving the introduction of other quantifiers.

In (43b) and (43c), we take treatment as a relation of three doctors to seven patients. We might instead regard (43) as a sort of daily (hourly, or whatever) summary, where it gives us totals for a number of separate treatment events. If those treatment events can involve multiple doctors and can involve multiple patients (two doctors together treating one patient, the twins with the measles being treated together by one doctor, etc.), then we might want to represent (43) as a statement about what happened in a number of cases, all tolled. If so, then it would seem that we want something like this pattern for unscoped quantification in $[nX: DX]\ [mY: PY]\ TXY$ (in the general case):

$$(47)\quad [nX: DX]\ [\forall x: xAX]\ [\exists V: VAX](xAV \wedge [\exists Y: PY]\ TVY)\ \wedge$$
$$[mY: PY]\ [\forall y: yAY]\ [\exists W: WAY]\ (yAW \wedge [\exists X: DX]\ TXW)$$

This allows that there were n doctors (total), even if they always acted individually or in teams of two in treating patients, and that there were m patients (total), even if they were treated individually or in pairs. If instead we assume that *treatment* is distributive in both argument places (all treatment is one-on-one), then this simplifies to:

$$(48)\quad [nX: DX][\forall x: xAX][\exists y: Py]\ Txy \wedge [mY: PY][\forall y: yAY][\exists x: Dx]\ Txy^{20}$$

The other complication occurs because for defined quantifiers, such as *at most n*, we also have cumulative readings, but the equivalences cited in connection with (43) do not hold. For example, in discussing the early trials of an experimental treatment, we might say:

(49) At most five doctors treated at most 30 patients.

There is clearly an unscoped, cumulative reading (that the total number of doctors is at most five and the total number of patients treated is at most 30). The scoped readings differ from that.

---

[20] In $[\forall x: xAX]\ [\exists V: VAX]\ (xAV \wedge [\exists Y: PY]\ TVY)$, the quantification over 'V' can drop out if the first argument place in TXY distributes, and $[\exists Y: PY]\ TxY$ will gain a distributing quantifier, producing $[\exists Y: PY]\ [\forall y: yAY]\ Txy$, which makes it equivalent to the simpler $[\exists y: Py]\ Txy$.

(49a) $\neg[>5X: DX_D] \neg[>30Y: PY_D]$ TXY
(49b) $\neg[>30Y: PY_D] \neg[>5X: DX_D]$ TXY

(49a) says that at most five doctors have this feature: they treated at most thirty patients. That means that if you consider some doctors who are six in number, say, then those doctors (collectively) treated more than 30 patients. That is not what we want for the cumulative reading of (49). Similarly, (49b) says that any patients who are more than 30 in number were treated by more than five doctors.

The cumulative reading is correctly captured as in (43a) (where we take *treatment* as a single relation between doctors and patients).

(49c) $\neg[>5X: DX_D] [\exists Y: PY_D]$ TXY $\wedge \neg[>30Y: PY_D] [\exists X: DX_D]$ TXY

Where we regard this as a summary of many treatments, we can use the more complicated form (based on (47)):

(49d) $\neg[>5X: DX_D] [\forall x: xAX] [\exists V: VAX] (xAV \wedge [\exists Y: PY_D]$ TVY) $\wedge$

$\neg[>30Y: PY_D] [\forall y: yAY] [\exists W: WAY] (yAW \wedge [\exists X: DX_D]$ TVW)

Thus we have ways of representing the semantic content of the cumulative readings of such sentences. (We have not indicated why such readings exist, i.e., how they are systematically generated in English. That is a project that I leave for linguists.)

RELATIONSHIP BETWEEN SINGULAR AND PLURAL QUANTIFICATION

It is worth noting the relationship between singular and plural quantification in simple sentences with monadic, distributive predicates. Consider:

(50) Most dogs bark.

We now have two ways of representing that:

(51) $[\mu x: Dx]$ Bx
(52) $[\mu X: [\forall z: zAX] Dz] [\forall z: zAX]$ Bz

Although the sentences look different, they are semantically equivalent.

If we can ignore the complication of semantic anomaly, which is not relevant in this kind of case, our semantics for quantified sentences can be this:

Singular quantification: $\mathbf{C}$, $\mathbf{P}$, $\mathbf{R}$ $|= [Qv: H]$ G iff some individuals I are v-satisfiers$_{C,P,R}$ of G, some individuals J are the v-satisfiers$_{C,P,R}$ of H, and I are $\mathbf{Q}$ of J.

Plural quantification: $\mathbf{C}$, $\mathbf{P}$, $\mathbf{R}$ $|= [Qv: H]$ G iff some things I are such that $\mathbf{C}$, $\mathbf{P}$, $\mathbf{R}v/I |= $ G, some things J are such that J are the v-satisfiers$_{C,P,R}$ of H, and I are $\mathbf{Q}$ of J.

(Since these are distributive predications and there are no issues about semantic anomaly, we can use the semantic analysis of the proportional quantifier. Given these restrictions, that analysis applies to both types of quantification.) With these definitions, to show that (51) and (52) are equivalent, it suffices to show that, in general, the x-satisfiers of Fx are the same individuals as the X-satisfiers of $[\forall y: yAX]$ Fy, if F is a distributive predicate.

Proof Suppose that F is distributive.
I are *the* x-satisfiers$_{C,P,R}$ of Fx iff

every individual i among I is an x-satisfier$_{C,P,R}$ of Fx, and every x-satisfier$_{C,P,R}$ of Fx is among I iff

I are X-satisfiers$_{C,P,R}$ of $[\forall y: yAX]$ Fy, and whenever some things J are X-satisfiers$_{C,P,R}$ of $[\forall y: yAX]$ Fy, J are among I iff

I are *the* X-satisfiers$_{C,P,R}$ of $[\forall y: yAX]$ Fy.

A PROBLEM WITH CONJOINED TERMS

In Chapter 1 we indicated that there is a problem about the nature of conjoined terms. Let's make it completely explicit what that problem is and how our analysis deals with it. Consider:

(53) Alice and Betty are tall.
(54) Alice and Betty are classmates.

Although logicians traditionally analyzed (53) as (an ellipsis for) sentence conjunction, the use of *and* in (54) cannot derive from sentence conjunction. Furthermore, we can have a single compound subject with a conjoined predicate:

(55) Alice and Betty are tall and are classmates.

It seems very implausible to suppose that the subject terms in (53) and (55) are different, and the compound character of the subject term in (55) cannot be derived from sentence conjunction (for the same reason that it cannot for (54)). Thus many linguists and philosophers have pointed out a problem for the conjunctive analysis of (53).[21]

Some sentences, however, are ambiguous.

(56) Alice and Betty moved the table.

So we need to have two semantic analyses of the sentence. If this is not a subject ambiguity, then one might expect a predicate ambiguity, with both distributive and non-distributive readings of the predicate possible in this case.[22] There is good reason to think that this is not really an *ambiguity* in the predicate, however, since we can also have sentences like these:

(57) Joan moved the table, Mary moved the table, and later Alice and Betty moved it.

(58) Joan moved the table by herself, and Alice and Betty did it together.

(59) Alice and Betty moved the table, just as Joan did yesterday.

The verb anaphors in (58) and (59) especially make it difficult to see a singular/plural or distributive/non-distributive *ambiguity* in the predicate, since it is treated as a single predicate in (58) and (59).[23] With genuinely ambiguous verbs, one cannot use verb anaphors intending contrasting meanings of the verb, except as a joke.

(60) John cared for Alice, and so did Betty. (John loved her and Alice took care of her.)

---

[21] Massey 1976, 103, Dowty 1986, 98, Schwarzschild 1996, 14–15, Yi 2002, 25–6 (among many others) present similar arguments. Lasersohn 1996, 96–104, and Oliver and Smiley 2000, 294, contain a response to the most obvious attempt to patch up the conjunctive analysis.

[22] Dowty 1986, 98, for example, suggests that it is an ambiguity in the predicate. A plural predication '... are F' is distributive iff whenever some things are F, each of them is F. Otherwise it is non-distributive.

[23] Cf. Moltmann 1997, 52, where she has provided reasons to think that we cannot treat this distinction between distributive and non-distributive readings of a predicate as an ambiguity in the predicate. We can say "Alice, Betty and John lifted the table individually and collectively," and yet it appears that the single use of the predicate would not be consistent with the two modifiers if this difference were an ambiguity. Consideration of this sentence appears also to show (again) that this cannot be an ambiguity in the subject term ("Alice, Betty and John").

(61) On Monday, Arnold bought the farm, and Barnie did too. (Arnold died and Barnie made a real estate purchase.)

(63) Tiger Woods drove 300 yards at the first tee, and later I did (it) in a golf cart going around the course's parking lot.

This is true even when the meanings are related:

(64) On Thursday, Alice married two men and so did Reverend Watson. (Alice got married twice and Reverend Watson officiated at a gay marriage ceremony.)

And conjunction in series is even odd.

(65) On Thursday, Alice married John, Carla married David, and Reverend Watson married Betty and Frank.

But there is nothing odd or humorous about (57), (58) or (59).
A parallel set of considerations apply to quantified sentences.

(66) Some students are concerned (about . . .).

(67) Some students are surrounding Johnson Hall.

(68) Some students are concerned and are surrounding Johnson Hall.

Although the standard semantics for (66) would involve finding things that individually satisfy the predicates *x is a student* and *x is concerned*, that won't work for (67) or (68). And we have a related ambiguity in:

(69) Some students carried a flag.

If the difference between (53) and (54), between (66) and (67), between the two readings of (56), and between the two readings of (69) is not a difference in the semantic nature of the subject term and is not an ambiguity in the predicate, then what is it? It lies in whether there is a distributing universal quantifier associated with a predicate's (or a relation's) argument place. We solve the problems by taking sentences like (54) to be the "unmarked" case – (54) involves a non-distributive predication of a property (*are classmates*) to some things. A sentence like (53) will be more complicated semantically, having a distributing universal quantifier in its semantic analysis. The ambiguity in (56) and (69) is similarly due to the existence of readings that differ in whether or not there is an implicit distributing universal quantifier.

Godehard Link 1998, 51–2 and Roger Swarzschild 1996, 61–2 also take note of the ambiguity in sentences like (56) and (69). Swarzschild mentions it in the context of introducing a distributivity operator D. As he introduces it initially, it will not serve a general enough purpose, since a relation may have both distributive and non-distributive argument places. (*Each student arranged some stones in a circle.*) Without further elaboration, the operator D that he first introduces will apply to the entire clause it governs. Craige Roberts 1990, (159–62, 215–34) and Link 1998, 109ff have versions of the D operator that can be associated with argument places, and so have resources for marking this out, and Schwarzschild also elaborates his account in several ways. Distribution comes after much ado, however. Since for all of them all predication is ultimately singular, one must first construct a predication of a group or sum individual and then re-distribute that to its atomic constituents.[24]

There is no evident reason to employ a special D operator in the ultimate semantic representation rather than having a distributing universal play that role directly. Even if one were reluctant to adopt my non-singularist orientation to non-distributive predication, one could implement the idea of distributing universals within a semantic approach that treats non-distributive plurals as predications of sets or groups of some kind. For example, if you hold that (54) involves reference to a two-element sum-individual of some kind, whereas (53) involves predication of a property to the atomic constituents, then we can use whatever relation holds between atomic constituents and sum-individuals as the basis for formulating a distributing universal. If we use 'xEy' for the relationship that an atomic individual bears to the semantically relevant sum-individual (whether the theory requires that to be membership, atomic part, or something else), then we can represent distribution by a distributing universal. First, consider a non-distributive sentence:

(70) Some classmates are surrounding Johnson Hall.[25]
       [$\exists x$: x is a group & C^*x] R^*xj

[24] Actually, Schwarzschild does not always distribute to atomic constituents. We discussed that earlier in this chapter. Also, see Winter 2000, esp. 60–6, for reasons why only atomic distribution is needed.

[25] We use C^* rather than C because the predicate of the group is generally different than the corresponding predicate of individuals. For example, no set surrounds a building, and although a mereological sum might be thought to surround a building, it can't be a classmate or be classmates. Whatever the process of group formation is, it will require changing the predicate as well as changing the subject.

Plural sentences with distributive predications are then distinguished by the presence of the distributing universal.

(71) Some students are surrounding Johnson Hall.
[∃x: x is a group & [∀y: yEx] Sy] R*xj

(72) Some students are tall.
[∃x: x is a group & [∀y: yEx] Sy] [∀y: yEx] Ty

The presence or lack of distributing universals and the ordinary considerations of quantifier scope then account for relevant differences between sentences and for relevant ambiguities. No special operators are needed; the distributing quantifiers take their place.

The proposal to treat distributive predication as the more complex case, marked by the presence of a distributing universal, might not seem appealing from a traditional perspective. Traditional first-order logic has no means at all for accommodating non-distributive predication, and linguists have generally followed logicians by treating the underlying semantic metalanguage as a fundamentally singularist metalanguage that lacks non-distributive predication. This leads to the requirement for plural predication to be represented by singular predication to sum individuals or sets or groups. If we represent all plural predication by singular predications to groups of some kind (the general practice), then it will not seem at all natural to take plural predication as the basic case, with distributive predication explained by the presence of a distributing universal.

However, I urge that we take non-distributive plural predication and plural quantification as the basic case. If we take our underlying logic or our language for semantical analysis to be one that, like English, allows non-distributive plural predication, we eliminate layers of artifice from the semantics of plurals. Distribution is represented by a quantifier, and the ordinary facts about quantifier scope account for the ambiguity in (56) and (69) as well as the other facts about distribution.[26]

The simpler and intuitively satisfying solution to the problems associated with non-distributive plural predication are an important consideration in favor of this reorientation. Rather than changing the subject (from some students to a group, for example) and correlatively changing the predicate, we incorporate non-distributive predication in a fundamental way.

---

[26] Rayo 2002 presents a similar treatment of distribution.

They are surrounding the building.
They are classmates.
They come from many different countries.
The fugitives are among them.

We understand these perfectly well without translating them into sentences in which 'They' (or 'them') refers to some single thing rather than to more than one. We can then formulate the account of distribution without carrying on an additional process of group formation that really distorts the picture about what the true subjects of predication are.

5

Set Theoretic Semantics

The semantics of Chapter 3 provides a systematic interpretation for the sentences of a language with non-distributive predication and plural reference and quantification. The present chapter is not really needed. However, set theory has become so much the semantic standard, that some people will feel more satisfied about the interpretability of plurals when they see a set-theoretic semantics. In addition, a semantics in this form may facilitate some comparisons with related work of others. So I will develop a set-theoretic semantics here; in any case, that will enable us to consider again the limitations of the set-theoretic approach in the case of plurals.

SET THEORETIC REPRESENTATION OF NON-DISTRIBUTIVE PREDICATION

Since we will now allow ourselves reference to sets, there is an obvious semantics for a non-distributive predication like:

(1) Alicia, Betty and Carla are meeting together.
(2) F⌊a, b, c⌉

The sentence (2) is true iff FX is true relative to an assignment of {Alicia, Betty, Carla} to X. A model will assign a set of sets of individuals to a monadic predicate, its (plural) extension in the model, and we can use 'FX_M' to refer to the set of sets that is the plural extension of the predicate FX in a model M. If a_M, b_M, c_M are the individuals that a model M assigns to terms 'a', 'b' and 'c', then

'F⌊a, b, c⌉' will be true in a model M iff $\{a_M, b_M, c_M\} \in FX_M$.

If Alice, Betty, Carla, Doreen and Ellen surrounded the Chancellor, then {Alice, Betty, Carla, Doreen, Ellen} will be one of the sets whose members jointly satisfy 'X surrounded the chancellor'.[1] The fact that this is a non-distributive predicate means that there is no guarantee that each of the subsets (of a set of surrounders) will be a set of things that jointly satisfy that predicate or that any individual person satisfies that predicate. Even if Alice, Betty, Carla, Doreen and Ellen surrounded the Chancellor, it does not follow that Alice and Betty did. They may have been standing together to the Chancellor's left, for example. And of course it does not follow that Alice did.

This leaves us with a choice to make concerning predicates that are distributive. Since a plural term can occur in a single sentence in both distributive and non-distributive argument positions, and since plural variables will do so as well, we need to be able to give a semantics for distributive and non-distributive predication that allows that. Since the plural extension of a non-distributive predicate is a set of sets, our semantics will work most uniformly if we also make the plural extension of a distributive predicate a set of sets. Consider the predicate Sx, *x is a student* (and the plural SX, *X are students*). In standard (singularist) treatments of first-order logic, a semantics would assign a set of individuals in a model's domain to Sx.[2] If K is such a set of individuals (the set of students) in an ordinary model **M**, then we have two evident possibilities for the plural extension in our semantics. Using SX_M to stand for the plural extension of the predicate in a model **M**:

"Plural-set" interpretation of 'SX': SX_M would be $\wp(K) - \{\emptyset\}$

"Unit-set" interpretation of 'SX': If a, b, c, . . . are the members of K, then SX_M would be $\{\{a\}, \{b\}, \{c\}, . . .\}$

Either choice provides us with a set of sets as the extension of 'X are students'.

The plural-set option might seem natural, since every subset of a set of students is also a set of students. However, there is good reason to prefer the unit-sets (singletons) choice for the interpretation of sentences with names and without quantifiers.

As we have seen, some predicates allow for satisfaction either by a single individual or by several individuals. 'X lifted the table' can

---

[1] Although availing ourselves of set-theoretic resources, we should not go so far as to say that the set surrounds the Chancellor or even that a set satisfies the predicate 'X surrounded the Chancellor', though the latter may be too tempting to avoid.

[2] Actually, a semantics often assigns a set of one-tuples of individuals to a monadic predicate.

be true of a single (strong) individual or of many (perhaps weaker) individuals (in a joint effort). We need to distinguish distributive and non-distributive plural claims involving such predicates. For example:

(3) Alice, Bob and Carla lifted the table.

can be true in virtue of either a non-distributive or a distributive satisfaction of the predicate. We can distinguish these by saying, for example:

(4) They lifted the table collectively (together) and did not lift the table distributively (individually).

The plural-set choice for the interpretation of non-distributive predicates would have the unfortunate result of leading us to have two ways for the set {a, b, c} to be a member of the extension of 'X lifted the table'. Both their lifting it individually and their lifting it together would be represented by that set's being in the extension of the predicate, and our semantics would provide no way to distinguish importantly different cases. In particular, these cannot be distinguished:

(5) They lifted the table distributively (individually) and lifted the table collectively (together).

(6) They lifted the table distributively (individually) and did not lift the table collectively (together).

In both these cases, {a}, {b}, {c} and {a, b, c} would all be members of the plural extension of the predicate, if we chose the plural-set interpretation for distributive predicates. The unit-set interpretation of distributive satisfaction, though, will distinguish these cases semantically, with {a, b, c} being an element of the extension in models that verify (5) but not so for (6). Thus we will choose the unit-set approach to the interpretation of distributive satisfaction of predicates, and purely distributive predicates will always have a set of singletons as the plural extension.

We also need a way to syntactically mark the distinction between distributive and non-distributive predication in the formal language itself. As we have seen, marking each argument place with 'D' or 'C' to indicate whether the argument place is to be taken distributively or non-distributively with respect to that use of the predicate is not totally clear, unless we introduce ways to indicate the scope of the distributivity. So we continue to use such sentences only as a convenient shorthand, when scope is clear enough.

(7) $L\lfloor a,b,c\rceil_C \land \neg L\lfloor a,b,c\rceil_D$

These subscripts are no part of our formal language. Our better notation is to use the predicate 'x is among Y' (or 'x is one of Y') in a distributing universal quantifier marking the distributive case, thus providing a way to mark the ambiguous scope of the distributing universal:

(8) They lifted the table, but no one person among them lifted it.

(9) $L\lfloor a,b,c\rfloor \wedge [\forall x: x$ is a person among $\lfloor a,b,c\rfloor] \neg Lx$

(10) They lifted the table, but it is not the case that each person among them lifted it.

(11) $L\lfloor a,b,c\rfloor \wedge \neg [\forall x: x$ is a person among $\lfloor a,b,c\rfloor] Lx$

With C and D subscripts, we would distinguish two types of relationship of a plural term to a predicate.

'$F\lfloor a, b, c\rfloor_C$' will be true in a model **M** iff $\{a_M, b_M, c_M\} \in FX_M$

'$F\lfloor a, b, c\rfloor_D$' will be true in a model **M** iff $\{\{a_M\}, \{b_M\}, \{c_M\}\} \subseteq FX_M$

These two relationships are also simple consequences of marking distribution by a distributing universal quantifier.

'$F\lfloor a, b, c\rfloor$' will be true in a model **M** iff $\{a_M, b_M, c_M\} \in FX_M$

'$[\forall x: xA\lfloor a, b, c\rfloor] Fx$' will be true in a model **M** iff $\{\{a_M\}, \{b_M\}, \{c_M\}\} \subseteq FX_M$ (i.e., iff each of $\{a_M\}, \{b_M\}, \{c_M\} \in FX_M$).

In general, a model will interpret an n-place predicate as a set of n-tuples of sets of items in the domain. So if the only liftings represented in a model **J** are these

Seven students (together) lifted Bernie.
Carlos lifted Bernie.
Alice lifted three tables (at once)

then the interpretation in **J** would be a set including these three pairs:

$\langle\{s1, s2, \ldots, s7\}, \{Bernie\}\rangle$
$\langle\{Carlos\}, \{Bernie\}\rangle$
$\langle\{Alice\}, \{t1, t2, t3\}\rangle$

(Here 'sn' stands in for a name of a particular student in the model, and 'tn' for the name of a particular table.)

QUANTIFIERS

The simplest kind of quantified sentence for us is a sentence involving only non-distributive predicates.

Seven classmates are meeting (together).

'$[7X: CX]$ FX' is true in a model **M** iff some set S is such that $S \in F_M$ and $S \in 7_M(C_M)$.[3] (The members of S are meeting together and the members of S are seven classmates.)

Here '7_M' stands for a function that selects the seven-membered sets that are members of the set it applies to. (For any set k, $7_M(k) \subseteq k$, every member of $7_M(k)$ has seven members, and every seven-membered member of k is a member of $7_M(k)$.)

We must allow for multiple quantification, and that requires that we introduce a function **R** that makes assignments to free variables. For plural variables, **R** assigns some set of things to each variable of the language. For a singular variable, **R** will assign a unit set to the variable. To give the semantics for multiple quantification, we must consider alternative ways of assigning sets of individuals to variables, so we need to define:

Rv/s is the assignment to variables that is just like **R** except that it assigns s to v (where v is a variable and s is some non-empty set).

Then we can give the conditions in which a clause is true, relative to a model **M** and an assignment **R** to the variables. (For example, an open sentence 'X are classmates' will be satisfied by an assignment of {Alice, Betty, Carlos} to X iff Alice, Betty and Carlos are classmates, i.e., {Alice, Betty, Carlos} $\in C_M$.)

To interpret quantifiers, we can define the extension of an open sentence in a model, relative to an assignment of a variable, and relative to a particular variable. For example, consider the model **J** (indicated above) and an assignment **R** to variables that assigns {Alice} to X and {Bernie} to Y. The extension of LXY relative to X according to **J** and **R**, $LXY_{J,R,X}$, would be {{s1, s2, . . . , s7}, {Carlos}}, since s1, s2, . . . , s7 lifted Bernie (together) and Carlos lifted Bernie (and that is all), according to the model. $LXY_{J,R,Y}$ would be {{t1, t2, t3}}, since those are the things that Alice lifted (at once). In general, an extension is a set

---

[3] Strictly speaking, $\langle S \rangle \in F_M$.

of sets. For a plural variable ν and a sentence G, we define the extension of G (in model **M** relative to variable-assignment **R**) as follows:

$$E \in G_{M,R,\nu} \text{ iff } M, R\nu/E \models G. \ (G_{M,R,\nu} \subseteq \wp(D)-\{\emptyset\})[4]$$

The quantificationally relevant extension must be defined differently for singular variables, and this is the principal place where the difference between the two kinds of variables will show up. Roughly put (and with the help of brackets), in the case of a singular variable ν, we want $G_{M,R,\nu}$ to include all unit sets of [things that satisfy G] whereas with plural ν, we want all [sets of things] that satisfy G.

The set representing the property of being a student will be a set of (one-tuples of) unit (singleton) sets. Nothing in that set is seven-membered. When we consider a quantificational sentence like 'Seven students are meeting', however, we need semantic access to a seven-membered set of individuals (students). So when ν is a singular variable, we define $G_{M,R,\nu}$ in the following way:

$$E \in G_{M,R,\nu} \text{ iff } E \neq \emptyset, \text{ and } \forall d \in E, M, R\nu/\{d\} \models G. \ (G_{M,R,\nu} \subseteq \wp(D)-\{\emptyset\})$$

Note that we have two things that might be called the *extension* of a distributive predicate F. One is the unit-set interpretation of Fx, a set of singletons that **M** associates with F, F_M. The other is a set of sets of individuals $Fx_{M,R,x}$, where $Fx_{M,R,x} = \wp(\{i: \{i\} \in F_M\})-\{\emptyset\}$. Although we saw good reason to take the unit-set interpretation (F_M) of the extension of a distributive predicate for the purposes of interpreting unquantified sentences, we must also have access to the plural-set interpretation ($Fx_{M,R,x}$) of the extension for the purpose of interpreting quantified sentences.

The easiest way to see why we must give different treatment to the singular and plural variables here, is to think about the difference between these two sentences:

> Seven classmates are meeting (together).
> Seven students are meeting (together).

Seven classmates are classmates together; it is the seven people together who satisfy the predicate 'X are classmates'. The sentence about classmates is true if some seven-membered set is both a set of classmates

---

[4] Note that we allow that $G_{M,R,\nu}$ may be empty, but it is not possible that $\emptyset$ is a member of $G_{M,R,\nu}$.

and a set of people meeting together. But each one is a student. Each satisfies 'x is a student'. A quantifier must select a subset of $G_{M,R,v}$ as its interpretation (the seven-membered sets that are classmates (together) or the seven-membered subsets of the set of students, for example). A quantifier Q in a model **M** (we will write Q_M) selects a subset of $\wp(D)-\{\emptyset\}$. In fact, for any set $k \subseteq \wp(D)-\{\emptyset\}$, $Q_M k \subseteq k$.

Now we are in a position to give the semantics for our basic non-proportional quantifiers, for example, $\exists$ (*some*), κ (*many*), σ (*several*) and simple numericals.[5]

> For variable v, and quantifier Q (from among $\exists$, κ, σ, and the simple numericals (1, 2, etc.)):
>
> **M**, R$|= [QN: G]$ H iff some set s is such that $s \in H_{M,R,v}$ and $s \in Q_M(G_{M,R,v})$.

The universal quantifier $\forall$ will be defined:

> $[\forall v: G]$ H $=$ df$\neg[\exists v: G]$ $\neg$H

Look briefly at how our semantics works for sentences mixing distributive and non-distributive predication.

> Seven students are meeting (together).
>
> $[7X: [\forall y: yAX]$ $Sy]$ MX
>
> **M**, R$|= [7X: [\forall y: yAX]$ $Sy]$ MX iff some set s is such that $s \in MX_{M,R,X}$ and $s\in 7_M([\forall y: yAX]$ $Sy_{M,R,X})$.

Consider the semantics for $[\forall y: yAX]$ Sy.

> **M**, R$|= [\forall y: yAX]$ Sy iff **M**, R $| = \neg[\exists y: yAX]$ $\neg Sy$ iff it is not the case that some set k is such that $k \in \neg Sy_{M,R,y}$ and $k \in \exists_M(yAX_{M,R,y})$.
>
> $k \in \neg Sy_{M,R,y}$ iff $\forall d \in k$, **M**, R$y/\{d\}| = \neg Sy$.
>
> $k \in yAX_{M,R,y}$ iff $\forall d \in k$, **M**, R$y/\{d\}| = yAX$.
>
> $k \in \exists_M(yAX_{M,R,y})$ iff $k\in yAX_{M,R,y}$. (The existential quantifier function on a non-empty set of sets is the identity function.)
>
> **M**, R$| = \neg[\exists y: yAX]$ $\neg Sy$ iff it is not the case that some set k is such that $\forall d \in k$, **M**, R$y/\{d\}| = \neg Sy$ and $\forall d \in k$, **M**, R$v/\{d\}| = yAX$;

---

[5] The quantifiers that are defined here are the basic (existence-entailing) non-proportional quantifiers. Basic (existence-entailing) proportional quantifiers (*most, 1/3, some* interpretations of *all*, for example) will require a separate definition, and we will define additional quantifiers in terms of the basic quantifiers, as in Ch. 3.

i.e., iff no set k is a set of non-students and a set of things among X; i.e., iff no non-student is among X; i.e., iff every individual among X is a student (according $\mathbf{M}$ and $\mathbf{R}$).

$[\forall y: yAX]$ $Sy_{\mathbf{M},\mathbf{R},X}$ is the set of all such sets; i.e., the set of all (non-empty) sets of students. So $7_{\mathbf{M}}([\forall y: yAX]$ $Sy_{\mathbf{M},\mathbf{R},X})$ is the set of all seven-membered sets of students. Thus $\mathbf{M}, \mathbf{R}| = [7X: [\forall y: yAX]$ $Sy]$ MX iff some set s is such that $s \in MX_{\mathbf{M},\mathbf{R},X}$ and $s \in 7_{\mathbf{M}}([\forall y: yAX]$ $Sy_{\mathbf{M},\mathbf{R},X})$; i.e., some set s is a member of the set of sets of individuals meeting together and a member of the set of seven-membered sets of students.

PROPORTIONAL QUANTIFIERS

As we saw in Chapter 3, we must give a different interpretation to proportional quantifiers. "Most (all) jazz musicians" cannot mean "jazz musicians who are most (all) in number." The quantifier indicates a portion (most or all) of some specified reference class of individuals, and so we need to build in the reference to that class. And since there may be no appropriate reference class in the case of some non-cumulative predications, we need to recognize the possibility of semantic anomaly.

When Q is a proportional quantifier, $[QX: AX]$ has an interpretation only when some things are identifiable as "the As". As we noted in Chapter 3, this always happens when A is cumulative, but it may also happen for purely contingent reasons. For example, the sentence

All students meeting together in the next room are wearing hats.

is acceptable when there is only one meeting in the next room, even though it would not be acceptable if there were several separate meetings. As in Chapter 3, we parallel natural language, allow for the syntactic acceptability of such sentences, and provide for cases in which they are semantically anomalous.

Let's identify a condition K that must be fulfilled if semantic anomaly is to be avoided with proportional quantifiers. If G is any clause with plural variable v and extension $G_{\mathbf{M},\mathbf{R},v}$:

K: $\exists S$, $S \in G_{\mathbf{M},\mathbf{R},v}$ such that $\forall S', S' \in G_{\mathbf{M},\mathbf{R},v}, S' \subseteq S$; i.e., $\cup(G_{\mathbf{M},\mathbf{R},v}) \in G_{\mathbf{M},\mathbf{R},v}$.

If Q is a proportional quantifier, then $[QX: GX]$ has a well-defined interpretation relative to a model $\mathbf{M}$ only if $G_{\mathbf{M},\mathbf{R},X}$ fulfills condition

K. Then we can give the semantics for proportional quantifiers like 'all' ($\Lambda^\exists$) and 'most' (μ) as follows:

> If $G_{M,R,\nu}$ fulfills condition K, then
>
> $S \in \Lambda^\exists{}_M (G_{M,R,\nu})$ iff $S \in G_{M,R,\nu}$ and all members of $\cup\, G_{M,R,\nu}$ are in S;
>
> $S \in \mu_M (G_{M,R,\nu})$ iff $S \in G_{M,R,\nu}$ and most members of $\cup\, G_{M,R,\nu}$ are in S.

The general semantic clause governing quantifiers (and, ultimately, other clauses of the semantics) needs to recognize the possibility of semantic anomaly.

> For plural variable ν, and proportional quantifier Q (e.g., $\Lambda^\exists$ and μ), if $G_{M,R,\nu}$ fulfills condition K, then $M, R| = [Q\nu: G]$ H iff some set s is such that $M, R\nu/s | = H$ and $s \in Q_M(G_{M,R,\nu})$.
>
> If ν is plural and $G_{M,R,\nu}$ does not fulfill condition K, then $[Q\nu: G]$ H is semantically anomalous with respect to M and R (when Q is a proportional quantifier).

THE FORMAL LANGUAGE AND SEMANTICS

The syntax is the same as for the formal language of Chapter 3.

A model **M** on a domain **D** will represent some sentences as true. If a sentence has free variables, then it may be represented as true relative to an assignment of values to the variables.

> If c is an individual constant, then $c_M \in \mathbf{D}$.
>
> If P^n is an n-place relation, then $P^n{}_M \subseteq (\wp(\mathbf{D})-\{\varnothing\})^n$.
>
> If Q is a quantifier, then Q_M is a partial function such that for any $E \subseteq \wp(\mathbf{D})-\{\varnothing\}$, $Q_M(E) \subseteq E$ (or Q_M is undefined for E).[6]

To treat quantifiers as part of the logical vocabulary, we must constrain the functions assigned to quantifiers so that for each quantifier word, every **M** assigns the same function to it; e.g., if $E \subseteq \wp(\mathbf{D})-\{\varnothing\}$:

> $S \in \exists_M (E)$ iff $S \in E$. ($\exists_M$ is the identity function.)
>
> $S \in \kappa_M (E)$ iff $S \in E$ and many things are in S.
>
> $S \in \sigma_M (E)$ iff $S \in E$ and several things are in S.

[6] Q_M is undefined if Q is a proportional quantifier and E does not fulfill condition K.

$S \in 7_M$ (E) iff $S \in E$ and seven things are in S.
etc.

For a proportional quantifier, the condition is more complicated.

$S \in \mu_M$ (E) iff $S \in E$, and $\exists S^*$, $S^* \in E$ such that $\forall S'$, $S' \in E$, $S' \subseteq S^*$, and most of S^* are in S; i.e., iff $S \in E$, $\cup(E) \in E$, and most of $\cup(E)$ are in S.

Terms
An interpretation of a term with respect to **M** and a function **R** (that assigns values, non-empty subsets of **D**, to variables) is some non-empty set S such that $S \subseteq D$.
For an individual constant c, if $c_M = d$, then $c_{M,R} = \{d\}$.[7]
For a variable v, $v_{M,R} \subseteq D$. If v is a singular variable, then $v_{M,R}$ is a singleton set.
For a term $\lfloor T_1, \ldots, T_n \rfloor$, $\lfloor T_1, \ldots, T_n \rfloor_{M,R} = T_{1M,R} \cup \ldots \cup T_{nM,R}$.

Clauses
Atomic: **M, R**$\models (B^n \, T_1 \ldots T_n)$ iff $\langle T_{1M,R}, \ldots, T_{nM,R} \rangle \in B^n{}_M$.

M, R $\models T_1 \, A \, T_2$ iff $T_{1M,R} \subseteq T_{2M,R}$.

$\neg$: If G is semantically anomalous with respect to **M** and **R**, then $\neg$G is semantically anomalous. Otherwise, **M, R** $\models \neg$G iff it is not the case that **M, R** $\models$ G.
$\wedge$: If G is semantically anomalous or H is semantically anomalous with respect to **M** and **R**, then (G $\wedge$ H) is semantically anomalous. Otherwise, **M, R** $\models$ (G $\wedge$ H) iff **M, R** $\models$ G and **M, R** $\models$ H.

Singular quantification: For singular variable v and quantifier Q, if G is semantically anomalous or H is semantically anomalous, then [Qv: G] H is semantically anomalous. Otherwise, **M, R** $\models$ [Qv: G] H iff some set s is such that $s \in H_{M,R,v}$ and $s \in Q_M(G_{M,R,v})$.

Plural quantification with non-proportional quantifiers: For plural variable v and non-proportional quantifier Q (for example, $\exists$, κ, σ, and the simple numerals (1, 2, etc.)), if G is semantically anomalous or H

---

[7] Although we can think of an individual constant as referring to an individual, when we evaluate the constant's role in sentences, we must always consider the singleton set containing that individual. This is a peculiarity of this set-theoretic semantics that does not exist in the semantics without set theory.

is semantically anomalous, then [Qv: G] H is semantically anomalous. Otherwise, $\mathbf{M}, \mathbf{R} \models$ [Qv: G] H iff some set s is such that $s \in H_{M,R,v}$ and $s \in Q_M(G_{M,R,v})$.

Plural quantification with proportional quantifiers: For plural variable v, and proportional quantifier Q ($\Lambda^{\exists}$ or μ, for example), if G is semantically anomalous or H is semantically anomalous, then [Qv: G] H is semantically anomalous. Also, if $G_{M,R,v}$ does not fulfill condition K,[8] then [Qv: G] H is semantically anomalous. Otherwise, $\mathbf{M}, \mathbf{R} \models$ [Qv: G] H iff some set s is such that $s \in H_{M,R,v}$ and $s \in Q_M(G_{M,R,v})$.

Closed sentence S: $\mathbf{M} \models$ S (S is true in model $\mathbf{M}$) iff for all $\mathbf{R}$, $\mathbf{M}, \mathbf{R} \models$ S.

Logical truth: S is a logical truth iff for all models $\mathbf{M}$, $\mathbf{M} \models$ S.

RELATIONSHIP BETWEEN SINGULAR AND PLURAL QUANTIFICATION

In Chapter 4 we indicated that it is important to prove that there is a relationship between the two different representations of a simple distributive quantification:

Many dogs bark.
[κx: Dx] Bx
[κX: [∀z: zAX] Dz] [∀z: zAX] Bz

The sentences are semantically equivalent. To show that the two versions of 'Many dogs bark' are equivalent, it suffices to show that these are the same set, for any distributive predicate F:

$Fx_{M,R,x}$
[∀y: yAX] $Fy_{M,R,X}$

Ignoring the complication of semantic anomaly, which is not relevant in this kind of case, our semantics for quantified sentences is this:

$\mathbf{M}, \mathbf{R} \models$ [Qv: G] H iff some set s is such that $s \in H_{M,R,v}$ and $s \in Q_M(G_{M,R,v})$.

---

[8] K: $\exists S, S \in G_{M,R,v}$ such that $\forall S', S' \in G_{M,R,v}, S' \subseteq S$. $(\cup(G_{M,R,v}) \in G_{M,R,v}.)$

The full proof here becomes a bit more cumbersome than the corresponding proof in Chapter 4, but the following outline should suffice. If F is distributive, then $Fx_{M,R,x} = [\forall y: yAX] Fy_{M,R,X}$.

Proof: $S \in Fx_{M,R,x}$ iff $\forall d \in S$, M, $Ry/\{d\} \models Fx$
  iff $\forall d \in S$, $\langle\{d\}\rangle \in F_M$
  iff $S \in [\forall y: yAX] Fy_{M,R,X}$.

THE SET-THEORETIC APPROACH AND THE GOAL OF SEMANTICS

The set-theoretic approach just outlined will lead to paradox if we take it as a very general approach to semantics. Since every quantification requires a set, a sentence such as:

(17) Some things are the non-self-membered sets.

will create a problem. That sentence is true, but the semantics requires that there be a set of non-self-membered sets in order for it to be true. Of course, the formal correlate of it will be true in some models:

(18) $\exists X \forall y (yAX \leftrightarrow (Sy \wedge y \notin y))$

It can be true in a model as long as the set that the semantics requires for the truth of the sentence is not itself a thing in the model (or at least is not something that 'S' applies to in the model). But then the semantics requires that there be a set that 'Sx' does not apply to, and so 'Sx' does not mean 'x is a set', [9] and so we have not really verified the original sentence.[10] Put another way: if we insist that every set that the semantics requires is a set in our model, we will get a contradiction if we try to make (17) true in a model.

If a semantics is just a technical device for showing that some language is interpretable in some model or other (to show consistency of some sentences, for example), then it is not necessary for predicates to have assignments in the model that give their true meaning. But

---

[9] Cf. Boolos 1998, 30ff., for related discussion.

[10] Having classes in addition to sets merely postpones the problem (cf. Lewis 1990, 65ff), if classes are individual things. If classes are not individual things, then introducing classes may just be a misleading way of adopting the plural solution. (See Ch. 2, 24, and Ch. 6, 146–7, for further discussion of classes "as many".)

when we are indicating how meanings of complex linguistic items are constructed from the meanings of simpler ones, and we hope to be able to include the very language that we speak in that, then we have a problem if the semantics requires that certain sets exist and also requires that the predicate that means 'x is a set' cannot apply to them. The set-theoretic semantics developed in this chapter crashes into the set-theoretic paradoxes, if we envision that semantics as something that at least leads the way towards a semantics for natural language.

This is a difficult issue, though. First, there are attitudes towards sets themselves that might cushion the collision. Sometimes sets are said to be *inexhaustible*, meaning that there can never be a fixed domain of all sets. Our semantics for (17) must reach out to a set that cannot be an individual in the domain of the interpreting model, but that fact might be seen as simply a symptom of a more general feature (bug?) of set theory, that "whenever we have formed a conception of quantification over some range of sets, we can define a set which isn't in this range."[11] Williamson 2003 argues very effectively against this kind of response when he considers views that would prevent us from talking about everything.

Second, though, is the very real question about what semantics achieves. We can focus on that by first considering some cases other than the case of set-theoretic semantics.

Event semantics. If Donald Davidson is right about the semantics of adverbs, then the semantics for 'John is walking slowly' involves quantification with respect to an event. ($\exists$e (e is a walking $\land$ John is an agent of e $\land$ slowly(e)). It seems, if we accept this, that we should conclude that the following principle is true in virtue of the meaning of 'John is walking slowly':

> E If 'John is walking slowly' is true, then at least one event exists.

Possible worlds semantics. If possible worlds semantics is right about the meaning of modality, then it would seem that the following principle is true in virtue of the meaning of 'I could have stayed home':

> P If ' I could have stayed home' is true, then at least one possible world exists.

---

[11] Linnebo 2004. This is his way of putting the view, which he attributes to Michael Dummett, Charles Parsons and Michel Glanzberg.

Tarskian semantics. If the ordinary Tarskian semantics gives the meaning of predicative sentences, then it seems that the following principle is true in virtue of the meaning of ' Alice is happy':

T If 'Alice is happy' is true, then at least one set exists.

The example based on the Tarskian semantics (**T**) is most relevant to our concerns (and we discussed the possible worlds example in Chapter 2). Few would say that the meaning of predicative sentences alone would verify **T**. Yet, according to the Tarskian semantics, the truth of the antecedent requires that there is a set of happy things. Let's call the principle "semantic realism".

> **Semantic realism:** If the semantics for S requires the existence of an entity e for the truth of S, then if S is true, e exists.

If the semantics actually tells us the meaning of the sentence, then presumably whatever entities are required in verifying models that correctly interpret the sentence must exist. So 'happy' must be associated with the set of happy things, if the Tarskian semantics provides the real meaning of the predicate.[12] I take this as a reason to think that Tarski's semantics does not give the meaning of predicative sentences but rather provides a formal model that illustrates some semantic properties. In particular, 'non-self-membered set' can't be associated with the set of such things, so semantic realism does not allow the possibility that the Tarskian semantics in terms of sets can give the actual meaning of 'non-self-membered set'.[13]

The semantics of Chapter 3 provides an approach to the semantics of plurals that may more plausibly be said to give the meaning of plural sentences. It will endorse the following principle:

> If 'Alice and Betty (together) lifted two tables (together)' is true, then at least one relation exists.

In Chapter 3 we associated each seriously plural (non-distributive or non-cumulative) predication with a property or relation. There we say that some things may have a property (like *being neighbors*) that is

---

[12] Presumably no one thinks of it in that way.

[13] Tarski identified other sources of paradox in semantics, and so he advocated for a strict metalanguage hierarchy; the semantics for a language is always expressed in some other language. That can't be very satisfying for any of us, but especially not for those of us who would envision a systematic semantics for natural language or who think that we can say that everything is self-identical.

associated with a predicate. Chapter 3 avoids set-theoretic paradoxes, but doesn't the assertion of the existence of properties involve us in perfectly analogous paradoxes? Consider the property of *not applying to (not being true of) itself*.

The answer on behalf of the semantics of Chapter 3 has several parts. First, one might give an answer like the inexhaustibility answer for sets. If we can make a firm distinction between the object language and the metalanguage, we identify the things **D** that are the individuals of the object language, and it is only in the metalanguage that we treat properties of things as additional individuals. Of course, when we consider the metalanguage itself as a plural language of the type we are considering, we then must consider the status of these properties. We must then introduce properties of those properties in the appropriate meta-metalanguage, etc., or we must have a theory of properties that is adequate for the semantics and that tells us that they cannot be treated as individuals.

Alternatively, we might interpret predicates by translation rather than by assigning properties (that are treated as individuals). One might explain translation as interpreting object-language predicates with predications, activities rather than objects. But what is predicated? A property? The answer can be that to talk of predicating something is misleading. In the limiting case of monadic plural predication, we say that some things <u>are</u> (or were or will be) in a certain way: they are neighbors, they are sitting in a circle, etc. Translation interprets by associating some such activity (the activity of predication, of saying that some things are somehow) with each predicate. Then, however, in defining logical truth we must consider all possible ways of translating or all ways of predicating, and (as we mentioned in Chapter 3) that specification is also troublesome.

The semantics of Chapter 3 provides a real advantage over the set-theoretic semantics in this chapter when we consider the semantics of natural language. We can develop a more homophonic semantics; we don't have to change the subject (to a set) and change the predicate (to a predicate of sets) when we interpret non-distributive plurals. So we have the right things filling theta-role positions. When we say that some students are surrounding Adams Hall, the students are the subject of the predication, not some other individual (like the set of students) that the students bear a relationship (like membership) to. If some students surround a building, then the students are the agents of the surrounding; our semantics should not force us to identify a property that is somehow related to surrounding but that has a set as its "agent". The semantics of Chapter 3 avoids the distorting change of subject and predicate that accompanies the development of a set-theoretic semantics, and so it is able to associate the actual agents (patients, etc.) with theta-roles rather than associating their set-theoretic surrogates.[14]

In addition, if a language for set theory itself is desired, then the semantics of Chapter 3 provides something with some potential. The paradoxes guarantee that relying on a set-theoretic semantics will produce difficulties of paradox or inexhaustibility if we try to use plurals as a language for set theory. We can avoid those problems with sets if we shift to a plural language with a semantics based on properties or on translation. This may not seem like much of a gain, but there is an asymmetry to consider here. It seems that we cannot give an adequate set-theoretic semantics for a language that would serve for a full theory of properties; but it seems that we can give an adequate property-theoretic semantics for a plural language that could serve for a full theory of sets.

Plural language has some advantages in metaphysics, in the semantics of ordinary language, and in the language for set theory itself. It is difficult to see any advantage in the set-theoretic approach to the semantics of plurals.

---

[14] There is some additional discussion of this issue in Ch. 2.

6

Among

The principal concern of this chapter will be to develop some axioms that express the fundamental features of the *among* relationship. In order to facilitate comparison with mereology, set theory and second-order logic, it is useful to develop *among* theory in a language that is simpler than the one discussed in Chapter 3. We will first indicate how we can eliminate singular variables. That may seem less familiar rather than more familiar, but we facilitate comparisons, especially to mereology, by having just one style of variable. For example, the main difference between *among* theory and some forms of mereology is just that we interpret those variables plurally and mereologists interpret them as singular. We can introduce singular variables as abbreviations. After indicating how to eliminate singular variables, we develop axioms that indicate the relationship between *among* theory and mereology.

Although *among* is interdefinable with *one of* on one understanding of the *one of* relation, we will see that there is reason to think that that is not the only understanding available for *one of*, and that will help to clarify some issues in the semantics of plurals, especially concerning the status of the plurally plural (the *perplural*).

We then consider the relationship of *among* theory to set theory and to second-order logic, and we very briefly discuss what reasons there are to think of *among* as a logical relationship.

In addition to providing a useful basis for the comparisons mentioned, the first-order plural theory of *among* may provide a base for a first-order way of talking about everything, contrary to Tim Williamson's claim that second-order logic is needed for such "generality absolutism". We will explore that issue.

THE ELIMINATION OF SINGULAR VARIABLES

The language of plurals developed in Chapters 1–3 includes singular and plural variables. Each argument position of a predication is either distributive or non-distributive, with the distinction between the variables available as one way to mark this difference. However, if we forthrightly embrace non-distributive predication as the "unmarked" case, and if we take the *among* relation to be basic, we can eliminate the use of singular variables, and this in turn facilitates the examination of the general logic of *among*. (For now we will develop this without singular terms. Those will be introduced later in the chapter.)

We have already indicated that these are equivalent:

$$[Qx: Fx]\ Gx$$
$$[QX: [\forall x: xAX]\ Fx]\ [\forall x: xAX]\ Gx$$

More generally, we can confine singular variables in our formal language to a very special context. Whenever we have a singular variable v, except in the context 'vAY', we can always have an associated distributing universal $[\forall v: vAX]$.[1] We can eliminate singular variables entirely by introducing the predicate X *is an individual* ('IX'), defined in the following way:[2]

$$IX =_{df} [\forall Y: YAX]\ XAY$$

When we have a quantified singular variable x in a sub-clause $\ldots x \ldots$, we can replace it by:

$$[\forall x: xAY]\ \ldots x \ldots$$

as indicated above. Then we can eliminate the singular variable:

$$[\forall X: XAY \wedge IX]\ \ldots X \ldots \qquad \text{(where the context} \ldots x \ldots \text{does}$$
not already have occurrences of X)

---

[1] We continue to take $\forall =_{df} \neg\exists\neg$.

[2] This definition seems to provide the resources for a response to Laurence Goldstein's challenge in Goldstein 2002, "The indefinability of 'one'." In effect, Goldstein takes plural quantification as primitive (as we are), and he argues that *one* is then not definable solely in terms of the logic. However, we here give a non-circular definition of IX in terms of the *among* relation. So if the *among* relation is available, then we have met the challenge to define *one*. 'IX' means X *is one individual*.

Our sole variables then are the plural variables, and distribution is explicitly represented by the presence of the distributing universal. We can use a plural quantifier to bind the plural variable Y appearing in 'XAY'. Applying this to a basic example:

[Qx: Fx] Gx
[QY: [∀x: xAY] Fx] [∀x: xAY] Gx
[QY: [∀X: XAY ∧ IX] FX] [∀X: XAY ∧ IX] GX

This elimination means that we can simplify the formal exploration of the *among* relation by using only plural quantifiers and variables.[3]

AXIOMS FOR "*AMONG* THEORY"

In developing axioms for *among*, we use only plural quantification and we allow for non-distributive predication. To facilitate comparison with standard formulations of mereology, we often use unrestricted quantifiers here, since only the universal and existential quantifiers are involved in the formal system. In typical English sentences, some sort of restriction to the kind of thing under discussion is a part of ordinary quantification. However, when we work at the level of generality of *among* theory, such restrictions to kinds are out of place in any case.

Our formal system has one primitive two-place relation A ("among") and one primitive quantifier ∃. (∃X can be thought of as "one or more things X are such that . . .", as in "One or more things are circularly configured" or "One or more things are making a racket in the other room.") The universal ∀ is defined in the usual way as ¬∃¬. The relation A is distributive in its first position: XAY is always equivalent to ∀Z ((IZ ∧ ZAX) → ZAY).[4] This fact, supplemented by an existence axiom, can provide the principal basis for the axiomatic system.

(**AX 1**)   ∀X ∀Y (XAY ↔ ∀W ((IW ∧ WAX) → WAY))
(**E**)   ∀X ∃Y (IY ∧ YAX)

---

[3] A sentence like "Some dogs are brown" is now ultimately represented by something that we might read as "Some individuals such that each individual among them is a dog are such that each individual among them is brown."

[4] This relation is also strongly distributive: XAY is always equivalent to ∀Z (ZAX → ZAY).

These two axioms alone enable us to prove that many principles of a classical mereology with atoms (see Simons, *Parts*, especially pp. 37, 41–3) apply to the *among* relation. Two definitions will be useful for that:

$$X \approx Y =\text{df } XAY \wedge YAX \qquad (X \text{ are the same things as } Y)$$
$$XOY =\text{df } \exists Z (ZAX \wedge ZAY) \qquad (X \text{ overlap } Y)$$

These two theorems then follow:[5]

M1: $\forall X \forall Y \forall Z ((XAY \wedge YAZ) \rightarrow XAZ)$
M2: $\forall X \forall Y (\forall W (WAX \rightarrow WOY) \rightarrow XAY)$

Proof of **M1**:

Suppose $XAY \wedge YAZ$	
$\forall W ((IW \wedge WAX) \rightarrow WAY)$	(**AX** 1)
$\forall W ((IW \wedge WAY) \rightarrow WAZ)$	(**AX** 1)
$\forall W ((IW \wedge WAX) \rightarrow WAZ)$	(logical consequence)
XAZ \qquad (**AX** 1)	

Proof of **M2**:

Suppose $\forall W (WAX \rightarrow WOY)$
 Suppose $IV \wedge VAX$
 VOY
 $\exists Z (ZAV \wedge ZAY)$
 Since ZAV and IV, VAZ
 $VAZ \wedge ZAY$
 VAY \qquad (**M1**)
$\forall W ((IW \wedge WAX) \rightarrow WAY)$
XAY \qquad (**AX** 1)

A related principle, the *strong supplementation principle* (Simons 1987, 29), is the contrapositive of **M2**. The *weak supplementation principle* (Simons 1987, 28):

$$\forall X \forall Y ((XAY \wedge \neg YAX) \rightarrow \exists Z ((ZAY \wedge \neg YAZ) \wedge \neg ZOX))$$

readily follows. This is commonly used as an axiom in formulations of mereology that take the concept of a proper part as basic.

---

[5] In proving theorems we will use informal reasoning with plural quantifiers. The plural existential and universal exploitation and introduction rules are perfectly analogous to those for singular quantifiers. See Yi 2005 for an axiomatic treatment of the logic of plurals that includes axioms for the underlying logic.

Alternatively, we can take **M1**, **M2** and **E** as our axioms and prove **AX 1**.

Proof of **AX 1** $(\forall X \forall Y (XAY \leftrightarrow \forall W ((IW \wedge WAX) \to WAY)))$ from **M1**, **M2** and **E**:

$\to$ From **M1** (transitivity)
$\leftarrow$ Suppose $\forall W ((IW \wedge WAX) \to WAY)$

> Suppose KAX
> $\exists W (IW \wedge WAK)$ (E)
> WAX (M1)
> $IW \wedge WAX$
> WAY
> $\exists W (WAK \wedge WAY)$
> KOY

So $\forall Z (ZAX \to ZOY)$
XAY (M2)

Thus the fundamental features of *among* that are made explicit by **AX 1** and **E** are equally captured by **M1**, **M2** and **E**,[6] and **M1**, **M2** and **E** are fundamental axioms of a mereology with individual atoms. Together with the comprehension axiom schema (to be introduced later), they constitute an axiomatization of mereology with atoms. Given any set of atoms, the interpretation is isomorphic to the field of subsets of that set, but excluding the empty set from the field (Simons 1987, 44). That structure is what we want for the interpretation of plural language (for any atoms). An important difference from the set-theoretic or mereological interpretation: we are talking about relations among the things that are in the subsets or that are "atomic parts" of a mereological sum, rather than relations among the subsets or the sums. We will not take the subsets or sums as additional individuals. The gain in ontological economy comes with a change in ideology – we need plural quantification and plural predication in our formal language and in our metalanguage. But once we have seen the pervasiveness of plural predication, it is natural to take plural (non-distributive) quantification as the standard case, with distributive quantification explicitly marked. And it is more than just natural. We maintain the subject and predicate of our sentences when we allow non-distributive predication rather

---

[6] Byeong-Uk Yi (personal communication) pointed out to me that **AX 1** and **E** are sufficient for the proof of **M1** and **M2**.

than changing to a singular subject and a (corresponding but) different predicate.[7] When I say 'They come from many countries,' or 'They are surrounding Adams Hall,' or 'They are seven in number (numerous),' I am talking about some individuals who non-distributively have these properties, not some individual things (sets or mereological sums) that have some corresponding distributive property.

The fact that our axioms also formalize a mereology with atoms might tempt one to read 'XAY' as 'X are part of Y'. It is best to resist this temptation. Our fundamental concept is expressed by "These are among those."

These students are among the best students I have taught.

If you are happy paraphrasing this in the following way:

These students are part of the best students I have taught.

then perhaps you can successfully read 'XAY' as "These are part of those," keeping it firmly in mind that the X and Y positions are both plural. I do not find the paraphrase to be very felicitous, and I suspect that the "part of" paraphrase has the potential to lead one down the path to singularism, transforming "These are among those" to "These are part of those" to "These are part of this." That would not be a correct interpretation of *among*; it would substitute a different relation (*part of*) for *among*. (I find it most natural to take the *part of* relation as a distributive relation of two individuals, *this* is part of *that*.)

THEOREMS

Reflexivity follows readily from **AX 1**.[8]
T1: $\forall X\, XAX$
Proof:
$\forall W((IW \wedge WAX) \rightarrow WAX)$
So XAX (**AX 1**)

[7] Oliver and Smiley 2001 also note the correlative change of subject and change of predicate, as does Burge 1977, though Burge does not adequately appreciate the non-singularist implications of this. Some individuals can be four in number, but no single thing can do that.
[8] Many of the proofs to follow are trivial, but I think that it is worthwhile to devote a little space to them because the use of a plural formal language is unfamiliar.

Since we have reflexivity (T1), transitivity (**M1**), and anti-symmetry[9] (from the definition of $\approx$), this is an axiomatization of a partial ordering, as expected. It would be misleading, however, to ask what *things* are partially ordered by the *among* relation. In most cases, an argument place in the relation is associated non-distributively with some things, not just a single thing. If we think of the *among* relation as generating a semi-lattice that represents the ordering, each node is associated non-distributively with some things. Only the nodes at the first level are associated with just one thing.

Our next theorem is strong distributivity of the first argument place of the *among* relation. **AX 1** says that X are among Y iff whenever a thing is among X it is among Y; T2 says that X are among Y iff whenever some things are among X they are among Y.

T2: $\forall X \forall Y (XAY \leftrightarrow \forall Z (ZAX \rightarrow ZAY))$
Proof: $\rightarrow$ transitivity of A (**M1**)
        $\leftarrow$ reflexivity of A (T1)
Extensionality principles are straightforward consequences of **AX 1** and T2.
Extensionality 1: $\forall X \forall Y (X \approx Y \leftrightarrow \forall Z (ZAX \leftrightarrow ZAY))$
Extensionality 2: $\forall X \forall Y (X \approx Y \leftrightarrow \forall Z (IZ \rightarrow (ZAX \leftrightarrow ZAY)))$

T3: $\forall X \forall Y (XAY \leftrightarrow \forall Z (ZOX \rightarrow ZOY))$
i.e., $\forall X \forall Y (XAY \leftrightarrow \forall Z (\exists W (WAZ \wedge WAX) \rightarrow \exists W (WAZ \wedge WAY)))$

$\rightarrow$ Suppose XAY
        Suppose $\exists W (WAZ \wedge WAX)$
        $\exists W (WAZ \wedge WAY)$ (**M1**)

$\leftarrow$ Suppose $\forall Z (\exists W (WAZ \wedge WAX) \rightarrow \exists W (WAZ \wedge WAY))$
        Suppose VAX
        $VAV \wedge VAX$
        $\exists W (WAV \wedge WAX)$
        so $\exists W (WAV \wedge WAY)$, i.e., VOY
    thus, $\forall X (VAX \rightarrow VOY)$
    So XAY (**M2**)

Several simple consequences of the definitions are worth noting.

T4: $\forall X \forall Y (XAY \rightarrow XOY)$

---

[9] $\forall X \forall Y ((XAY \wedge YAX) \rightarrow X \approx Y)$.

T5: $\forall X \forall Y (XOY \leftrightarrow YOX)$
T6: $\forall X \forall Y (IX \rightarrow (XAY \leftrightarrow XOY))$
T7: $\forall X \forall Y (XOY \leftrightarrow \exists W (IW \wedge WAX \wedge WAY))$
T8: $\forall X (IX \rightarrow \forall Y (YAX \rightarrow X \approx Y))$
T9: $\forall X \forall Y (X \approx Y \rightarrow \forall Z ((ZAX \leftrightarrow ZAY) \wedge (XAZ \leftrightarrow YAZ)))$

T10 says that there are disjoint things among X iff some things that are
among X are such that X are not among them (i.e., iff some things are
properly among X, i.e., iff X are at least two things, i.e., iff $\neg IX$).

T10: $\forall X (\exists W \exists Z (\neg WOZ \wedge WAX \wedge ZAX) \leftrightarrow \exists Y (YAX \wedge \neg XAY))$
$\rightarrow$ Suppose $\exists W \exists Z (\neg WOZ \wedge WAX \wedge ZAX)$, call them '$U$'
        and 'V'
        $\neg UOV \wedge UAX \wedge VAX$
            Case 1: XAU
            $\forall Y (YAU \rightarrow \neg YAV)$ (since $\neg UOV$)
            $\neg XAV$
            $\exists Z (ZAX \wedge \neg XAZ)$ (M2)
            Case 2: $\neg XAU$
            $\exists Z (ZAX \wedge \neg XAZ)$
        So $\exists Z (ZAX \wedge \neg XAZ)$

$\leftarrow$ Suppose $\exists Z (ZAX \wedge \neg XAZ)$, call them '$U$'
        $UAX \wedge \neg XAU$
        $\exists W (WAX \wedge \neg WOU)$, call them '$V$' (M2)
        $VAX \wedge \neg VOU$
        $\neg UOV \wedge UAX \wedge VAX$
        $\exists W \exists Z (\neg WOZ \wedge WAX \wedge ZAX)$

We can also define what it is for some things Z to be the sum of X
and Y:
$SXYZ =$ df $\forall W ((WOX \vee WOY) \leftrightarrow WOZ)$ (X and Y sum to Z)

T11: $\forall X \forall Y \forall Z (SXYZ \rightarrow \forall W ((WAX \vee WAY) \rightarrow WAZ))$

Although T11 holds, it is important to note that the following does
not hold:

$\forall X \forall Y \forall Z (SXYZ \rightarrow \forall W ((WAX \vee WAY) \leftrightarrow WAZ))$

(The failure of this is why we used 'O' rather than 'A' in defining $SXYZ$.)
If X are a and b and Y are c and d, then their sum Z are a, b, c, and d.
But b and c do not have the property of being among X or the property

of being among Y. However, when we restrict ourselves to individuals, we get the biconditional.

T12: $\forall X \forall Y \forall Z \, (SXYZ \to \forall W \, (IW \to ((WAX \lor WAY) \leftrightarrow WAZ)))$
(A consequence of T6.)

The universal closures of all of the following are additional theorems involving S:

$SXXX$
$(SXYZ \land SYXW) \to Z \approx W$ (commutativity)
$(SXYU \land SYZW \land SXWV) \to SUZV$ (associativity)
$SXYW \to (WAZ \leftrightarrow (XAZ \land YAZ))$
$(\neg XAY \land SXWZ) \to \neg ZAY$
$(\neg XOY \land SWYZ) \to \neg ZAX$
$XAY \leftrightarrow SXYY$
$(SYZW \land \neg XOZ \land XAW) \to XAY$
$(\neg YAX \land \neg YOZ \land SXZW \land SYZV) \to \neg VAW$

PRINCIPLES OF SAMENESS ($\approx$)

We already observed that extensionality is a trivial consequence of reflexivity (T1) and **AX 1**. We list it here as T13:

T13: $\forall X \forall Y \, (X \approx Y \leftrightarrow \forall Z \, (ZAX \leftrightarrow ZAY))$

But the following variant (with *properly among* in place of *among*) also holds, and is somewhat less trivial:

$\forall X \forall Y (\exists W (WAX \land \neg XAW) \to (\forall Z((ZAX \land \neg XAZ) \leftrightarrow (ZAY \land \neg YAZ)) \leftrightarrow X \approx Y))$

(This will be T15.) If some things are properly among X, then ((whenever some things are properly among X they are among Y, and whenever some things are properly among Y they are among X) iff X are the same things as Y). To prove this, we first prove the following lemma:

T14: $\forall X \forall Y (\exists Z (ZAX \land \neg XAZ) \to (\forall Z((ZAX \land \neg XAZ) \to ZAY) \to XAY)))$
Suppose $\exists Z \, (ZAX \land \neg XAZ)$
Suppose $\forall Z \, ((ZAX \land \neg XAZ) \to ZAY)$
   Suppose VAX

Case 1: $\neg XAV$
$VAX \wedge \neg XAV$
so VAY
VOY
Case 2: XAV
$ZAX \wedge \neg XAZ$ (instantiating our first assumption)
so ZAY
Also, ZAV (**M1**)
so $\exists Z\ (ZAV \wedge ZAY)$
VOY

Since VOY in either case,
$\forall Z\ (ZAX \to ZOY)$
So XAY (**M2**)

T15: $\forall X \forall Y\ (\exists W\ (WAX \wedge \neg XAW) \to$
          $(\forall Z\ ((ZAX \wedge \neg XAZ) \leftrightarrow (ZAY \wedge \neg YAZ)) \leftrightarrow X \approx Y))$
follows in an obvious way from T14.

T16: $\forall X \forall Y\ (X \approx Y \to XOY)$ (from T4)
T17: $\forall X \forall Y \forall Z\ ((X \approx Y \wedge Y \approx Z) \to X \approx Z)$ (from **M1**)
T18: $\forall X\ X \approx X$ (from T1)
T19: $\forall X \forall Y\ (X \approx Y \leftrightarrow Y \approx X)$
T20: $\forall X \forall Y\ (X \approx Y \leftrightarrow \forall Z\ (IZ \to (ZAX \leftrightarrow ZAY)))$
T21: $\forall X \forall Y\ (X \approx Y \leftrightarrow \forall Z\ (ZOX \leftrightarrow ZOY))$ (from T3)

ADDING OTHER PREDICATES

So far we have used only the relation *among* and other predicates and relations that can be defined in terms of *among*. We will wish to integrate this with other predicates, and this leads to the addition of two other axiom schemas that apply to sentences involving predicates of all sorts.

THE IDENTITY SCHEMA

All instances of the following schema must be true:

AS 1: $\forall X \forall Y\ (X \approx Y \to (FX \leftrightarrow FY))$

Every instance of this (where FX is any sentence without occurrences of Y, and FY is like FX but with all occurrences of X that are free within FX replaced by occurrences of Y) will be an axiom. This assures that the plural "identity" ($\approx$) functions fully like singular $=$. Singular identity can be defined as a special case, and it will obey all the usual laws.

$X = Y = \mathrm{df}\, X \approx Y \wedge IX$

Because the *among* relation is reflexive and transitive, it follows that singular identity ('$=$') is reflexive, transitive and symmetric.

COMPREHENSION

A comprehension schema adds significant power to our axiomatic system. We are not developing a hierarchy, as in set theory, where some things are members of something which is in turn a member of something else. There are just individuals. So it might seem natural to take the comprehension axiom schema to be the following:

$$\exists X \forall Y\, (IY \to (YAX \leftrightarrow FY))\qquad\text{(where X is not free in FY)}$$

But this needs a qualification. If nothing satisfies 'FY', then there will be no things such as these. So comprehension axioms, incorporating this existence condition, will be instances of the following schema:[10]

AS 2: $\exists Y\,(IY \wedge FY) \to \exists X \forall Y\,(IY \to (YAX \leftrightarrow FY))$ (where X is not free in FY)

The comprehension schema **AS 2** enables us to prove the singular version of the identity schema (singular Leibniz's Law) even if **AS 1** is not present.

LL: $\forall X \forall Y\,(X = Y \to (FX \leftrightarrow FY))$, i.e.,
$\forall X \forall Y\,((X \approx Y \wedge IX) \to (FX \leftrightarrow FY))$

First, we know from the definition of 'IX' that (even without **AS 1**):

$$(X \approx Y \wedge IX) \to IY$$

So to prove **LL**:
Suppose $X \approx Y \wedge IX$
Suppose FX
XAY
YAX

---

[10] Since not all predicates are cumulative, a version of **AS 2** that leaves out the restriction to individuals would be incorrect. We cannot say that if some people are meeting together, then there are some things X such that any things Y are such that Y are among X if and only if Y are meeting together. There is no such big meeting.

$IX \wedge FX$

$\exists Z \forall Y \, (IY \rightarrow (YAZ \leftrightarrow FY))$ AS 2

$IY \rightarrow (YAZ \leftrightarrow FY)$

$IX \rightarrow (XAZ \leftrightarrow FX)$

IY

$YAZ \leftrightarrow FY$

$XAZ \leftrightarrow FX$

$XAZ \rightarrow YAZ$ (from YAX and transitivity of A (M1))

Similarly, $YAZ \rightarrow XAZ$

$XAZ \leftrightarrow YAZ$

$FX \leftrightarrow FY$

So the standard singular form of Leibniz's Law is readily derived. That is weaker than **AS 1**, however. (If X and Y are the same things and X are meeting together, then Y are meeting together. That is a consequence of **AS 1**, but the singular form of LL will not serve to establish it.)

CONSEQUENCES OF COMPREHENSION

We can use **AS 2** in proving the theorem that if some things exist, then some things are such that all things are among them. This theorem is an important difference between *among* theory and set theory. (More on this follows in this chapter.)

T 22: $\exists X \, XAX \rightarrow \exists X \forall Y \, YAX$

Proof: Suppose $\exists X \, XAX$

$\qquad \exists Z \, (IZ \wedge ZAX)$ (E) Call them 'V'

$\qquad IV \wedge VAV$ (T1)

$\qquad \exists Z \, (IZ \wedge ZAZ)$

$\qquad \exists W \forall Z \, (IZ \rightarrow (ZAW \leftrightarrow ZAZ))$ (AS 2)

$\qquad \forall Z \, (IZ \rightarrow ZAW)$ (since, by T1, $\forall Z \, ZAZ$)

$\qquad \forall Y \forall Z \, ((IZ \wedge ZAY) \rightarrow ZAW))$

$\qquad$ So $\forall Y \, YAW$ (AX 1)

$\exists X \, XAX \rightarrow \exists X \forall Y \, YAX$

We can also prove that when X are some things and Y are some things, X and Y sum to some things Z uniquely.

T 23: $\forall X \forall Y \exists Z \, (SXYZ \wedge \forall W \, (SXYW \leftrightarrow W \approx Z))$

Proof: For any X and Y,

$\exists Z \, (IZ \wedge ZAX)$ (E)

So $\exists Z\,(IZ \wedge (ZAX \vee ZAY))$

So $\exists Z\,\forall W\,(IW \rightarrow (WAZ \leftrightarrow (WAX \vee WAY)))$ (**AS 2**)

Suppose $UOX \vee UOY$
Case 1: UOX
$\quad\exists V\,(IV \wedge VAU \wedge VAX)$ (T7)
$\quad$Call them 'V'
$\quad VAX$
$\quad$So VAZ
$\quad VAU \wedge VAZ$
$\quad UOZ$
Case 2: Similarly, if UOY, then UOZ
So UOZ
$\forall W\,((WOX \vee WOY) \rightarrow WOZ)$

Suppose UOZ
$\exists V\,(IV \wedge VAU \wedge VAZ)$ Call them 'V'
$VAX \vee VAY$ (since VAZ)
$UOX \vee UOY$ (since VAU)
$\forall W\,(WOZ \rightarrow (WOX \vee WOY))$
So $\forall X\,\forall Y\,\exists Z\,\forall W\,(WOZ \leftrightarrow (WOX \vee WOY))$. i.e., $\forall X\,\forall Y\,\exists Z\,SXYZ$

To prove uniqueness:
Suppose $SXYZ \wedge SXYV$
$\forall W\,(WOZ \leftrightarrow (WOX \vee WOY))$
$\forall W\,(WOV \leftrightarrow (WOX \vee WOY))$
$\forall W\,(WOZ \leftrightarrow WOV)$
$V \approx Z$ (T21)

Since we have proved the existence and uniqueness of sums, we can introduce functional notation for sums. (Although we stick with finitely long sentences in this definition, there is no reason why any X_i needs to be interpreted by only finitely many individuals.)

$$\varphi\Sigma(X_1, X_2, \ldots X_n) = \mathrm{df}\,\exists Z, Y_1, Y_2, \ldots Y_{n-2}\,(SX_1X_2Y_1 \wedge SX_3Y_1Y_2 \wedge$$
$$SX_4Y_2Y_3 \wedge \ldots \wedge SX_nY_{n-2}Z \wedge \varphi Z)$$

From either T22 or T 23, we also have:

T 24: $\forall X\,\forall Y\,\exists Z\,(XAZ \wedge YAZ)$

And we have the following theorem concerning S:[11]

---

[11] This corresponds to the "distributivity" principle in Landman 2000, 97.

T 25: $\forall X \forall Y \forall Z \forall W ((SXYZ \wedge WAZ) \rightarrow$
$\qquad (WAX \vee WAY \vee \exists X' \exists Y' (X'AX \wedge Y'AY \wedge SX'Y'W)))$

Proof:

Suppose $SXYZ$ and WAZ and $\neg WAX$ and $\neg WAY$.

$\qquad \exists V, VAW$ and $\neg VOY$. (since $\neg WAY$ and **M2**)

$\qquad VAZ$ and $\neg VOY \qquad$ (since VAW and WAZ)

$\qquad VOX$. $\qquad\qquad$ ($SXYZ$, def. S)

Since VOX and VAW, $\exists X^* (X^*AX \wedge X^*AV \wedge X^*AW)$. So,

$\exists X^* (IX^* \wedge X^*AX \wedge X^*AW)$ **(E)**

$\exists X' \forall V^* (IV^* \rightarrow (V^*AX' \leftrightarrow (V^*AX \wedge V^*AW)))$ (comprehension)

Similarly

$\exists Y' \forall V^* (IV^* \rightarrow (V^*AY' \leftrightarrow (V^*AY \wedge V^*AW)))$

$X'AW$ and $Y'AW$, so

$\forall V^* (IV^* \rightarrow ((V^*AX' \vee V^*AY') \rightarrow V^*AW))$

Now, for the other direction, suppose that IV^*, V^*AW and $\neg V^*AX'$

$\qquad \neg V^*AX$

$\qquad V^*AZ \qquad$ (since V^*AW)

$\qquad V^*AY \qquad$ (T 12)

$\qquad$ so $V^*AY' \qquad$ (since V^*AW and V^*AY)

So $\forall V^* (IV^* \rightarrow (V^*AW \rightarrow (V^*AX' \vee V^*AY')))$

Thus $\forall V^* (IV^* \rightarrow (V^*AW \leftrightarrow (V^*AX' \vee V^*AY')))$

i.e., $SX'Y'Z$

Thus our theorem: $\forall X \forall Y \forall Z \forall W ((SXYZ \wedge WAZ) \rightarrow$
$\qquad (WAX \vee WAY \vee \exists X' \exists Y' (X'AX \wedge Y'AY \wedge SX'Y'W)))$

Another simple consequence of comprehension is an analogue of the ZF pairing axiom.

T 26: $\forall Z \forall W ((IZ \wedge IW) \rightarrow \exists Y \forall X (IX \rightarrow (XAY \leftrightarrow (X = Z \vee X = W))))$

TERMS

Now we are in a position to deal with singular terms and compound terms within the context of the system developed in this chapter. Since we have eliminated singular variables, except as abbreviations, we need to develop our logic for individual constants in a way that makes the right connection with appropriate plural variables. A sentence φa with individual constant 'a' must now be understood as entailing $\exists X$ ($IX \wedge \varphi X$) (where X is a variable not already occurring in φa). We will need an additional axiom schema. For any individual constant α, this is an axiom:

AS3: $I\alpha$

Thus any sentence φα can be written equivalently as $I\alpha \wedge \varphi\alpha$. Also, where α is an individual constant and Fα is any sentence without occurrences of X, this will be an axiom:

AS4: $F\alpha \rightarrow \exists X\ FX$

The use of an individual constant is thus existentially committing. (A "free-logic" variation would not include **AS4**.)

For compound terms, we need to introduce an axiom that indicates how they are to be understood. We had indicated in our semantics that $\lfloor \nu, \mu \rceil$ is to be understood as representing the sum of ν and μ. Since we have defined the sum predicate S and proven the existence and uniqueness of sums, we can use the following as our axiom for compound terms:

ACT: $\forall X \forall Y\ SXY \lfloor X, Y \rceil$

So, for example, to show that $XA \lfloor X, Y \rceil$, we need only to show that $\forall Z\ (SXYZ \rightarrow XAZ)$, and that follows from T1 and T11. (XAX and $\forall Z\ (SXYZ \rightarrow \forall W\ (WAX \rightarrow XAZ))$.) The following fundamental theorem is equivalent to **ACT**:

ACTO: $\forall X \forall Y \forall W\ ((WOX \vee WOY) \rightarrow WO \lfloor X, Y \rceil)$

Given the definition of Σ, all instances of the following are provable.
   $\forall X_1, X_2, \ldots X_n\ (\lfloor X_1, X_2, \ldots X_n \rceil \approx \Sigma\ (X_1, X_2, \ldots X_n))$
Finally, in analogy to the summation concept, we can define others.

The *difference* of X and Y are Z ($X - Y \approx Z$), or, perhaps more aptly put, Z *complement* Y *among* X: $DXYZ =$ df $\forall W((WAX \wedge \neg WOY) \leftrightarrow WAZ)$

When XAY, no complementers of Y among X exist. The following theorem indicates that the complementers exist in all other cases:

T 27: $\forall X \forall Y \forall Z\ (\neg XAY \rightarrow \exists Z\ (DXYZ \wedge \forall W\ (DXYW \leftrightarrow W \approx Z)))$

Proof:
Suppose $\neg XAY$
$\exists Z\,(IZ \wedge ZAX \wedge \neg ZAY)$ (AX 1)
$\exists Z\,\forall W\,(IW \to (WAZ \leftrightarrow (WAX \wedge \neg WAY)))$ (AS 2)
Call them 'Z'

$\forall W\,(IW \to (WAZ \to WAX))$
ZAX (AX 1)
$\forall W\,(WAZ \to WAX)$ (T2)
$\forall W\,(IW \to (WAZ \to \neg WAY))$
$\neg ZOY$ (T7)
$\forall W\,(WAZ \to \forall V\,(WOV \to ZOV))$ (T3, T5)
Since $\neg ZOY$,
$\forall W\,(WAZ \to \neg WOY)$
So $\forall W\,(WAZ \to (WAX \wedge \neg WOY))$

To prove the other direction:

> Suppose $WAX \wedge \neg WOY$
> $\forall V\,(VAW \to (VAX \wedge \neg VOY))$ (T2, T3)
> $\forall V\,(VAW \to (VAX \wedge \neg VAY))$ (T4)
> $\forall V\,(IV \to (VAW \to (VAX \wedge \neg VAY)))$
> $\forall V\,(IV \to (VAW \to VAZ))$ (feature of Z)
> WAZ

So $\forall W\,((WAX \wedge \neg WOY) \to WAZ)$
Thus $\exists Z\,\forall W\,(WAZ \leftrightarrow (WAX \wedge \neg WOY))$ i.e., $\exists Z\ DXYZ$

Proving uniqueness:
Suppose that $DXYZ$ and $DXYV$
$\forall W\,((WAX \wedge \neg WOY) \leftrightarrow WAZ)$
$\forall W\,((WAX \wedge \neg WOY) \leftrightarrow WAV)$
But then $\forall W\,(WAZ \leftrightarrow WAV)$
So $V \approx Z$ (T 13)

Product (intersection) of X and Y: $PXYZ =$ df $\forall W\,((WAX \wedge WAY) \leftrightarrow WAZ)$
No product (intersection) will exist when $\neg XOY$.

T 28: $\forall X\,\forall Y\,\forall Z\,(XOY \to \exists Z\,(PXYZ \wedge \forall W\,(PXYW \leftrightarrow W \approx Z)))$
Proof:
Suppose XOY
$\exists W\,(IW \wedge WAX \wedge WAY)$ (T7)

$\exists Z \forall W \ (IW \rightarrow (WAZ \leftrightarrow (WAX \land WAY)))$ **(AS 2)**
Call them 'Z'

$ZAX \land ZAY$ **(AX 1)**
$\forall W \ (WAZ \rightarrow (WAX \land WAY))$ (T2)

For the other direction, suppose that $VAX \land VAY$

$\forall W \ (IW \rightarrow ((WAX \land WAY) \rightarrow WAZ))$
$\forall W \ (IW \rightarrow (WAV \rightarrow WAZ))$
VAZ (T2)

$\forall W \ ((WAX \land WAY) \rightarrow WAZ))$
Thus $\exists Z \forall W \ (WAZ \leftrightarrow (WAX \land WAY))$, i.e., $\exists Z \ PXYZ$

Proving uniqueness:
Suppose that PXYZ and PXYV
$\forall W \ ((WAX \land WAY) \leftrightarrow WAZ)$
$\forall W \ ((WAX \land WAY) \leftrightarrow WAV)$
But then $\forall W \ (WAZ \leftrightarrow WAV)$
So $V \approx Z$ (T 13)

The universal closures of all of the following are additional theorems involving P.
PXXX
$(PXYZ \land PYXW) \rightarrow Z \approx W$
$(PYZW \land PXWV \land PXYU) \rightarrow PUZV$
$PXYZ \rightarrow XAZ$
$XAY \leftrightarrow PXYX$
$(PXYZ \land XAZ \land YAZ) \rightarrow X \approx Y$

ONE OF

Most discussions of the logic or semantics of plurals use the fundamental relation *x is one of Y* rather than our relation *X are among Y*. I have been understanding *x is one of Y* in a way that makes these interdefinable. Using 'XKY' for 'X is one of Y':

$XKY =_{df} XAY \land IX$ $(IX =_{df} [\forall Z: ZAX] \ XAZ)$
$XAY \leftrightarrow [\forall Z: ZKX] \ ZKY$

We define the *one of* relation in terms of *among*, and the *among* relation is reflexive and transitive. The *one of* relation inherits those properties (if a bit degenerately, in the case of transitivity). The *is one of* relation is just a special case of *among*.

However, it seems that some uses of x *is one of Y* rely on a different understanding of that relation that would not allow for the definition of *is one of* in terms of *among*. Some treatments of plurality differentiate between singular and plural argument places and singular and plural terms in a fundamental way, and the *one of* relation involves a singular first argument and a plural second argument. Then reflexivity for the *is one of* relation is not straightforwardly formulable, and transitivity would seem to need to introduce the plurally plural in order to be formulable, and once that is done, might be judged false. Partly there is a syntactic issue, since this other way of taking 'is one of' requires that the argument positions in 'x is one of y' be filled by terms of different "levels": for example, in a common notation, 'x is one of yy'. But in any case, the comprehension axiom requires that there be single-item "pluralities", so yy might be such a single-item plurality. Even then, on the alternative approach being considered here, if 'x is one of yy' is true, it will still not be the case that 'x' and 'yy' are assigned the same value. Rather, 'x' is assigned an individual, and 'yy' is assigned a single-item "plurality". Thus this relation is not reflexive. Also, it is not transitive. From 'x is one of yy' and 'yy is one of zzz', we cannot conclude that x is one of zzz. Even if yy and zzz are both single-item pluralities, it will not be the case that x is one of zzz. An individual assigned to 'x' will differ from the single-item plurality assigned to 'yy' to satisfy 'x is one of yy', and it is that single-item plurality, not the atomic individual, that will be one of some plurality of pluralities that is assigned to 'zzz'.

We can use 'Q' for the hierarchical 'one of' relation just discussed. We can define a relation *among* in terms of Q, but it will be a different relation than the one we have been discussing. Use 'M'.

$$xxMyy = df [\forall z: z \, Q \, xx] \, z \, Q \, yy.$$

'M' will stand for a relation that is reflexive and transitive, like A, but it will relate pluralities of individuals rather than plurally relating individuals. We might say that a plurality xx collects some individuals X.

One could now define a distinct relation 'one of' in terms of M in the way that I defined K in terms of A. Use 'N'.

$$xxNyy = df [\forall zz: zzMxx] \, xxMzz \wedge xxMyy$$

N is a different relation than Q and a different relation than K. Q relates an individual x to a plurality yy. N relates a one-item plurality xx to a plurality yy. N is reflexive and degenerately transitive, but Q is not.

What is the difference between A and M and between K and Q and N? A and K involve plural predications and Q, M and N involve singular predications applied to pluralities. The Q relation differs from K because it builds plurality-creation into the relation. A plurality is a single thing that collects the individuals; the approach based on Q builds singularization into the fundamental semantic relation.

To put that another way. If we want to define Q in terms of A and K, we must add some kind of singularizing relation, like 'xx collects X', where xx is a plurality that collects some things X. Then:

$$x Q yy = \mathrm{df}\, x A X \wedge yy \text{ collects } X$$

yy would be a singular representative of X. I would need to add singularization to A and K in order to define Q (and M and N).

Our goal in developing an understanding of plurals is to see what we can do without such plurality creation, i.e., singularization.

PERPLURALS

We are now in a position to look closely at what sense we can make of the idea that there is phenomenon of the perplural (plurally plural) in addition to the plural. In Chapter 2 we saw that the case for a linguistic need was not compelling; we have other ways of interpreting sentences that might at first seem to be plurally plural. Now that we have a more solid understanding of our primitives, we can see whether an understanding of the plurally plural is a natural outgrowth of an understanding of plurals. Another look at that issue will reveal something significant about the choice of *among* rather than *one-of* as our fundamental semantic relation.

Allen Hazen's case for the perplural (Hazen 1997) involves a central example:

As a semi-serious example, pretend our plural endings on nouns are iterable: then we could assert the existence of infinitely many cats by saying something like this:

There are some catses such that for each cats among thems there are some cats among thems including at least one more cat.

(Note that the first occurrence of 'are' is perplural and the second merely plural, that 'each' is being used in construction with a plural noun, and that 'some' is used both plurally and perplurally.)

Consider an attempted formalization of that sentence employing perplurals using 'A' as we have defined it in this chapter to stand for the *among* relation.

$$\text{(Inf)} \quad \exists XX \, [\forall Y: YAXX] \, [\exists Z: ZAXX] \, (YAZ \wedge \neg ZAY)$$

Double variables like 'XX' are used for the plurally plural, but there is no real linguistic hierarchy here, since all variables are assigned, as values, some cats, whether the variable is single or double. This sentence is automatically false, since $XXAXX$. If we want to say something true, then we cannot using 'A' in (Inf) to represent the *among* relation we have employed or to represent the *one-of* relation as we have defined it, represented by 'K' above, for two reasons. First, like the A relation, the K relation is reflexive. Also, the relation in (Inf) must apply to values for 'Y' and 'Z' that are not atomic individuals in order to achieve the definitional goal, and 'K' requires a reference to an individual in the first argument place (if the statement is to be true).

How are we to understand 'among' in Hazen's example? As suggested in the last section, we could take it as combining singularization and *one-of*, the relation represented by 'M' that we defined in terms of the relation represented by 'Q'. That is, $yQxx$ iff some things Y are such that yKY and xx (is a single thing that) collects Y. $xxMyy$ iff $[\forall x : zQxx] \, zQyy$. Then

$$\text{(InfQ)} \quad \exists xxx \, [\forall yy: yyQxxx] \, [\exists zz: zzQxxx] \, (yyMzz \wedge \neg zzMyy)$$

This, however, undermines the claim that there are distinctive perplurals. On this understanding, perplurals turn out to be ordinary plurals applied to objects that have "members" (or other constituents), like the singular representative yy of some things Y or the thing yy that collects some things Y, and we don't really have a separate phenomenon of perplurals. If we mean by perplurals that they are pluralities of pluralities, and if a plurality is itself some thing, then perplurals are just plurals of these special objects.

What is novel in Hazen's example is the way of forming general terms to apply to these pluralities. We introduce the general term 'cats' (singular) and 'catses' (plural) to apply to some thing that is a plurality of cats and to some things that are pluralities of cats. But for a cats to be one of them, it must be one plurality; and for there to be some of them, there must be at least one. That is why a sentence like (InfQ) must employ an *among* relation (M) that has singularization built in; it is defined in terms of the Q-relation and is not our *among* relation (A).[12]

Our way of understanding plurals provides no evident basis for understanding perplurals as a phenomenon separate from ordinary plurality. The language of perplurals can be understood if we build in singularizing assumptions. Given those singularizing assumptions, perplurals are expressible by ordinary plurals applied to the "higher-level" objects that the singularizing process introduces. If we do not make the singularizing assumptions, then there is no evident way to understand perplurals in the way that Hazen intends.

This does not rule out the possibility that there are other ways to understand perplurals. However, if we take our understanding of *among* and refuse to introduce sets, pluralities or other singularizers, then the most obvious routes to perplurals are closed.

RELATIONSHIP TO SECOND-ORDER LOGIC

George Boolos argued that we can use the logic of plurals as a basis for understanding monadic second-order logic. I want to make a more targeted claim. For some purposes, a plural first-order language will have some of the advantages that are ordinarily associated with second-order logic. I will indicate ways in which we can use plural quantification to achieve goals that monadic second-order quantification achieves. I will then confront some criticisms of Boolos's project and consider whether they apply to my project.

The guiding idea is this. Consider a second-order quantification:

$\exists F\, Fx$

In the version of our system with singular variables, this would "correspond" to:

$\exists Y\, xAY$

---

[12] I suppose that this approach would actually introduce an infinite hierarchy of *is one of* relations, for plural second arguments, perplural second arguments, etc.

yQ_1xx

xxQ_2zzz

$zzzQ_3wwww$

Monadic second-order quantification corresponds to quantification into the second argument place of the *among* relation.[13] Our language is a plural first-order language that can express what is said in monadic second-order logic. (There is a difference in that nothing corresponds to the empty set in the language of plurals. But that is not an important difference.) We can state significant principles that correspond to principles ordinarily formulated in monadic second-order logic.

For example, building on *among* theory, we can state the general principle of mathematical induction as an axiom rather than as an axiom schema. Assume that we have 0 and the successor relation *Sxy*: *x is a successor of y,* and we have the other Peano axioms. Then the induction schema of ordinary first-order Peano arithmetic can be replaced by the following first-order, plural axiom, where our atoms (individuals) are the natural numbers:[14]

$$\forall X \, ((0AX \wedge \forall y \, (yAX \rightarrow \forall z \, (Szy \rightarrow zAX))) \rightarrow \forall yAX)$$

(If we introduce a functional notation, say '*sx*' for the successor of *x*, then the clause '$\forall z \, (Szy \rightarrow zAX)$' can be replaced by '$syAX$'.) If we add this to the other axioms for Peano arithmetic, we have a categorical characterization of arithmetic, as in second-order logic.[15]

Similarly, we can enlarge our domain and state the *axiom of completeness* of real analysis (that whenever there is an upper bound among some things, there is a least upper bound among them):[16]

$$\forall X \, (\exists x \forall y \, (yAX \rightarrow y \leq x) \rightarrow \exists x \, (\forall y \, (yAX \rightarrow y \leq x) \wedge \forall z$$
$$(\forall y \, (yAX \rightarrow y \leq z) \rightarrow x \leq z)))$$

When added to the other axioms of real analysis (which involve only singular variables), we have an axiomatization that is categorical and has only uncountable models (as in second-order logics).

Because we can formulate the Peano Axioms, including the induction axiom, in our plural language, we know that compactness fails for this

[13] Here I am comparing my approach to a standard interpretation of second-order logic that treats second-order quantification over monadic predicates as corresponding to quantification with respect to sets or classes of individuals. Interpretations of second-order quantification that treat monadic second-order quantification as quantification over properties are not being considered.

[14] If our domain includes some things in addition to natural numbers, then we must qualify this:

$$\forall X \, ((0AX \wedge \forall y \, (yAX \rightarrow \forall z \, (Szy \rightarrow zAX))) \rightarrow \forall y \, (y \text{ is a natural number} \rightarrow yAX)).$$

[15] Cf. Shapiro 2001, 46.   [16] Cf. ibid.

system of plural logic. Consider infinitely many formulas S consisting of the Peano axioms, including the plural induction axiom, together with the following formulas (where 'c' is a new individual constant and 's' stands for the successor function):

$$c \neq 0, c \neq s0, c \neq ss0, \ldots$$

Whenever formulas S' among S are finite in number, S' are satisfiable. But S are not satisfiable in any model. And since compactness fails, completeness must also fail. No finitely long proof enables us to show that S are inconsistent.[17]

Within the context of a plural language (including the comprehension schema), we can expect to be able to develop a considerable portion of mathematics, including real analysis. We should expect this to correspond to what is developed in so-called[18] *second-order arithmetic*.[19] Since second-order arithmetic involves only sets that are not members of further sets, plural references can replace the set-theoretic references of second-order arithmetic. The only difference then is in the absence of anything corresponding to an empty set in *among* theory. It seems that that would be at most a technical inconvenience, not a serious impediment to the development of mathematics.[20]

If we can speak plurally of ordered pairs, we can further develop the expressive power of plural logic (or monadic second-order logic) in the context of mathematics. When we can speak of ordered pairs, plural logic and monadic second-order logic come to have the expressive power

---

[17] Cf. Shapiro 2001, 47.

[18] I say 'so-called' here only because second-order arithmetic is ordinarily formulated as a two-sorted first-order theory. The two sorts of variable are interpreted by natural numbers and by sets of natural numbers. This is second-order in the sense that it involves sets of first-order objects, and it is not higher order because no sets of sets interpret any variables. See Simpson 1999 for a presentation and for references.

[19] The appropriate system here seems to be the full (impredicative) second-order arithmetic. Nothing in *among* theory itself would motivate a restriction to any of the sub-systems that Simpson 1999 considers. Allen Hazen (1993) finds this to be an objection to the plural understanding of second-order logic: "... since there is no way of making sense of the relevant restrictions to the comprehension principles on the pluralist reading ... The pluralist is then in the anomalous position of holding that someone (the predicativist) who accepts *part* of second-order logic is ontologically committed to *more* than someone who accepts all of it!" But when someone makes a distinction, whether among some things or among some claims, they may well be committed to more, as the basis for that distinction. It is hard to see how this objection could have any force.

[20] The numbers cannot be constructed set-theoretically from the empty set as they often are. But that applies to second-order arithmetic as well as to plural, first-order arithmetic. We can take as the natural numbers any things that satisfy the Peano axioms.

of full second-order logic. We might just stipulate that ordered pairs of things in our domain are also in our domain; I know of no special problems in doing so. But some might prefer that they be constructed from more basic resources.

If natural numbers are the only objects and we have defined arithmetic operations, then it is simple to encode ordered pairs. In order to say that some pairs $\langle a, b \rangle$, $\langle c, d \rangle$ and $\langle e, f \rangle$ have a property F, we need to be able to identify a property of single things that can be decoded as carrying that information. For example, if we consider the number $n = 2^a * 3^b$, it meets the usual conditions for a definition of an ordered pair $\langle a, b \rangle$: if $m = 2^c * 3^d$, then $n = m$ iff $a = c$ and $b = d$. Any property of ordered pairs corresponds to some property of numbers that have 2 and 3 as their (only) prime factors. Similar encoding (in terms of prime factorization) extends to other ordered n-tuples.

Because of this encoding capability, if we can express arithmetic truths in a plural language (or in monadic second-order logic), we can develop the power of full second-order logic with respect to that domain.

The simple method involving prime factorization is not available for objects in general. However, it seems that methods developed by Burgess and Hazen[21] can be adapted for encoding pairs in a more general way, as long as we are sure that the basic objects (atoms) are infinite in number.

Suppose that there are infinitely many atoms[22] and that we can identify two relations, M1 and M2, that meet certain conditions:

> they are 1-1 relations
> each is defined for every atom (the domain of each is everything)
> each maps the items of the domain into a proper part of the domain (thus the need for infinitely many atoms)
> their ranges do not overlap

Then each atom **a** will have an M1-image (M1(**a**)) and an M2-image (M2(**a**)). An ordered pair $\langle a, b \rangle$ will then correspond to the unordered pair M1(**a**) and M2(**b**), and we can predicate properties of $\langle a, b \rangle$ by predicating the corresponding properties of the unordered pair of M1(**a**) and M2(**b**). Similar ideas will enable us to define n-tuples of atoms for $n > 2$.

---

[21] Cf. Lewis 1991, 121–33. Also, Hazen 1997 and Hazen 2000.

[22] Burgess, Hazen and Lewis (Lewis 1991, appendix) also consider modifications for talking about relations in worlds with atomless gunk. We have been considering plurals (some things), and so have been ignoring gunk. We will continue to be neutral about the existence of gunk.

Without assuming at least that unordered pairs[23] are things, we wouldn't have a direct way of talking about something that corresponds to the ordinary extension of a relation (a set of ordered pairs), however. Suppose that **Rab**, **Rcb**, **Rad** and ¬**Rcd**. In isolation, talking about the things M1(**a**) and M2(**b**) can stand in for talking of the ordered pair ⟨**a**, **b**⟩; but talking about M1(**a**) and M1(**c**) and M2(**b**) and M2(**d**) won't give us the information about what is related to what. We would need some composite objects to make the appropriate differentiations that ⟨**a**, **d**⟩ is included but ⟨**c**, **d**⟩ is not, for example. We might say that the unordered pair {M1(**a**), M2(**d**)} is one of the things involved in the interpretation of R but {M1(**c**), M2(**d**)} is not. But this method can't give us what we need for the full encoding of relations unless we take pairs (or some other composites) as objects and can identify suitable relations M1 and M2. Using this method and taking unordered pairs as objects will then give us a reduction of ordered pairs to unordered pairs for the relevant domain. Hazen and Burgess provide a method that uses the mereological parthood relation as a basis for identifying suitable relations and identifying suitable composites in a fully general way.

In any case, my goal is to develop the language of plurals, not the language of second-order logic.

CRITICISMS OF PLURALS

Charles Parsons is critical of Boolos's idea that monadic second-order logic can have a plural interpretation.[24] Boolos's approach includes a semantic clause that defines second-order quantification and relates each second-order variable to some things, and our semantics (Chapter 3) has followed this, relating each plural variable to some things. About Boolos's approach, Parsons says (1990, 299): 'It is hard to agree with Boolos in finding that the treatment of second-order variables in this definition does not offer scope for the notion of a value comparable to what it offers to the notion of a value of an individual variable.'

---

[23] Burgess and Hazen are working in a context where mereology is available, and so they employ fusions where we employ unordered pairs here.

[24] In "Everything," Williamson 2003, Tim Williamson also criticizes the use of plurals in giving an account of second-order logic. Those criticisms are interesting, but they provide no direct reason to think that a generality absolutist cannot use a language with non-distributive plurals rather than higher-order language in expressing her view. Further discussion follows.

But Boolos is interpreting these variables as plural variables, and so it is very hard to see why we should expect them to have a̱ (single) value. Rather, a plural variable may be related to many things; that is what makes it plural. When I say 'They are meeting together', I do not intend 'they' to refer to some single thing. Plural pronouns don't have a single value, and there is no reason why plural variables need to have one either. To say otherwise is just to manifest the singularist prejudice (see Chapters 1 and 2).

Singularism also seems to be the principal motivator for Parsons' further criticisms of Boolos's account of second-order quantification. Parsons favors (1990, 299):

an ontological intuition a little different from but complementing Quine's, according to which ontological commitment is carried by the expressions that play the role of subjects in language and thus indicate what one is talking about. In a primitive second-level predicate, second-order variables or expressions that can be substituted for them play that role. The same is evidently true of plural expressions in Boolos's paraphrases of second-order formulae, as I have indicated above. Boolos has not, in my view, made a convincing case for the claim that his interpretation is ontologically non-committal [i.e., that it is not committed to anything that is a single value for plural variables].

The first thing to say is that we can regard plurals as committing one to the things "that play the role of subjects . . . and thus indicate what one is talking about." Saying '*They* are surrounding the building' commits me to the existence of *them*. Or we can take the more Quinean criterion, that we are committed to the things with respect to which we existentially quantify. Saying that some students are surrounding a building commits one to students and to things surrounding a building.[25] (Perhaps plural quantification is clearer about ontological commitment than second-order quantification is, since it quantifies only into argument (noun) positions.) Parsons has given us no reason to think that every subject term must be singular, and so no reason to think that using a plural variable commits one to some single thing that is its interpretation. (Boolos's probable response to this seems to be anticipated in the very title of Boolos 1984: "To be is to be the value of a variable (or to be some values of some variables).")

---

[25] Allen Hazen (1993, 136–7) also seems to presume that if quantifiers are ontologically committal, then the use of a plural quantification ("some students are surrounding the building") must commit one to the existence of a single thing to which the predicate applies.

Parsons continues (1990, 300):

> An advocate of Boolos's interpretation in an eliminative structuralist setting
> could grant my claim about ontological commitment, but then take a position
> analogous to the Fregean: second-order variables indeed have pluralities as their
> values, but these are not objects [i.e., a plurality is not a single object]. . . . There
> will still be, as with Frege's concepts, the irresistible temptation to talk of
> pluralities as if they were objects, as we have already noted above.

It seems to me that the advocate of Boolos's interpretation should not
take the first step, of conceding that a second-order variable takes a
plurality as its value. On the pluralist interpretation of second-order
logic, a second-order variable can be related to many things, and if so,
no single thing is its semantic value; in particular, if a plurality is a single
thing, then it is not the semantic value. One might be able to speak of
pluralities and resist the temptation to regard them as single things, as
I believe Peter Simons usually does, for example (despite Parsons' claim
that this temptation is irresistible). But to talk of pluralities will at least
be misleading, and so it is better to resist the very first step that Parsons
offers, that of talking of pluralities, even if one tries at the same time
to say that they are not objects. Once we set aside singularist prejudice,
that first step is really not very tempting anyway. Resisting it just means
reminding oneself that if some things are many in number, then they
are not one in number.[26] You might be able to put them in a box that
is one in number, but they are still many things, even if they are all in
the same box. And they definitely aren't the box.

In recent work Pierre de Rouilhan[27] seems to fall into the same gutter.
He urges that a variable, even a plural one, must have a single value,
even if that value is a multiplicity, and then he goes on to wonder
what these multiplicities are. That is the singularist myopia, and I think
that we can best avoid the stumbles it leads to by avoiding talk of
multiplicities, pluralities and manifolds. If talking about a multiplicity
of people makes you think that you are talking about some thing other
than some people, then you should avoid that kind of talk. You won't
need it for the understanding of plurals.

[26] There is an ambiguity here. Each of the (many) things is one in number, even
though they (together) are not one in number. But presumably that is not the source of
any misunderstanding.
[27] Rouilhan 2002. On p. 194, he says that the Geach–Kaplan sentence "affirms the
existence of a *collection* of critics," then goes on to call such collections *multiplicities*.
Then he asks, "What is a 'multiplicity' in this sense?"

Bertrand Russell's talk[28] of two conceptions of *class*, *classes as many* and *classes as one*, seems similarly misleading. Once we have allowed talk of sets or classes, it will be very hard (though perhaps not impossible) to avoid treating them as objects (sets as one), and it will be nearly impossible to avoid being thought to have done so. So I am largely in agreement with Parsons that the first step, talk of pluralities or manifolds or multiplicities that are not objects, or talk of sets as many, is likely to lead to true singularism. Parsons embraces singularism; I would avoid that first step.[29]

Seeing the affinity between plurals and second-order logic in the representation of sentences like the Geach–Kaplan sentence and the Peano Axiom, some might be tempted to go in the other direction and argue that second-order logic is the basis for an account of plurals. But second-order logic provides no basis for understanding non-distributive predication in the simpler cases like those of Chapter 1. There is nothing predicative about the plural reference in 'They are surrounding Adams Hall.' The pronoun refers non-distributively to some things, and there is no evident way to bring second-order logic to bear in a successful analysis. Nor is there any need.

James Higginbotham 2000 says many correct things about plurals, and he also notes the inadequacy of any second-order analysis of demonstrative plurals in simple non-distributive predications. However,

---

[28] Russell 1903, 69. "In a class as many, the component terms [individuals], though they have some kind of unity, have less than is required for a whole. They have, in fact, just so much unity as is required to make them many, and not enough to prevent them from remaining many." I suppose that Russell is poking fun at himself here. In any case, why should any unity at all be required to make them many?

[29] Richard Cartwright 1994 makes a similar point.

It is one thing for there to *be* certain objects; it is another for there to be a *set*, or set-like object, of which those objects are the members. Russell intended to respect the distinction, I think, in his talk of the class *as many* and the class *as one*; it was no triviality, and in fact was soon held to be doubtful, that the "class as one is to be found wherever there is a class as many." But the terminology is badly chosen. For a class as many is inevitably taken to be *a* class as many, *an* object distinct from the many it comprises; and the very distinction intended is thereby threatened ....

In Cartwright 2001, he favors the use of 'collection' as a singular term that should not be understood to stand for some single individual, in other words, that should be understood to function in the way that Russell seems to have wanted for 'class as many'. Cartwright is certainly not misled by his use, and he sets the stage so carefully that perhaps no one else will be misled by his use either. But once one introduces such a term, it becomes difficult to avoid true singularism and difficult to limit misunderstanding. Few others should try it.

he concludes that we should take 'they' and 'them' to be referring to classes as many. Except for a lingering singularism, though, there is no reason to say this rather than to say that plurals refer non-distributively to some things. Saying that a plural pronoun refers to a class as many either identifies one class that a plural refers to or it doesn't. If it does, it makes the singularist mistake. If it doesn't, then there is no reason to say it.

WILLIAMSON ON EVERYTHING, PLURALS AND SECOND-ORDER LOGIC

We have seen that one feature of the logic developed here is the theorem that some things are everything (if anything at all exists). This in itself has little metaphysical bite, since it merely says that some things in the quantificational domain are everything in the quantificational domain. Trivial, as a logical theorem should be. The question of whether we can ever coherently speak a language with absolutely unrestricted quantifiers is not answered by the existence of that theorem.

Timothy Williamson calls the more metaphysically contentful position that there are such things as everything "generality absolutism," and he argues for this view (mainly by arguing against its denial, generality relativism). I am in sympathy with his conclusion, and I think that the language of plurals may be relevant here, providing a language for generality absolutists.

Near the end of his discussion, Williamson argues, to the contrary, that the generality absolutist can and must use second-order logic to formulate his view non-paradoxically, and he argues that Boolos's plural interpretation of second-order logic is not adequate. However, even if one accepts his argument that Boolos's interpretation of second-order logic is inadequate,[30] that does not mean that plurals are not useful for the generality absolutist. In fact, plurals provide a first-order alternative for the generality absolutist's avoidance of paradox when the plurals are directly employed (i.e., without the mediation of second-order logic).

---

[30] Sorting out the criticisms involves considering different interpretations of second-order logic. Clearly Boolos has in mind the standard interpretation in the logical tradition, where second-order quantification "corresponds to" quantification over sets. Williamson considers modal contexts, where second-order quantification "corresponds to" quantification over properties. We do not need to sort out all of those issues here.

The Generalized Paradox

Here is a slight variation of Williamson's derivation of a Russellian sort of paradox for anyone who is a generality absolutist employing singularist first-order logic as the only language. If 'P' is some first-order predicate, 'F' is schematic for a verb of natural language, and 'I(F)' refers to a (property, set or other) single entity that interprets the verb, then we can formulate the following principle:

(1) For everything o, if I(F) interprets P, then P applies to o (under interpretation I(F)) iff o Fs.

For example:

∀o, if the set of tall things interprets P, then (P applies to o iff o is tall).

∀o, if the property of being tall interprets P, then (P applies to o iff o is tall).

or whatever you take the appropriate interpretation of a predicate to be. The important thing here is that we are taking the interpretation of a predicate to be a thing.

Now define the verb 'R' (in terms of some particular object-language predicate P):

(2) For everything o, o Rs iff either o does not interpret P or o interprets P and P does not apply to o (under o).

This amounts to saying that o Rs iff o does not interpret P or o is a heterological interpretation of P (i.e., o is not an interpretation of P under which P applies to o). Applying (1) to R:

(3) For everything o, if I(R) interprets P, then P applies to o (under I(R)) iff either o does not interpret P or o interprets P and P does not apply to o (under o).

Since an interpretation is something (according to the singularist position being explored here), the generality absolutist must allow it as a value of o. So:

(4) If I(R) interprets P, then P applies to I(R) (under I(R)) iff either I(R) does not interpret P or I(R) interprets P and P does not apply to I(R) (under I(R)).

Equivalently:

> (4′) If I(R) interprets P, then P applies to I(R) (under I(R)) iff P does not apply to I(R) (under I(R)).

This entails that I(R) cannot be the interpretation of a predicate P. But it is. It is the interpretation expressed by 'either o does not interpret P or o interprets P and P does not apply to o under o', i.e., o is not an interpretation of P or o is a heterological interpretation. The generality absolutist employing singularist first-order logic as the only language is led to (4′) and can provide no principled reason to exclude I(R) as an interpretation of a predicate, and so we have a paradox for such a position.

Williamson's response

After criticizing alternatives to generality absolutism, Williamson develops the idea that second-order logic can be a way out of the paradox. The response to looming paradox is to avoid treating interpretations as individual entities. Instead of saying that J is an interpretation of a predicate P such that P applies to o, we make J into a verb and say that P Js o. "No such things as interpretations have been postulated."[31] Then in giving the semantics, we must replace quantification "over" interpretations by second-order quantification into the position held by such verbs. We can use second-order quantification for saying "Some J*is such that P J* o," for example.

In connection with this, Williamson criticizes the Boolos understanding of second-order logic in terms of plurals and so concludes that plural quantification does not provide an adequate basis for avoiding paradox. This is too hasty a conclusion, even if we grant that all of the criticisms of Boolos's plural account of second-order logic are correct.

Plural, first-order response

Suppose that instead of taking the detour through second-order logic, the generality absolutist employs a first-order plural language directly. Let us say, for example, that if the red things interpret a predicate P, then P applies to o iff o is red. This uses a dyadic relation 'X interpret P' where the first argument place is a non-distributive plural argument position. Now, instead of second-order quantification, we can have plural

---

[31] Williamson 2003, 454.

first-order quantification when we do something that corresponds to quantifying over interpretations. We can say, for example, that "Some X^* are such that X^* interpret P." The paradox will not arise.[32]

We can go back and see why the paradox does not arise.

> (1pl) For every individual o, if X interpret P, then P applies to o iff o is among X.

Some individuals X interpret a (monadic, distributive) predicate (if anything does), and we say that the predicate applies to each of the individuals among X. Now define 'R' in terms of a particular predicate P:

> (2pl) For everything o, o Rs (R applies to o) iff either o does not interpret P or P does not apply to o.

(Note that we cannot define this in quite the same way as before:

> (2*) For everything o, o Rs iff either o does not interpret P or (o interprets P and P does not apply to o).

The clause 'o interprets P and P does not apply to o' yields an immediate contradiction in conjunction with (1pl). If o interprets P, then P applies to o, since o is among o.)

Now let K be the things of which R is true (i.e., an individual o Rs iff o is among K), and apply (1pl) and (2pl) to K:

> (3pl) For everything o, if K interpret P, then P applies to o iff either o does not interpret P or P does not apply to o (i.e., iff o is among K).

Sentence (3pl) simply applies the fact that K are the things that R applies to. There is no way to proceed from here to get a contradiction. K is not a suitable substituend for o, since o is singular. What follows, for each individual thing o, is that if K interpret P, then either o does not interpret P or P does not apply to o; in other words, if 'R' is the "translation" of P, then no single thing can (by itself) interpret P. If we employ plurals, then we do not need to require that an interpretation is

---

[32] Alternatively, if we take the view that some ordered pairs interpret our formal language, we can say:

If S interpret the language L, then P applies to d in L iff (P, d) is among S.

This employs plural predication in a slightly different way to develop an alternative to Williamson's second-order approach. This idea was suggested by Gabriel Uzquiano (conversation).

an individual; rather, some individuals interpret a predicate, and so the paradox is avoided.

As we saw in our development of a systematic semantics, we can develop this idea beyond the case of monadic predicates, interpreting each object-language plural variable by some things. We can then quantify over alternative interpretations of such variables ("Some things $K^* \ldots$", etc.). The semantics thus shows how the generality absolutist can talk about everything without recourse to second-order logic. With either Williamson's approach or ours, the generality absolutist goes beyond first-order singularist logic in order to state her position. We stay first-order but introduce plurals; Williamson employs higher-order logic while denying that we can employ plurals as a way of understanding that use of higher-order language.

Williamson objects to using plurals as the basis for developing a generality-relativist alternative, giving five "reasons to doubt that plurals are ultimately what we want for generalizing into predicate position." However, we are using plurals directly, not using them as a translation of a quantification into predicate position; we develop our plural semantics independently, not as a translation of second-order logic. So this objection has no direct force against our approach.

Nevertheless, we should look at his objections to see if he identifies any real advantage of a second-order approach over a plural approach.

Objection 1: Plurals are not predicative. Reading 'Px' as 'it is one of them' is too indirect.
Answer: Nothing in our approach would suggest that plurals are predicative, and our approach to this issue is at least as direct and natural as Williamson's, so this amounts to nothing for us. (Williamson himself suggests that this is no more than a hint of trouble for the plural interpretation of second-order logic.)

Objection 2: Dealing with unsatisfied predicates makes the plural interpretation of second-order logic awkward. Nothing corresponds to the empty set, and so we have an awkward additional clause about the empty case all the time.
Answer: This is minor, as Williamson himself indicates. But in any case, it has only to do with the awkwardness of using plurals to translate second-order logic, and it has no relevance to our direct approach.

Objection 3: Quantification into n-place predicate position has no natural reading for n greater than one. Plurals provide a direct translation of monadic second-order logic (quantification in predicative positions) and not for quantification into relational positions. To get the more general second-order logic, we need plural quantification over ordered n-tuples. This is unnatural.

Answer: Two things.

Williamson, like us, would need to employ ordered n-tuples in the systematic semantics for his language, so there is no real advantage for his approach here.

This is again at most relevant to the translation of second-order logic into plurals, but not relevant to us, since we do not rely on the existence of any such translation (or, for that matter, on the existence of second-order logic) as a part of our use of plural language to express generality absolutism.

Objection 4: The plural reading gives unwanted results when modal operators are introduced (pp. 456–7).

Answer: Williamson's objection here indicates that he takes second-order quantification to "correspond to" quantification over properties rather than sets. (He indicates that we need a "more intensional, predicative reading of second-order quantification than plurals seem to provide" p. 457.) That is not Boolos's interpretation or a standard interpretation in logic or mathematics generally. We follow the more standard approach of giving an extensional account of the semantics of predicates. This will not immediately embed in modal contexts. We speak of some things interpreting a predicate, and the treatment of modality would require us to talk about things interpreting a predicate relative to a possible world, or some such thing. More needs to be done to give a semantics that goes beyond the bare extensional account. Exactly how to do that and understand what you are doing is an issue both for a plural language and for a language that allows second-order quantification. There are questions in either case, and I see no special advantage to Williamson's approach here. We must leave the problem of understanding modality for more extended consideration, but I see no reason to think that there is any problem of principle that applies to the interpretation of modals involving plurals that is not paralleled in trying to understand modals involving second-order logic.

In particular, Williamson says that "it is hard to make sense of the plural reading of the second-order quantifiers without validating this principle":

$$\forall F \, \forall G \, (\forall x \, (Fx \leftrightarrow Gx) \rightarrow \Box \, \forall x \, (Fx \leftrightarrow Gx))$$

With plurals, there are two analogues of this principle, and with a natural modal extension of our language, one is validated (or at least nearly so) and one is not.

$$\forall X \, \forall Y \, (\forall z \, (zAX \leftrightarrow zAY) \rightarrow \Box \, \forall z \, (zAX \leftrightarrow zAY))$$

That will presumably be valid (though some questions about what to say in worlds in which not everything among X exists would need to be resolved). Another principle:

$$\forall X \, \forall Y \, (\forall z \, ((zAX \leftrightarrow Fz) \wedge (zAY \leftrightarrow Gz) \wedge (Fz \leftrightarrow Gz)) \rightarrow \Box \, \forall z \, (Fz \leftrightarrow Gz))$$

will not be validated. However things stand with second-order logic, this is no problem for a plural language.

Objection 5: The plural reading of second-order logic has no natural generalization to higher level quantification. By a generalization of Russell's paradox, we need $(n + 1)$–order logic to define logical consequence in n-order logic.

Answer: We can define logical consequence for standard, singular first-order logic with a first-order plural metalanguage. What do we need for the semantics of a first-order plural language? The approach that I have been suggesting seems vulnerable, since it introduces properties and relations in the interpretation of plural predications. It is not clear how to give the semantics for some plural predicates ('X are meeting together' or 'X lifted a piano') otherwise. However, the (extensional) semantics for purely singular predication can be given without reference to properties: if a monadic predicate is purely singular (i.e., distributive), then we can say that some things interpret it. If an n-place relation is purely singular (distributive at all argument places), then we can say that some n-tuples interpret it. If we have Williamson's goal of interpreting an ordinary singular first-order language that allows everything in its domain, then we can do so in a plural language that is not higher-order. We interpret the formal language in a plural language that we understand.

We need the reference to properties and relations only for the systematic semantics of predicates of that interpreting plural language, predicates that are potentially non-distributively satisfied (in one or more argument positions). Chief among these would be 'X interpret predicate p' and 'X are among Y'. Williamson's point here may be that if we consider the language in which we give the semantics for plurals, and the language in which we give the semantics for that language, etc., we have no way of settling on just what semantic resources are needed. But with his approach, we require only higher and higher order languages, each generated in the same way from the previous one.

On the other hand, in endorsing second-order and higher-order logic without either an ordinary first-order interpretation (first-order quantification over sets or properties) or a plural interpretation, Williamson is requiring the generality absolutist to rely on something that is at most dimly understood, even at the initial step. There seems to be little advantage in that.

More work is needed on this issue, but there seems to be at least a *prima facie* case that plurals may be at least as suitable as second-order logic for the expression of generality absolutism.

RELATIONSHIP TO SET THEORY

Broadly, *among* theory differs from set theory in that there is no analogue of the empty set, and there is just one relation, *among*, that is an analogue of both the membership and the subset relation. Because *among* theory is not singularist, no hierarchy builds in the way that it does in set theory. Whether we use plural or singular quantifiers, non-distributive or distributive predicates, we are still talking about whatever are the individuals of our domain and not about any other things that collect them.

The set theoretic hierarchy is itself an item of mathematical interest, and it is a tool for modeling in mathematics, so we cannot expect *among* theory to have the mathematical reach that set theory has. Nevertheless, it would be valuable to know when set theory is needed and what can be done without it, if only to understand set theory's contribution better.[33]

We noted that we have the natural extensionality principles (T13, T20); our broad comprehension principle also provides an analogue of pairing (T26)[34] and provides for much more than the separation axiom

---

[33] Burgess 2004 expresses a similar sentiment: "Irreducibly plural quantification amounts to the very last stop before the introduction of sets. If we are to understand what is most distinctive about set theory, we must understand what it adds to and how it goes beyond the mere plural; and to understand *that* we must understand the plural and its logic."

[34] T 26: $\forall Z \forall W((IZ \wedge IW) \rightarrow \exists Y \forall X(IX \rightarrow (XAY \leftrightarrow (X \approx Z \vee X \approx W))))$

Using singular variables as well as plural, we can restate this:

$$\forall z \forall w \exists Y \forall x (xAY \leftrightarrow (x = z \vee x = w))$$

provides. Set theory's axiom of replacement says that given a set and a function, the image of that set under the function exist. The analogue for *among* theory also holds.

$$\forall X \, [(\forall x, y, z \, ((Rxy \wedge Rxz) \to y = z) \wedge \exists x, y \, (xAX \wedge Rxy)) \to$$
$$\exists Z \, \forall y \, (yAZ \leftrightarrow \exists x \, (xAX \wedge Rxy))]$$

In fact, even without the restriction to functions, this is a simple consequence of the comprehension schema.

$$\exists y \, \exists x (xAX \wedge Rxy) \to \exists Z \, \forall y \, (yAZ \leftrightarrow \exists x \, (xAX \wedge Rxy))$$

We do not want to have an empty set axiom, a union axiom is unnecessary, and we do not have a power set axiom that generates a hierarchy. (Trivial analogues of the union and power set axioms follow immediately from **AX 1**: $\forall X \forall Y (\forall W ((IW \wedge WAY) \to WAX) \leftrightarrow YAX))$. There is no axiom of infinity and requiring that there are infinitely many things would require introducing additional resources of some kind. For example, adding the Peano axioms would generate an infinite domain of objects. Infinity of the domain is not required by *among* theory but it is consistent with it.

The axiom of choice has plural analogues, as David Lewis has noted.[35] These two choice schemas are similar to Lewis's:

first choice schema
$$\forall X \{ [\forall y \, (yAX \to \exists z \, Ryz) \wedge$$
$$\forall x_1, x_2, z \, ((x_1 AX \wedge x_2 AX \wedge x_1 \neq x_2 \wedge Rx_1 z) \to \neg Rx_2 z)] \to$$
$$\exists Z \, \forall y \, (yAX \to \exists w (wAZ \wedge Ryw \wedge \forall v ((vAZ \wedge Ryv) \to v = w)))\}$$

If we are willing to employ quantification over ordered pairs, then we can translate this into an axiom (as opposed to a schema):
[$\forall Y : Y$ are some ordered pairs] $\forall X \{ [\forall y \, (yAX \to \exists z \langle y, z \rangle AY) \wedge$
$\forall x_1, x_2, z \, ((x_1 AX \wedge x_2 AX \wedge x_1 \neq x_2 \wedge \langle x_1, z \rangle AY) \to \neg \langle x_2, z \rangle AY)] \to$
$\exists Z \, \forall y \, (yAX \to \exists w \, (wAZ \wedge \langle y, w \rangle AY \wedge \forall v \, ((vAZ \wedge \langle y, v \rangle AY) \to v = w)))\}$

second choice schema (if some things have a partial ordering with no last term, then there is a linear sub-ordering of those things with no last term)[36]

35 Lewis 1991, 71.   36 Ibid., 72.

$[\forall x \neg Rxx \wedge \forall x, y, z ((Rxy \wedge Ryz) \rightarrow Rxz)] \rightarrow$
$\forall Y \{\forall x (xAY \rightarrow \exists z (zAY \wedge Rxz)) \rightarrow$
$\exists Z [ZAY \wedge \forall x (xAZ \rightarrow \exists y (yAZ \wedge Rxy)) \wedge \forall x, y ((xAZ \wedge yAZ) \rightarrow$
$(Rxy \vee Ryx))]\}$

This can be similarly translated into an axiom with a quantification over ordered pairs. We also can give a simpler schema that exploits the fact that some properties of things are non-cumulative, but it has no evident translation into a non-schematic single axiom.

third choice schema

$[\exists X \, FX \wedge \forall X \, \forall Y ((FX \wedge FY) \rightarrow (X \approx Y \vee \neg XOY))] \rightarrow$
$\exists Y \, \forall X (FX \rightarrow \exists! z (zAX \wedge zAY))$

Any of these three versions of the axiom of choice can be added as an additional axiom schema. They seem evidently true, but they seem not to follow from anything that we have so far built into *among* theory.

In presenting the theorems of *among* theory, we noted the theorem that some things are all the things there are, whereas a corresponding set-theoretic claim, that there is a set that includes all the things there are, is problematic. We should also note that in set theory with urelements, if there is a predicate '*x* is an urelement', then the following analogue of T22 may be true:

$\exists y \, y$ is an urelement $\rightarrow \exists z \, \forall y$ (*y* is an urelement $\rightarrow y \in z$)

But set theory has many more things than just the urelements, so with set theory it must always be true that no things are everything.[37]

FURTHER RELATIONSHIP TO SET THEORY

If we see a first-order plural logic as our base language, then an interesting issue for us is what we would need to add to build set theory from natural principles. John Burgess has developed this idea (Burgess 2004), and his work is very illuminating about just what set theory adds to plurality.[38]

---

[37] There is another relationship between plurals and set theory. Rayo and Uzquiano (1999) have developed the idea (from Boolos) that a logic of plurals can be used as the formal metalanguage for set theory, thus allowing sets but enabling us to talk about some sets even when there is no set of them. Linnebo (2003) has criticized this. We pursue a related idea in the next section.

[38] Burgess builds on the work of others. See Burgess 2004 for references.

This section indicates how to develop some of his ideas within the context of our notation and our understanding of plural quantifiers.[39] Interested readers can then pursue this issue in his paper and its sources.

In moving from plurals to sets, we need two primitives. We will use 'u $\equiv X$' for the dyadic relation "u is the set of all and only X". (In other words, each member of u is among X, and each individual among X is a member of u. u collects X.) We could use set membership as a primitive instead (as we implicitly did in our gloss of '$\equiv$'), or we can introduce it:

$$u \in v \leftrightarrow \exists X(v \equiv X \wedge uAX)$$

Our first axiom is then the axiom of extensionality:

EXT: $(u \equiv X \wedge v \equiv Y) \rightarrow (u = v \leftrightarrow X \approx Y)$

Because our plural variables are interpreted by some (one or more) things, this axiom does not say anything about the empty set. We need to give that a separate introduction. We will use the primitive expression 'ø' to denote the empty set, and introduce an existence axiom:[40]

$$\exists u\ u = ø$$

We can then define the predicate 'Set(u)':

$$Set(u) = df\ \exists X\ u \equiv X \vee u = ø$$

We can then add an axiom that requires that 'ø' refers to the empty set:

$$u = ø \leftrightarrow (Set(u) \wedge \neg \exists X\ u \equiv X)$$

The standard set-theoretic version of extensionality, in terms of $\in$, then follows from **EXT** once we add '$\equiv$' and 'ø' to our primitives and define '$\in$'.[41]

$$(Set(u) \wedge Set(v)) \rightarrow (\forall w(w \in u \leftrightarrow w \in v) \leftrightarrow u = v)$$

---

[39] Burgess interprets the plural existential quantifier as "0 or more things . . ." rather than "one or more things . . .". This means that there will be some small differences between his approach and ours, especially concerning the treatment of the empty set. The following discussion adapts his to our differences in notation.

[40] This differs from Burgess's presentation because of his different interpretation of the existential quantifier. If we wished to have a system that did not take on any specific existential commitments at this point, we could instead have a conditional axiom: $\exists v \exists X v \equiv X \rightarrow \exists u\ u = ø$. (If there are any sets, then there is an empty set.)

[41] Burgess says, "The introduction of plurals, and the definition of $\in$ in terms of $\equiv$ have, so to speak, permitted what lies beneath extensionality in its conventional formulation to be exhibited explicitly . . . ."

As Burgess points out, the fact that domains can be restricted makes the definition of a set substantive; he identifies it as the *Axiom of Heredity* rather than as a definition. It requires that whenever 'Set(u)' applies to some thing (in the domain of discourse), all of its members exist in the domain of discourse.

We can see immediately the familiar problem in taking set theory as the theory of plurals. Although this is a basic theorem for plurals (too trivial to even be worth listing, since $X \approx X$):

$$\forall X \, \exists Y \; Y \approx X$$

a corresponding existence claim for sets will lead to paradox (given our comprehension axiom for plurals):[42]

$$\forall X \, \exists y \; y \equiv X$$

We cannot always replace "Some Fs . . . " by "Some set of Fs ____".

Burgess points out that we can use plurals in conjunction with the notion of *limitation of size*, and then motivate the set-theoretic axioms of *separation* and *replacement* in terms of this.[43] The idea of limitation in size is that some things will form a set if there are not too many of them. The following principle is an evident consequence of this idea:

Separation: $Y \mathrm{A} X \rightarrow (\exists u \; u \equiv X \rightarrow \exists v \; v \equiv Y)$

If Y are among X, and X form a set, then X are not too many to form a set, so Y are not too many to form a set.[44] Given what we have so far established, this is interderivable with the following:

$$\mathrm{Set(u)} \rightarrow \exists v \, (\mathrm{Set(v)} \wedge \forall w (w \in v \leftrightarrow (w \in u \wedge w \mathrm{A} Z)))$$

If we replace '$w\mathrm{A}Z$' by 'Φw', then we have a schema that corresponds to traditional formulations of separation.

Similarly, we can motivate *replacement*.

$$(u \equiv X \wedge \exists f \, (f \text{ maps } X \text{ 1--1 onto } Y)) \rightarrow \exists v \; v \equiv Y^{[45]}$$

If X are not too many to form a set and X can be mapped 1--1 onto Y, then Y are not too many. We can also get some non-conditional

---

[42] Given comprehension, $\exists X \forall v (v \mathrm{A} X \leftrightarrow \neg v \in v)$.

[43] See Burgess 2004 for references to earlier developments of this idea.

[44] This formulation of the separation axiom does not entail that there is an empty set. Because of Burgess's different treatment of plural quantifiers, his formulation does.

[45] Quantification with respect to a function can be understood as plural quantification with respect to ordered pairs.

existence axioms if we have the right views about how many are too many; if two are never too many to form a set, then we get the pairing axiom, and if infinitely many are not too many, then we get the axiom of infinity. Plurals provide a way of talking about some things being two in number, infinite in number, or too many, independently of their forming sets, and so provide a nice way to state these ideas as motivators for set-theoretic principles.

Burgess also considers the reflection principle (Bernays) as a basis for more of set theory, when employed in the context of a logic of plurals. The idea of the reflection principle is that for any statement S that is true, there is some set t such that S is true when the domain of quantification is restricted to t. (This might seem obviously false, since a statement like 'X don't form a set' might be true of some things, and within any set t, any things you pick will form a set (*separation*). But the relativization must be complete if it is to be applicable, and so 'X don't form a set that is within t' must be the fuller relativization. It may be true of some things in a set t that the set of those things is not in t.)

The reflection principle can also be thought of as growing out of a slightly more contentful version of the *limitation of size* conception of sets. Roughly put, the motivating idea is that as long as some things are not so many that we can't even talk about how many they are, then they are not too many to form a set.[46]

We can define t-relativization simply. Each quantifier is restricted to members of t, so we can reintroduce restricted quantifiers and replace as follows.

$\forall u$ is replaced by $[\forall u : u \in t]$[47]
$\exists u$ $[\exists u : u \in t]$
$\forall X$ $[\forall X : [\forall u : uAX]u \in t]$[48]
$\exists X$ $[\exists X : [\forall u : uAX]u \in t]$

If Φ is any sentence, then Φ^t is the sentence that is like Φ except that each quantifier is replaced by the corresponding t-relativized quantifier. Then the *Axiom of Reflection* is:

$$\Phi \rightarrow \exists t \, \Phi^t$$

---

[46] See Burgess 2004 for a more carefully laid out set of concepts that might connect the reflection principle and limitations of size.

[47] More fully, $[\forall u : [\exists Y : t \equiv Y]uAY)]$. Equivalently, $\forall u \, (\exists Y(t \equiv Y \wedge uAY) \rightarrow \ldots)$.

[48] Equivalently, $[\forall X : [\exists Y : t \equiv Y]XAY]$ or $\forall X(\exists Y(t \equiv Y \wedge XAY) \rightarrow \ldots)$.

Following Bernays, Burgess suggests that when we combine this with extensionality, separation, the empty set axiom,[49] and the definitions already provided, we can derive all of the usual existence axioms of ZF. See Burgess 2004 for discussion and further references.

IS *AMONG* A LOGICAL CONSTANT?

The question of what is a part of logic and what is not a part of logic is vexed, and I am not certain exactly what to count as relevant.[50] However, by one clear criterion, the *among* and *identity* relations are a part of logic. And it seems that *among* has as much claim to be a part of logic as *identity* does.

The idea that logical constants are characterized by indifference to structure has a considerable pedigree. Lindenbaum and Tarski, 1934 (see Sher, p.61):

> Every relation between objects (individuals, classes, relations) which can be expressed by purely logical means is invariant with respect to every one-one mapping of the 'world' (i.e., the class of all individuals) onto itself.

Mostowski, 1957, says that a logical quantifier "does not allow us to distinguish between different elements of [the universe]."

Building on these ideas, Gila Sher (1991) formulates some individually necessary (and, according to her, jointly sufficient) conditions for something's being a logical constant. Only one of these conditions is important for us, the condition that a logical constant must be interpreted in a way that makes it invariant under isomorphic structures. Logic is about the necessary truths that are formal truths; the particular features of the individuals involved in the interpretation of a claim must not matter to the question of whether a logical constant applies or not, only their structural relationships can matter. On this criterion, an ordinary predicate 'Fx', for example, is not a logical constant because it does not require isomorphic interpretations in distinct models. (Models can have the same domain size and yet assign different numbers of individuals to the predicate 'F'.) However a quantifier like 'most' is a

---

[49] Burgess's own version does not have (or need) a separate empty-set axiom, because of his different treatment of plural quantification.

[50] See Linnebo 2004 for a related discussion.

logical constant, because the semantics for "Most A are B" relies solely on a comparison of the number of As with the number of As that are B. Any models that are isomorphic in their interpretation of A and B will yield the same truth-value for "Most A are B". If two models are isomorphic with respect to the non-logical elements of a sentence, the truth-value of the sentence must be the same in the two models.

Clearly the *among* relation meets this condition. Any isomorphism between two domains will support corresponding claims about what things X are among things Y. Nothing about the particular features of individuals is relevant in the semantics for *among*; in fact, if we consider all that can be said with *among* as our only primitive predicate or relation, only the size of the domain will make any difference in what is true. In so far as this is the reason to regard identity as a logical relation, we can also regard the *among* relation as a logical relation.

7

THE: The Basic Logic

In this chapter and the next we will indicate how plural definite descriptions are to be represented in our formal language. The bottom line is simple: definite descriptions are quantifier phrases, and 'the' can be represented as a quantifier. Based on that, it might seem that two chapters on this one quantifier is unjustified. However, a number of important facts about plurals interact in interesting ways in the treatment of definite descriptions, and so we need to make this a separate topic. In particular, the consideration of uses of 'the' with plurals and with mass terms will lead us to a brief comparison of plural quantification with mass quantification. We also include an application of the account of definite descriptions to a puzzle about the plural *de re* developed by Philip Bricker, and to some examples that Remko Scha introduces in motivating his influential account of definite descriptions.

Chapter 8 will consider the special context sensitivity of definite descriptions and look at some different approaches that we can consider there. That is important in itself and as a preliminary to Chapter 9, where we will look at the issue of whether (and if so, how) definite descriptions provide us with the fundamental resource for representing the content of so-called *E-type* pronouns.[1]

In all of this, having the resources for a discussion of plural definite descriptions makes it easier to see general features of phenomena involving definite descriptions and pronouns.

PLURAL 'THE'

The students are wearing hats.

The students are surrounding the building.

---

[1] Gareth Evans called attention to these, especially in Evans 1977 and 1980.

The students come from many countries.

The students wearing hats are athletes.

The students wearing hats are teammates.

The students who are teammates are wearing hats.

The students who are teammates are wearing similar hats.

All of the students are happy.

Most of the students are forming a line at the ticket counter.

Joan paid the students $100 each.

Joan distributed $2,000 to the students (in accord with their individual travel needs).

These examples of plural definite descriptions include both distributive and non-distributive predicates, both within the definite description and in the main verb of the sentence. We want to accommodate all of these uses in our account of definite descriptions.

The fundamental approach here will be to develop the semantics for plural definite descriptions along the lines of a Russellian theory of singular definite descriptions as developed by Stephen Neale. (The work of Richard Sharvy is also an important influence in our account.) In particular, I will develop an account that treats 'the' as a quantifier that can be analyzed in terms of the existential and universal quantifiers, and I will not include separate treatment of a distinctive referential description. (If you think that there are referential descriptions – I am not talking about those.)[2] My initial account of plural definite descriptions will have the Russell–Neale account of singular definite descriptions as a limiting case (where all predicates are purely distributive and cumulative).[3]

In the ordinary singular case, we might represent definite descriptions this way:

(1) The doctor is rich.
(2) [$\imath x$: Dx] Rx

---

[2] Neale and others have effectively argued against the idea that a distinctively referential description needs a separate definition. See, e.g., Neale 1990, ch. 3 and Kripke 1977. I have argued similarly in McKay 1984.

[3] In Ch. 8 we will take the basic model developed in this chapter and make it more context-sensitive.

Following Neale, I wish to hold that a singular sentence with a description is equivalent to another sentence involving universal and existential quantifiers:

(3) $[\imath x: Dx]$ Rx is equivalent to $[\exists x: Dx \wedge [\forall y: Dy]\ y = x]$ Rx

This is an adaptation of Russell's account of definite descriptions to the environment of restricted quantification. This new environment significantly changes things, however. Russell was at pains to point out that English definite descriptions, like indefinite descriptions, do not correspond to any unified element of their logical representation.[4] With unrestricted quantification this is true.

(4) *The D is R* is equivalent to $\exists x\ (Dx \wedge \forall y\ (Dy \rightarrow y = x) \wedge Rx)$

No unified part of the representation corresponds to the noun phrase *The D*, just as nothing corresponds to the noun phrase *Some D* in the representation of *Some D is R* with unrestricted quantifiers, '$\exists x\ (Dx \wedge Rx)$'. In such representations, the quantifier phrases can be interpreted as "frames" for predicates (a frame for 'Rx' in this case), but are not syntactic units. We, however, can use restricted quantifiers to create quantifier phrases (syntactic units) that correspond to the quantified noun phrases in English.[5] Whether we use '$[\imath x: Dx]$' or its equivalent in terms of existential and universal quantification ('$[\exists x: Dx \wedge [\forall y: Dy]\ y = x]$'), the English noun phrase corresponds to a unit, the quantifier phrase, in the formal representation.

Sentence (1) indicates that there is exactly one contextually available doctor, and it is rich. I want to show how this follows from a general account of descriptions that allows them to be used with plurals and non-distributive predicates.

When we use 'the' with plurals, we intend to be referring to all of the contextually available individuals satisfying the restricting predicate.

(5) The students are in the library.

(6)[6] $[\imath X: SX_D]\ LX_D$

[4] See Russell 1905.

[5] See Neale, pp. 38–49.

[6] Where a subscript indicates that a predicate 'FX_D' is distributive, it indicates that a distributing universal is suppressed. So it is shorthand for '$[\forall z: zAX]\ Fz$' or (if we use only plural quantifiers) '$[\forall Z: IZ \wedge ZAX]\ FZ$'. We can use the subscript when the scope of the distributing universal is clear, thus avoiding some clutter in the formulas.

We can try to use Neale's account as a model. Since we have two universal quantifiers, we need to think about which universal quantifier (if either) will work. Using the plural sameness relation developed in Chapter 4, we can try to apply the Russell–Neale model in the following way:

$$(7)^7 \quad [\exists X: SX_D \land [\Lambda Y: SY_D] \, Y \approx X] \, LX_D$$
$$(8) \quad [\exists X: SX_D \land [\forall Y: SY_D] \, Y \approx X] \, LX_D$$

(7) says:

> (9) Some students such that all of the students are them are in the library.

(8) says:

> (10) Some students X such that whatever students Y you pick, Y are X, are in the library.

The first captures what we want, and the second doesn't. In the case in which Al, Bill and Carla are all of the students, the second requires, for example, that Al and Bill are Al, Bill and Carla if it is to be true. However, the second can be revised to give us the right meaning.[8]

$$(11) \quad [\exists X: SX_D \land [\forall Y: SY_D] \, YAX] \, LX_D$$

The plural definite description requires that any students you might pick are among X. And once we see this definition, we can also see that a parallel definition will also work for Λ.

$$(12) \quad [\exists X: SX_D \land [\Lambda Y: SY_D] \, YAX] \, LX_D$$

These expansions seem to indicate that the definite description has the idea of totality at its core. The idea of using totality (rather than identity) as the core concept in the account of definite descriptions is due to Sharvy.[9] Since we have already identified the *among* relation as a fundamental logical relation, and since singular identity is defined in terms of this, really as a special case of *among*, this is a congenial result. The generalization of definite descriptions employs this *among* relation, and the singular definite description (with identity) will be a special case.

---

[7] This is equivalent to the simpler $[\Lambda^3 Y: SY_D] \, LX_D$. ('$\Lambda^3$' really is the plural definite description operator.) The form in (7), though, is more directly comparable to the use of the other universal quantifier.

[8] Helen Cartwright 2000, 233–4, presents the same truth-conditions for plural definite descriptions.

[9] Sharvy 1980.

'ALL OF THE A'

Sometimes we employ 'the' in connection with other quantifiers, especially proportional quantifiers. Although I have used sentences like:

(13) Most students are surrounding Adams Hall.

(14) $[\mu X: SX_D]\, RXa$

as examples employing plural quantification with a non-distributive predicate, this sentence may strike you as a bit odd.[10] That sentence needs a clear context in which it is salient who all of the relevant students are. This is to be expected, since 'most' is a proportional quantifier that needs a clear reference class. People I have discussed this with are usually at least somewhat more comfortable with the following sentence:

(15) Most of the students are surrounding Adams Hall.

$[\imath X: SX_D][\mu Y: YAX]\, RYa$

i.e.

(15a) $[\exists X: SX_D \wedge [\forall Z: SZ_D]\, ZAX][\mu Y: YAX]\, RYa$

or

(15b) $[\exists X: SX_D \wedge [\Lambda Z: SZ_D]\, ZAX][\mu Y: YAX]\, RYa$

On our semantics, this is equivalent to the shorter $[\mu X: SX]\, RXa$ (given the distributive character of 'SX', which makes anomaly impossible), but the use of the definite description has a pragmatic effect, signaling reference to some particular contextually available students. Thus it clearly signals that the conditions for the felicitous use of a proportional quantifier have been met.[11]

---

[10] Helen Cartwright finds these to be "ungrammatical" (Cartwright 1996, 50). I don't find (3) ungrammatical, but it seems slightly off key without prior context.

[11] As noted in Ch. 3, Helen Cartwright has also noticed that some quantifiers are much improved when 'of the' is inserted to make a "quantified partitive," and that failure of cumulativity in the predicate plays a role. See Cartwright 2000, 242. However, she has not distinguished proportional and non-proportional quantifiers in the way that we have, and so she does not get a full and accurate diagnosis of the problem. She also goes too far in saying that " 'All' demands a distributive predicate as verb phrase." By distinguishing two universal quantifiers (Λ and $\forall$) and recognizing that Λ is a proportional quantifier,

IMPROPER PLURAL DESCRIPTIONS

If we go back to the situation in which three separate meetings of students are taking place in the park, and in which no particular meeting has special salience, the following sentence becomes problematic:

(16) The students meeting together in the park are wearing t-shirts.

(16a) $[\imath X: SX_D \wedge MX]\ WX_D$

The sentence is acceptable in a situation in which there is only one meeting. But in the situation we are considering, with multiple, independent meetings, the conditions for the definite description are not met. No students are "the students meeting together in the park." 'MX' is not a cumulative predicate, so there can be some things I that satisfy it and some things J that satisfy it without there being things K such that K are *the* things that satisfy it. (I and J together do not satisfy the predicate.) For this reason, *The students meeting together in the park* can be an improper description.[12]

When a plural definite description is improper, the two different expansions, employing different universals, get different semantic evaluations:

(16b) $[\exists X: SX_D \wedge MX \wedge [\wedge Z: SZ_D \wedge MZ]\ ZAX]\ WX_D$

we can get a much finer diagnosis. Clearly her restriction is too severe. The following would be correctly represented with $\wedge$:

> All (of the) students are meeting together in the chapel.
> All (of the) students are fraternity brothers.
> All (of the) students are surrounding the building. (Think of answering "Which students are surrounding the building?")
> All (of the) students who met together are surrounding the building. (Acceptable if there was just one salient meeting.)

The following would be correctly represented with $\forall$ (see Ch. 3, 74–5):

> All companies that compete have common interests.
> All students who have a class together know each other.

See Ch. 10 for further discussion of the distributive character of 'all'.

[12] Cartwright 2000, 231–2, also discusses the fact that a failure of cumulativity can have the consequence that a definite description that contains the predicate is improper.

If there is more than one meeting, then our semantics makes the universal (Λ) clause, the maximality clause in (16b), anomalous, and so the quantified sentence has no truth-value.[13]

(16c) $[\exists X: SX_D \wedge MX \wedge [\forall Z: SZ_D \wedge MZ] ZAX] WX_D$

In this case, the conditions for the maximality clause are not met. There is no way to pick some X to be students meeting together in the park such that no matter how you select Z to be students meeting together in the park, Z will be among X. No students meeting together in the park include all such students. (The predicate is not cumulative.) So if we were to select this as the expansion of the definite description sentence, then we would say that the definite description sentence is false (not anomalous) in this situation.

I have no strong view about whether English sentences with improper plural descriptions are false or anomalous. Either view can be readily accommodated, though I will give some reasons to prefer the model (16b) as the right way to deal with anomaly.

First, let's consider a possible simplification for those who would like all sentences to have truth-values. Semantic anomaly occurs (in the semantics we have now) when we have a proportional quantifier Q with a non-cumulative predicate P in a situation in which there are some things I that satisfy P and some things J that satisfy P, but I and J sum to individuals that do not satisfy P. If we use $\forall$ in our account of definite descriptions and confine proportional quantifiers to the context $[QX: XAY]$, then we can have definite truth-values for all sentences. For instance, instead of

(17) $[\mu X: SX_D] RXa$

for "Most students are surrounding Adams Hall," we will always write

(18) $[\imath X: SX_D][\mu Y: YAX] RYa$

(*Most of the students are surrounding Adams Hall*), where the definite description explicitly picks out the individuals we are to take *most* of. Then, if we use the $\forall$ account of the definite description, we will always get a definite truth-value for the sentence. When the predicate within the definite description is non-cumulative, the definite description may be improper. When it is not a proper description, the sentence will be

---

[13] The same remarks apply, even more directly, to the equivalent $[\Lambda^\exists Z: SZ_D \wedge MZ] WX_D$.

false, not anomalous (given this account). So if there are several student meetings going on, then a sentence "Most of the students meeting together ... " will be false rather than anomalous on this approach.

Although we will not adopt that here, it suggests itself as an interesting possibility if we wish to banish semantic anomaly in the formal language. I will continue to assume that we get anomaly rather than falsehood when the maximality condition for a proportional quantification is not met. I will not assume that sentences like (17) must be rewritten as sentences like (18).

Returning to the case of expressions explicitly of the form "Q of the A", where Q is proportional, we can find some reason to prefer an analysis of definite descriptions on the model of (16b) rather than (16c). If someone says

(19) All of the students who are meeting together in the park are fraternity brothers.

the definite description will be a proper description if and only if there is just one meeting of students in the park (or we have some other contextual restriction that indicates which meeting we are talking about). If there are (equally salient) multiple student meetings, this will be an anomalous definite description, and I will take the sentence to be semantically anomalous as a result. (Note that if there are two meetings, (19) seems anomalous even if all of the students who are involved in the meetings are fraternity brothers. We don't know which students are being talked about in (19).)

Since I want to regard the semantic anomaly as stemming from the description rather than from the quantifier itself, I am adopting the approach modeled on (16b), where the definite description's maximality clause is analyzed in terms of 'Λ' rather than '$\forall$'. This approach has the consequence that when there are several meetings going on, with one meeting consisting of seniors, the following is anomalous:

(20a) Some of the students meeting together are seniors.

But the following will be true:

(20b) Some students meeting together are seniors.

That seems right to me. (20a) would be false rather than anomalous if we treated 'the students' in (20a) as a governing description and we modeled our descriptions on (16c). That result doesn't seem right to me.

PECULIAR DEFINITE DESCRIPTIONS

We should briefly note a peculiarity. We have said that plural definite descriptions involving non-cumulative properties can be improper definite descriptions when the conditions for the maximality clause are not met. We have a more subtle problem with the "small" category of predicates that are non-distributive and cumulative: predicates like *X are at least three in number*, *X have at least $100 among them*, etc. Let's consider a sentence with a definite description and a restrictive relative clause containing such a predicate:

(21) The students who are at least three in number are in the classroom.

According to either account of plural definite descriptions (using Λ or ∀), (21) will be true iff there are at least three students and all (contextually relevant) students are in the classroom (since the sum of all the students who are three or more in number is all students).

In fact, though, such definite descriptions are always peculiar (as long as we stick to the reading of 'who are at least three in number' as a restrictive relative clause).[14] This is a very strange way to say that there are at least three students, and it is also a very strange way to say that all students are in the classroom. These can be said much more briefly and directly in other ways, and a simple conjunction will serve to say both.

(21a) The students are at least three in number and all students are in the classroom.

A sentence like (21), but with a non-restrictive relative clause, is another way of saying what (21a) says. (21), though, requires some inference to recognize that the students *X* who include any students *Y* who are at least three in number are all of the students. Thus (21) is peculiar; it is hard to see how one would choose (21) to express this.[15]

---

[14] It is tempting to read this as a non-restrictive relative clause for the very reason that it is so peculiar when read restrictively.

[15] Helen Cartwright briefly considers an example like this, without ever fully stating it. She considers the predicate 'people with $0.25 or more among them'. She regards descriptions with such predicates as "legitimate". Cartwright 2000, 233.

THE SINGULAR DEFINITE DESCRIPTION

No matter which version of the plural definite description we use, the standard (Russellian) account of the singular definite description in terms of the existential and the universal comes out easily as a special case. Plural definite descriptions can have non-distributive clauses as the restriction of a quantifier phrase or as the main clause of a sentence.

(22) The students who met together in the park are now surrounding Adams Hall.

(23) $[\imath X: SX_D \wedge MX] RXa$

We have offered two different analyses that might plausibly represent this.

(24) $[\exists X: SX_D \wedge MX \wedge [\forall Z: SZ_D \wedge MZ] ZAX] RXa$
(25)[16] $[\exists X: SX_D \wedge MX \wedge [\Lambda Z: SZ_D \wedge MZ] ZAX] RXa$

When all predicates are (even weakly) distributive,[17] however, sentences of the forms (26)–(29) are equivalent (as we noted in Chapters 3 and 6):

(26) $[\forall X: CX_D] BX_D$
(27) $[\Lambda X: CX_D] BX_D$
(28) $[\forall x: Cx] Bx$
(29)[18] $[\forall X: CX \wedge IX] BX$

So (30)–(33) are also equivalent, since the first argument position of the *among* relation is always distributive:

(30) $[\forall Z: CZ_D] ZAX$
(31) $[\Lambda Z: CZ_D] ZAX$
(32) $[\forall z: Cz] zAX$
(33) $[\forall Z: CZ \wedge IZ] ZAX$

---

[16] Or $[\Lambda^{\exists} X: SX_D \wedge MX] RXa$.

[17] A predicate P is *weakly distributive* iff whenever some things are P, each of them is P. A predicate P is *strongly distributive* iff whenever some things X are P, any things Y among X are P. (The predicate *are greater than four in number or less than two in number* is weakly distributive but not strongly distributive. I know of no uncontrived examples that differentiate.)

[18] We use this representation (instead of (28)) when only plural quantification is permitted. See Ch. 6.

Thus when we have singular quantification, simply applying the above analysis of definite descriptions to the singular case would lead us to analyze a sentence of the form

(34) $[\imath x: Cx]\, Bx$

(35) $[\imath X: CX \wedge IX]\, BX$

in the following way:

(34a) $[\exists x: Cx \wedge [\forall z: Cz]\, zAx]Bx$

(35a) $[\exists X: CX \wedge IX \wedge [\Lambda Z: CZ \wedge IZ]\, ZAX]\, BX$[19]

(35b) $[\exists X: CX \wedge IX \wedge [\forall Z: CZ \wedge IZ]\, ZAX]\, BX$

But zAx is true for an assignment of values to z and x if and only if $z = x$ is true, if z and x are singular variables. Correspondingly, $IX \wedge [\forall Z: CZ \wedge IZ]\, ZAX$ is true on an assignment iff some individual is assigned to X such that every individual that is C is identical to that individual. So our analysis, extended to the singular case, is equivalent to Neale's Russellian analysis.

(36) $[\exists x: Cx \wedge [\forall z: Cz]\, z = x]\, Bx$

We have already noted that with basic quantifier expressions, when all predicates are distributive, the singular and plural quantified sentences are equivalent. (*Most dogs are brown* can be represented by '$[\mu x: Dx]\, Bx$' or by '$[\mu X: DX_D]\, BX_D$'. They will be equivalent.) Singular and plural definite descriptions, however, are not equivalent. (*The dog is brown* is not equivalent to *The dogs are brown*.) The definite description is a defined expression, defined in terms of the existential and a universal quantifier. The singular:

(37) $[\imath x: Cx]\, Bx$

is defined as

---

[19] There is a decision here. Consider a case where a student John lifted a table by himself and three other students lifted it together (and that is all the lifting that went on). Can we say "The student who lifted the table is tall" in virtue of John's height? If the singular definite description is proper in such a case, then we can take (35a) as a correct representation. If the singular definite description is not proper, because of the cooperating table-lifters, then we will need another analysis:

(35c) $[\exists X: CX \wedge IX \wedge [\Lambda Z: CZ]\, ZAX]\, BX$

(35d) $[\exists X: CX \wedge IX \wedge [\forall Z: CZ]\, ZAX]\, BX$

(35c) will be semantically anomalous, and (35d) will be false. I do not think that these would be appropriate analyses. In any case, though, all are available.

(38a) $[\exists x\colon Cx \wedge [\Lambda z\colon Cz]\; zAx]\; Bx$

(38b) $[\exists x\colon Cx \wedge [\forall z\colon Cz]\; zAx]\; Bx$

which can be defined as

(39a) [20] $[\exists X\colon CX \wedge IX \wedge [\Lambda Z\colon CZ \wedge IZ]\; ZAX]\; BX$

(39b) $[\exists X\colon CX \wedge IX \wedge [\forall Z\colon CZ \wedge IZ]\; ZAX]\; BX$

But the plural

(40) $[\imath X\colon CX_D]\; BX_D$

is defined as

(41) $[\exists X\colon CX_D \wedge [\forall Z\colon CZ_D]\; ZAX]\; BX_D$ or

(42)[21] $[\exists X\colon CX_D \wedge [\Lambda Z\colon CZ_D]\; ZAX]\; BX_D$

(41) and (42) are not equivalent to (39). Since BX and CX are both distributive, we have:

(41b) $[\exists X\colon [\forall W\colon IW \wedge WAX]\; CW \wedge [\forall Z\colon [\forall W\colon IW \wedge WAZ]\; CW]\; ZAX]\; [\forall W\colon IW \wedge WAX]\; BW$

(42b)[22] $[\exists X\colon [\forall W\colon IW \wedge WAX]\; CW \wedge [\Lambda Z\colon [\forall W\colon IW \wedge WAZ]\; CW]\; ZAX]\; [\forall W\colon IW \wedge WAX]\; BW$

Since BX and CX are distributive, (41) and (42) are equivalent, but they are not equivalent to (39). The uniqueness clause in (39) says that every individual that satisfies CZ is among the individual X (i.e., that there is just one individual satisfying CZ). Nothing in (40)–(42) produces that uniqueness; rather, we require that any individual*s* satisfying CZ are among (the individual*s*) X. That is the expected difference between singular and plural.

COMPARISON WITH MASS QUANTIFIERS

Richard Sharvy considered definite descriptions in general and developed the key idea that totality, rather than uniqueness, is a critical concept.

---

[20] Alternatively, we can take '$\imath$' as the singular variant of '$\Lambda^{\exists}$'. Then (37) is '$[\Lambda^{\exists}Z\colon CZ \wedge IZ]\; BX$', which is also equivalent to (39a).

[21] i.e., $[\Lambda^{\exists}Z\colon CZ_D]\; BX_D$

[22] Or, slightly more simply, $[\Lambda^{\exists}Z\colon [\forall W\colon IW \wedge WAZ]\; CW]\; [\forall W\colon IW \wedge WAZ]\; BW$.

We have considered plural definite descriptions within the context of an account of generalized quantifiers that allows for non-distributive plural predication, and our conclusion accords with this. Identity is a special case of totality, and so singular definite descriptions are a special case of the plural definite descriptions.

Sharvy wished to develop an even more general account of definite descriptions, applying to mass terms as well.

(43)   The gold in Utah is worth more than $100.

The treatment does seem analogous, at least, to what we have done.

(44)   Some stuff X is gold in Utah, and all gold in Utah is part of X, and X is worth more than $100.

Here we have mass quantifiers, with a 'part of' relation where we had 'among' in our analysis. As we saw in Chapter 6, the *among* relation is governed by principles that are formally analogous to the principles of mereology, and the principles of mereology are the principles of the *part of* relation. (Whichever basic axioms we use (AX1 or M1 with M2) the axioms are reinterpretable as fundamental axioms of mereology.)[23] So it may look like a fully general theory should be at hand.

However, as I indicated in Chapter 6, we should not try to replace the concept *among* by the concept *part of*, because the words 'X are part of Y' at least suggest, and perhaps require, that Y is a single thing that has X as a part or parts. In the case of plurals, we wish to avoid this singularist suggestion. To reinforce the caution here, consider that not everything that we want to say about some things applies equally to the mereological sum of those things. The mereological sum of the counties in Utah is the same as the mereological sum of the cities and townships in Utah. Nevertheless, we might wish to say contrasting things like these:

(46)   The counties in Utah are 15 in number.

(47)   The cities and townships in Utah are 100 in number, not 15.

(48)   The counties in Utah were named from 1917 to 1919.

(49)   The cities and townships in Utah were named from 1918 to 1921.

---

[23] The formalization for the *part of* relation for mass terms would not ordinarily include our existence axiom, which stipulates that there are individuals if there is anything.

(50) Richfield, Sevier County, and Utah are nested. (For any things x and y among these three, x is part of y or y is part of x.)

(51) Richfield, Emery County, and Utah are not nested.

The relevant mereological sum in all of these cases is Utah.[24] So it is difficult to see how mereology can do the job that is needed here. We would need to make incompatible predications of a single entity.

Sharvy himself argued that there is an "ordinary" sense of 'part' that makes each township a part of the denotation of 'the cities and townships of Utah' but not a part of the denotation of 'the counties of Utah' (p. 619: "x are part of y in this ordinary sense if x are *some of* y"). I would rather say each township is among the townships of Utah but not among the counties of Utah, and *among* (*is one of; are some of*) is not a *part of* relation. (Note that the words 'some of' are used in both count and mass examples, though as a plural in the first case and a singular in the second. *These are some of the bowls we are using; This is some of the soup we will serve.*)

Sharvy argues that the "part of" relation he is concerned with is not a materialist 'part of' relation. But then it is a different relation than the materialist 'part of' relation that is needed for the semantics of quantified mass terms. While ordinary usage might allow us to use 'part of' for this relation (and even that is questionable, see Chapter 6), it is better for us here to use different terms for the relations. Most importantly, we should recognize that the relation XAY that is central to the semantics of plurals does not require singularization of the second argument place.

When we say that most of the gold in Auckland is in two statues, that is consistent with saying that most of the things in Auckland that are made of gold are wedding rings. There are two distinct notions of totality, the totality of stuff and the totality of things. These share many general logical features, but the relations of the constituents to the totalities are distinct relations, and 'most' applies in different ways. The use of 'most' with a mass term means imposing a metric on a quantity; but the use of 'most' with count terms requires tallying individuals (in the finite case, at least). [25]

---

[24] None of this should be assumed to be geographically or historically accurate. In particular, the dates for naming are fabricated, and it has been merely assumed that Utah divides completely into cities and townships. If this is not true of the actual Utah, imagine a state called 'Utah' of which it is true. Possibility suffices for the point. The 'nested' example is from David Lewis (conversation).

[25] See Kurtz 1996 for some ideas along these lines.

The analysis of the use of 'the' with mass terms is structurally similar to the use of 'the' with count terms. But the notion of totality used with mass terms must be based on the notion *part of* rather than the relation *among*.

(52) The gold in Auckland is worth more than $100.

(53) Some gold in Auckland is such that all gold in Auckland is a part of it, and it is worth more than $100.

[∃x: Gx ∧ [∀y: Gy] y is part of x] x is worth more than $100

The items in this domain are quantities of stuff (Helen Cartwright's sense of 'quantity'), and the principles of an atomless mereology apply to the *part of* relation.

Conspicuously, we can identify the following analogous principles as another way in which the *among* relation and the *part of* relation differ. This principle is true:[26]

(54) For any things X, if X are the A's and X are the B's, then the A's are the B's.

$\forall X$, if $[\imath Y{:}AY]\ Y \approx X$, and $[\imath Z{:}BZ]\ Z \approx X$, then $[\imath Y{:}AY]$ $[\imath Z{:}BZ]\ Y \approx Z$.

But the corresponding principle for mereology is not true. We will use $f(X)$ to represent the fusion of X. Then the corresponding principle would be this:

(55) For any thing x, if x is the fusion of the A's and x is the fusion of the B's, then the A's are the B's.

$\forall x$, if $[\imath Y{:}AY]\ f(Y) = x$ and $[\imath Z{:}BZ]\ f(Z) = x$, then $[\imath Y{:}AY]$ $[\imath Z{:}BZ]\ Y \approx Z$.

That principle is false, as we saw in our visit to Utah. Things do not ordinarily have a unique decomposition into parts.

So we can conclude that the uses of 'the' with mass terms and with count terms are similar, in that they involve structurally similar notions of totality. But the relations of the constituents to the totalities are distinct relations, so there is no uniform representation of the general form of all uses of 'the', *contra* Sharvy.

---

[26] Strictly speaking, it is true if all of the descriptions are proper. If the descriptions are not proper, then it is either true or anomalous, depending on which approach we take to improper descriptions.

However, a development of the logic of mass terms should prove to be very much an analogue of our consideration of the logic of plurals. For example, there is a division between distributive and non-distributive predicates of masses, where a predicate is distributive if it meets this condition:

Whenever some stuff X is F, every (sufficiently large) part of X is F.[27]

This applies to terms like 'X is gold' or 'x is in San Francisco', but predicates like 'X is shaped into a ring' or 'X is spread over a large area' will not be distributive. Similarly, some predicates will be cumulative, but others, such as 'X is shaped into a ring' and 'X is gathered in one place' will not.

There will also be a distinction between non-proportional and pro-portional quantification with regard to felicity conditions. In a context in which there are many gold rings to consider, the phrase 'Most of the gold that is formed into a ring' will have no proper reference. (This is in contrast to 'Most of the gold that is formed into rings', which would consider a proportion of the totality of gold that is in rings.) Similarly, if there are separate quantities of gold in many places, then 'most of the gold that is gathered together' is not a proper description.

One might wish for more in the unification of quantifier concepts, that the concept *most* in 'Most students' is the same as the concept *most* in 'most gold'. However, we have a very substantial unification in the fact that the fundamental logical relation in one case is the relation *among* and the fundamental logical relation in the other case is the relation *part of*, and these are both governed by core axioms of the system developed in Chapter 6. In the plural case, we need some things to tally (provided by the existence axiom), and in the mass case, we require a metric on the masses under consideration.

PLURAL *DE RE*

Russell made a case for his account of definite descriptions by indicating how it could be used in resolving scope ambiguities. Philip Bricker (Bricker 1989) has identified related ambiguities that are best

---

[27] The qualification 'sufficiently large' is required, so that distributivity does not entail that no material has an atomic structure (i.e., that every kind of stuff is gunk).

resolved with resources that are equivalent to having plural definite descriptions and the *among* relation. (Bricker identifies the problem and indicates the general features of the solution in Bricker 1989.) In what follows, we consider that problem and indicate how the resources we have developed will solve it.

Consider the sentence

(56) Some person in the room must win a prize.[28]

On a standard disambiguation, this sentence will have two readings:

(56a) □ [∃x: Rx] Wx

(The *de dicto* reading: necessarily, some person in the room wins.)

The key point to keep in mind is that (56a) constrains possible worlds to have a winner in the room, but entirely different people can be in the room and, accordingly, different people can be winners, in different possible worlds. That contrasts with the following:

(56b) [∃x: Rx] □ Wx

(The *de re* reading: some person (actually) in the room has a certain property, of necessarily winning)

But Bricker has pointed out that there is another *de re* reading of (56).

(56c) The people in the room are such that necessarily, someone among them will win.

This does not predicate a property *de re* of any person (perhaps (56b) is false), but it does predicate a property *de re* of the people who are (actually) in the room – of necessarily having a winner among them. Thus this is *de re* with respect to the people in the room, but not *de re* with respect to any one of them. (These people are such that one of them must win, but it is not said that there is a *y* among them such that *y* has the property of necessarily winning.) Given the resource we have developed, the natural way to represent this is the following:

(56d) [ɿX: RX$_D$] □ [∃y: yAX] Wy

28 See Bricker 1989, 377.

The relationship to (56a) and (56b) can be seen more clearly if we represent them as:

(56e) $\Box$ [$\imath X$: RX_D] [$\exists y$: yAX] Wy

(56f) [$\imath X$: RX_D] [$\exists y$: yAX] $\Box$ Wy

((56e) is equivalent to (56a), and (56f) is equivalent to (56b).) (56d) can be viewed as an intermediate scope interpretation of (56).

This shows us something else. Even when non-distributive predication is not overtly involved, identifying a place for the non-distributive logical relation *among* may have a role in disambiguating even relatively simple sentences. (In earlier chapters, more complex sentences, like the Geach–Kaplan sentence, also showed the use for *among* and plural quantification.)

Related ambiguities come up in universally quantified sentences involving possibility.[29]

(57a) Any person in the room might win a prize.

(57b) Every person in the room might win a prize.

Here it is natural to take (57a) to express the reading with the most deeply embedded modal operator, since the word 'any' is an indicator that the universal has larger scope than the modal operator.

(57c) [$\imath X$: RX_D] [$\forall y$: yAX] $\Diamond Wy$

(57b) then has the following two readings:[30]

---

[29] See Bricker 1989, 375.

[30] There are some other readings for (57b), if we allow that some people might win a prize together (non-distributively).

(57i) $\Diamond$ [ΛX: RX_D] WX

It is possible that the people in the room will all win a prize together.

(57ii) [ΛX: RX_D] $\Diamond WX$

The people in the room are such that it is possible that they will all win a prize together.

These readings are made available since we allow non-distributive predication more generally. The "intermediate" reading is equivalent to (57ii):

(57iii) [$\imath X$: RX_D] $\Diamond$ [ΛY: YAX] WY

Still more scope variations are possible, and they would be possible readings for a similar sentence with 'all people' in place of 'every person' in (57b).

(57iv) $\Diamond$ [$\imath X$: RX_D] [$\forall Y$: YAX] WY

It is possible that, no matter what (combination of) people in the room you pick, those people win a prize together.

(57d) ◇ [ɪX: RX_D] [∀y: yAX] Wy

It is possible that the people in the room would all be prize-winners.

(57e) [ɪX: RX_D] ◇ [∀y: yAX] Wy

The people who are (actually) in the room are such that it is possible that they would all be prize-winners.

Some people may have different views about which of the three readings are available for which of the two English sentences. Perhaps all three readings are available for (57b), for example. But in any case there are at least these three distinct claims expressible by (57a) and (57b).

Bricker points out that, as one would expect, multiple readings are also available in temporal and doxastic contexts. The temporal example he gives has three readings that can be identified without introducing plural quantification. Let **P** be a past tense operator (*at some time in the past*).

(58)   Every book in the store was on sale.
(58a) **P** [∀y: By] Sy
(58b) [∀y: **P** By] **P** Sy
(58c) [∀y: By] **P** Sy

However, there is an additional disambiguation of (58c) that can be made clear with the help of plural quantification.

(58d) [ɪX: BX_D] [∀y: yAX] **P** Sy
(58e) [ɪX: BX_D] **P** [∀y: yAX] Sy

If **P** means 'at some time in the past', then an interpretation of (58c) needs to indicate whether it is being said that the books were on sale at the same time or not. The difference between (58d) and (58e) indicates that. ((58b) also has additional readings, but the presence of multiple tense operators raises issues that we cannot consider without a much more thorough consideration of how to represent tense. We won't do that here.)

(57v) [ɪX: RX_D] [∀Y: YAX] ◇ WY

No matter what (combination of) people in the room you pick, it is possible that those people will win a prize together.

(57vi) [ɪX: RX_D] ◇ [∀Y: YAX] WY

The people in the room are such that it is possible that no matter which (combination) of them you pick, those people will win a prize together.

The readings in this footnote are additional to the readings considered in the main body.

(59)   Ralph believes that someone in the house committed the murder.

(59a) Ralph believes that [ɿX: HX_D] [∃y: yAX] Cy

(59b) [ɿX: HX_D] Ralph believes that [∃y: yAX] Cy

(59c) [ɿX: HX_D] [∃y: yAX] Ralph believes that Cy

Clearly these are three distinct readings that are available for (59).

We also need to be able to deal with cases of multiple modality.

(60)   It might have been the case that some person in the room had to win.

(60a) ◇ [ɿX: RX_D] [∃y: yAX] □ Wy

(60b) ◇ [ɿX: RX_D] □ [∃y: yAX] Wy

(60c) ◇ □ [ɿX: RX_D] [∃y: yAX] Wy

(60d) [ɿX: RX_D] ◇ □ [∃y: yAX] Wy

(60e) [ɿX: RX_D] ◇ [∃y: yAX] □ Wy

(60f) [ɿX: RX_D] [∃y: yAX] ◇ □ Wy

These are all distinct possible interpretations of the English sentence (60). Our tool for identifying readings and clearly separating them seems to work well.

RELATIONSHIP TO SCHA'S DISCUSSION OF DEFINITE DESCRIPTIONS

Remko Scha's work on distributive, collective and cumulative quantification[31] has been important and influential. His approach to definite descriptions seems to be directly opposed to ours, since he holds that definite descriptions are not quantifiers and are not subject to the same scope influences as quantifiers. However, taking definite descriptions as quantifiers in the way that we do, we can (and indeed need to) say much the same thing that Scha says about key examples he discusses, and with our approach we can identify genuine scope ambiguities that involve definite descriptions (as we have already done).

Scha presents three "geometric" examples for consideration:

(61)   The squares contain the circles.

---

[31] Scha 1981.

Diagram A

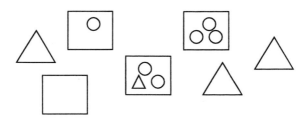

(62) The sides of rectangle 1 run parallel to the sides of rectangle 2.

(63) The sides of rectangle 1 cross the sides of rectangle 2.

Diagram B

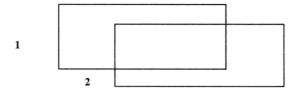

Scha says that the following are paraphrases of these:

(61a) Every circle is contained in some square.

(62a) Every side of rectangle 1 runs parallel to some side of rectangle 2, and every side of rectangle 2 runs parallel to some side of rectangle 1.

(63a) Some sides of rectangle 1 cross some sides of rectangle 2.

I would wish to say very much the same thing as Scha about the fact that these are interpreted very differently. The difference is not due to any issue of quantifier analysis or quantifier scope in the initial English sentences. I would represent them all as involving two plural definite descriptions, and the sentences would be equivalent no matter what the order of the descriptions was.

(61b) [ɪX: CX] [ɪY: SY] Y contain X

(62b) [ɪX: X are sides of R1] [ɪY: Y are sides of R2] X run parallel to Y

(63b) [ɪ X: X are sides of R1] [ɪY: Y are sides of R2] X cross Y

We get the varying interpretations of these (61a–63a) because there are different lexical conditions on the plural predicates. Plurals are related to their singular counterparts in different ways, so that these plurals are used to make different kinds of claims about the things under discussion.

Y contain X: [∀x: xAX] [∃y: yAY] y contains x

X run parallel to Y: [∀x: xAX] [∃y: yAY] x runs parallel to y ∧ [∀y: yAY] [∃x: xAX] y runs parallel to x

X cross Y:[32] [∃x: xAX] [∃y: yAY] y crosses x

This relationship between singular predicates and their non-distributive plural counterparts varies with context, and so we should not take these, as Scha seems to, as fixed meaning postulates for the plural use of these verbs. The meanings above are apt for the particular examples that Scha gives, but cannot be relied on as general constraints on the meanings of these verbs in plural cases.[33] Nevertheless, in giving a uniform syntactic analysis of the sentences involving definite descriptions and in accounting for the differences in meaning by a difference in the way that the plural predicate relates to its singular counterpart, we can agree with Scha.

Unlike Scha, though, we treat definite descriptions as quantifiers. Scha assigns only a non-distributive reading to plural definite descriptions, and thus seems not to be able to admit the distributive ambiguity in sentences like

(64) The boys lifted a 200-pound weight.

In addition, he claims that definite descriptions take only small scope, though this is manifestly false.

(65) Every year the students in my class surprise me.

(66) Each student met with the faculty members of her or his department.

The standard distributive interpretations are not available in these geometric examples only because they represent impossible, or at least very unlikely, situations.

---

[32] This may need to be specified as plural to get the meaning right. That does not affect the main discussion here.

[33] See Roberts 1987, Landman 1989, Schwarzschild 1996 and Landman 2000, 121, for examples where these meaning postulates do not apply.

Thus our approach seems to have all of the virtues of his in these geometric examples and several advantages, both in its treatment of the particular cases and in its over-all theoretical scope and simplicity. We have a systematic way of treating distributivity phenomena and systematic ways of representing scope distinctions. In addition, our plural quantification at least provides the resources for clearly representing the different ways in which the plural relations "these contain those," "these cross those," and "these are parallel to those" relate to their singular counterparts. The fact that these are different raises questions about the lexical and pragmatic facts that underlie these differences, but that is beyond our scope here.

8

THE: Context Sensitivity

The definite description quantifiers that we have introduced in the formal language are understood in the following way.

> $[\imath X: CX]\ BX$ is understood as $[\exists X: CX \wedge [\Lambda Y: CY]\ YAX]\ BX$ or, equivalently, as $[\Lambda^\exists X: CX]\ BX$. (*The shipmates are in mutiny.*)
>
> $[\imath x: Cx]\ Bx$ is understood as $[\exists X: CX \wedge IX \wedge [\Lambda Y: CY \wedge IY]\ YAX]\ BX$ or equivalently $[\exists x: Cx \wedge [\forall y: Cy]\ y = x]\ Bx$ or $[\Lambda^\exists x: Cx]\ Bx$.[1] (*The captain is bold.*)

This provides for distinct but related ways of understanding singular and plural definite descriptions, with the singular a special case of the plural but not equivalent to the plural (even when the predicates are distributive).

Many uses of definite descriptions, though, are "incomplete." That is, the explicit definite description does not uniquely specify an individual or, in the plural case, some maximally inclusive individuals; we rely on context to provide the additional resources that make the description uniquely applicable. Two processes of contextual supplementation are important here. One is *predicate supplementation*: a brief definite description stands proxy for a longer definite description that can be constructed by adding predicates that are explicit in the discourse context. The other is *domain restriction*: the context restricts the domain for the definite description, with uniqueness achieved within that smaller domain.[2] These processes are not mutually exclusive. Both can be at work in the interpretation of definite descriptions. However, there are features of definite descriptions that do not seem to be

---

[1] This last abbreviates $[\Lambda^\exists X: CX \wedge IX]\ BX$. This can be true only if there are some things (or some thing) J that satisfy '$CX \wedge IX$' such that all things that satisfy '$CX \wedge IX$' are among J. But then J must be just one thing and the only C.

[2] See Neale 1990, 95ff for a discussion of *explicit* (predicate supplementation) and *implicit* (domain limitation) approaches.

explained well by either of these approaches or by their combination. Definite descriptions seem to be more sensitive to context than other quantifiers are.[3]

PREDICATE SUPPLEMENTATION AND DOMAIN RESTRICTION

Let's first consider an example where predicate supplementation seems like the obvious explanation for what is going on.

> (1) My daughter is at Swansea School, and the headmaster is a very distinguished person.

Although the words 'the headmaster' do not give us a uniquely specifying definite description, there being many schools with headmasters, it is clear from context that we can understand this as *the headmaster at Swansea School*, and the description will be proper if there is exactly one of those. The description 'the headmaster' goes proxy for a fuller definite description 'the headmaster at Swansea School'. In this case, the linguistic resources for completing the description are fully explicit in the context.

However, in many cases context provides no specific words that can serve as completers for the description, and so it is more attractive to understand these as cases of domain limitation. According to this second approach, context delimits the domain in such a way that, within that domain, the description is uniquely specifying. Contextually indicated quantifier domain limitation is of course the norm for other quantifiers too,[4] so the fact that we have this in the case of definite descriptions should be no surprise.

> (2) John had his broken arm checked yesterday. He was impressed with the examination room and the equipment, and the doctor predicted rapid healing.

The three definite descriptions are all understood to be unique within the domain under consideration, the individuals involved in the examination situation.

---

[3] The approach to be developed here has some affinity to some ideas of Craige Roberts 2003, though ultimately I am advocating even more flexibility.

[4] Cf. Neale 1990, 95ff.

We can have both of these processes (contextually indicated predicate completions for definite descriptions and contextually indicated domain restrictions) in play separately or together in various examples involving descriptions. However, even with both of those processes available to explain how definite descriptions get their reference, there are two problems.[5]

PROBLEM 1: LACK OF UNIQUE SPECIFICATION

Many definite descriptions seem incomplete in more significant ways. The context does not provide linguistic resources that can be inserted to complete the description (in the way that 'at Swansea School' was available in our first example) and nothing in the context limits the domain in a way that would produce uniqueness. Here are two perfectly normal uses of definite descriptions.

(3) One day, a man and a boy were walking along a road, and the man said to the boy: 'Would you like to be king?'[6]

(4) A jogger bumped into me yesterday. The jogger was wearing a baseball cap.

Obviously, the use of 'the man' in (3) does not require that there was only one man walking along a road with a boy one day. In (4), the appropriate use of the definite description does not require that there is just one jogger or even that there was just one jogger yesterday. We immediately understand that this refers to a jogger who bumped into me yesterday. So far that is the accommodation that the predicate supplementation process provides. But even if 'jogger who bumped into me yesterday' is not uniquely specifying, that will not make the second sentence of (4) inappropriate.

In the second sentence of (4), I use the definite description to refer to the individual that is the basis for my asserting the first sentence, even if there were other joggers (perhaps little noticed or long forgotten) who bumped into me yesterday. If we are to maintain something like the Russell–Neale–Sharvy analysis for such definite descriptions, with

---

[5] Predicate supplementation might be viewed as a special case of domain limitation. But that is not an important matter for our purposes.

[6] This example is from Gareth Evans (Evans 1985, 131). See Ch. 9 for further discussion of Evans's treatment of this example.

a uniqueness or maximality clause, we must allow for this further way that descriptions can be incomplete. Nothing said about the individual is uniquely specifying, but a particular individual is the basis for the claim.

We might regard this as domain limitation, but there is nothing in the context that explicitly indicates how the domain is limited (so that within the domain there is only one jogger I bumped into yesterday and the definite description can then be proper). Nothing in the first sentence of (4) indicates which jogger is being discussed. The predicates 'x is a jogger' and 'x bumped into me yesterday' may apply to many, though I go on to talk about just one. We can understand such definite descriptions as applying to the individual that was the speaker's basis for the previous claim, but no part of the claim itself indicates what individual that is. If we are to understand this as domain limitation, it seems that one limitation must be to what the speaker has in mind or to whatever is the basis for the speaker's prior claim.

We have a corresponding problem with plural definite descriptions.

(5) Some students met together in the park, and now **the students** are playing well together.

Even if we understand 'the students' in the second clause as a kind of proxy for 'the students who met together in the park', our use of the definite description does not require that the literal maximality condition is met. There may be other students who met together in the park, but the description in the second clause will refer to the students who were the basis for the claim in the first clause. We must understand the context as limiting the domain for the second to what the speaker has in mind.

Domain limitation issues apply to other quantifiers as well as to definite descriptions, so it might be argued that the analysis in terms of other quantifiers stands untroubled. But there seems to be a difference. For example:

(4') A jogger bumped into me yesterday. A jogger who bumped into me yesterday such that every jogger who bumped into me yesterday is identical to her was wearing a baseball cap.

The second sentence of (4') makes a claim that only one jogger bumped into me yesterday. (4) is clearly not committed to that. We cannot simply say that the definite description is subject to the same domain restrictions as the quantifiers that are used in analyzing it.

(5′) Some students met together in the park, and now some students who met in the park and who are such that all students who met in the park are among them are playing well together.

If there was more than one meeting (of students in the park yesterday), then (5′) will be false (or at least inappropriate) in a way that (5) is not. Even if domain limitation is relevant to definite descriptions and other quantifiers, somehow the use of other quantifiers does not succeed in limiting the domain in the way that the definite description does.

We will return to this issue after consideration of another kind of example that poses a problem for the domain limitation account.

PROBLEM 2: MULTIPLE DOMAINS

The following example raises a problem for the domain limitation approach.

(6) John bought some books. He put **the books** on the shelf next to some other books he bought.

This seems like an acceptable use of the definite description. To maintain a version of the domain limitation approach, it seems that we have to say that there are different domains for different quantifiers within the second sentence. We cannot see the contextual limitations on the definite description as a restriction on our general domain of discourse, applying throughout the sentence. That is awkward. The alternative, that the definite description is to be understood as something like 'the books he bought that were the basis for what I just said', may initially seem more attractive in this case.

Recent work by Craige Roberts provides an idea that might serve as the basis for a sensible development of the domain limitation approach so that sentences like (6) are no longer so problematic.[7] The domain restriction for definite descriptions seems to be very local to the conversational context in which the description is used; the use of the description must bear a certain relationship to prior context, but other quantifiers

---

[7] Roberts 2003. I am kidnapping her idea, not just borrowing it. She puts it to use in a very different account of definite noun phrases.

in the sentence ("some other books he bought") are not subject to the same restriction to such a local context. Our examples (5) and (6) might then be seen as plural illustrations of some of the features of this context dependence.[8]

It suffices for our immediate purposes to say that some notion of contextual availability is needed to say how definite descriptions differ in use from other quantifiers. In light of examples like (4)–(6), we would have to say that the account must allow that what is contextually available for an utterance u of a definite description may be less than the total domain of individuals available for other quantification. Accordingly we cannot simply take 'the' to be defined in terms of uniqueness within a sentence's full interpretive domain. The use of 'the' has a special connection with contextual availability, and our semantic conditions really indicate that we are defining definite descriptions in terms of existential and universal quantification in a (possibly) more restricted domain – a domain of things that are made especially available in the discourse context.[9] Adapting Roberts' idea to a fundamentally Russellian account of plural definite descriptions that includes plural definite descriptions, it seems that we could say the following.

Given a context C, an appropriate use u of a definite phrase 'the Fs' refers to some things X such that:

(i) X are available for u in C and X are Fs[10]
(ii) $\forall Y$ such that Y are available for u in C and Y are Fs, $Y \wedge X$

The definite description differs from other quantifiers in that other quantifiers do not share the same restriction to what is locally contextually available. Putting this another way, we could say that other quantifiers seem to be slightly less flexible in the way that their domains are limited in conversation.

The oddness of the following indicates how this context sensitivity is a special feature of definite descriptions:

---

[8] Roberts develops a general account of singular descriptions that provides more detail concerning this contextual dependence.

[9] *Weakly familiar*, in Roberts' terms.

[10] Roberts would say 'contextually entailed to be F' where I say 'F' (though she speaks only of the singular case). However, it seems to me that an account in terms of entailment is a mistake. When I speak of *the Fs*, I speak of the contextually available things that are F, not merely of those such that the discourse already entails that they are F.

(6*) John bought some books. Some books that are all books that he bought are such that he put them next to some other books he bought.

Although (6) does not seem contradictory, (6*) does. Using the existential and universal quantifiers does not so readily allow the kind of domain flexibility that the interpretation of (6) requires, reinforcing the idea that the context-dependence and domain flexibility of descriptions exceed that of other quantifiers.

This is not to say that there cannot be multiple domains for quantifiers within a sentence that does not contain definite descriptions. Stanley and Williamson[11] provide the following examples:

(7) A group of evangelists met in the square, whereupon everyone converted someone.

(8) Someone angered everyone by being overly joyful.

(9) Nobody cared that nobody came.[12]

(10) As the ship pulled away from the dock, every man waved to every woman, every woman waved to every man, and every child waved to every child.

(11) When we looked out of the window, everyone saw everyone putting up their umbrellas.

My proposal allows that quantifiers, including definite descriptions, can have different domains within a sentence. However, it still seems that definite descriptions are more readily limited by a certain conversational process: a speaker characterizes, perhaps non-uniquely, a situation that he or she wishes to discuss, then goes on to use definite descriptions in speaking of the individuals that play unique roles within that situation. Sentences (3)–(6) all illustrate this process. In sentence (6), the situation that serves as the resource situation for the definite description is ultimately embedded in a larger situation.[13] If we introduce a subscript δ for quantifiers to indicate that they are restricted to the domain of what is conversationally available for definite descriptions to refer to, then we

---

[11] Stanley and Williamson 1995.

[12] Attributed to Peter Ludlow.

[13] This differs in several important ways from the proposal that Roberts makes. The differences require an extended discussion that I defer to other occasions. Here I use just her idea that separate domains may be required for the interpretation of definite descriptions and the interpretation of other quantifiers in a sentence.

could try to give the truth-conditions for a use of a definite description in the usual way, but with these suitably restricted quantifiers:[14]

'The Cs are B' is true iff $[\exists_\delta X: CX \wedge [\Lambda_\delta Y: CY] YAX] BX$

'The C is B' is true iff $[\exists_\delta X: CX \wedge IX \wedge [\Lambda_\delta Y: CY \wedge IY]$ $YAX] BX$ or equivalently $[\exists_\delta x: Cx \wedge [\forall_\delta y: Cy] y = x] Bx$

However, this index needs to be different for every occurrence of 'the', since what counts as contextually available constantly shifts. In addition, the other quantifiers within a sentence might differ in their domain, so that different indices are appropriate. So we will instead use a numerical index, where the numerical index can be taken to indicate the domain of objects that are contextually available at the point where the index is used. If we analyze a definite description, the two quantifiers appearing in the analysis, the existential and the embedded universal, must have the same index.

Stanley and Williamson (1995, 294) argue that because of the general domain-variability of quantifiers, "definite descriptions should be treated as unitary quantifier expressions, rather than analysed away in terms of their Russellian expansions." The argument is based on the judgment that in a sentence like

(12) There is exactly one bottle, and every bottle is in the refrigerator.

the two quantifiers might have distinct domains. If so, then (12) cannot be a paraphrase of

(13) The bottle is in the refrigerator.

Our analysis is not subject to this objection, since it analyzes a definite description in terms of correspondingly indexed existential and universal quantifiers.

What the speaker has in mind, the situation under discussion, limits the domain for a subsequent definite description. However, it is important to note that this limitation is not a part (even implicitly) of the descriptive (predicative) content of the definite description. The domain limitation is contextually conditioned rather than actually described.

---

[14] Roberts says that the existence and uniqueness claims are presuppositions of the use of a definite description. I see no reason not to think that they are part of the truth-conditions.

Our discussions are constrained by prior discourse without thereby being about prior discourse.

For this approach to be successful, contextual availability must be interpreted with considerable flexibility. We accommodate by finding ways to interpret the context or fill in the content of a description so that what the speaker is saying will make sense. Thus a speaker who just says

(14) The students are very nervous today

"out of the blue," will be interpreted as having some appropriate situation in mind, and that limits what students are eligible for consideration, even if we cannot immediately tell what that situation is. And introduction of new predicates will often widen or shift the context to include satisfiers of the new predicates, thereby providing new domains for definite descriptions (and other quantifiers as well).

> (15) Alice was angry with her students yesterday because they had not prepared for class. The students complained that she had given them too much to do. I think that the students are probably just lazy, because I had a similar problem with the students I taught last year.

Interpreting the last definite description ('the students I taught last year') requires expanding the domain of contextually available referents. I introduce a predicate with a scope that requires such broadening ('students I taught last year'), including a conversational anchor ('I') that relates the expanded domain to the conversation. Putting this another way: I am discussing a larger situation, in this case one that includes the situation that was relevant for the earlier definite description.

From a formal standpoint, I propose to continue to define the operator 'ι' as we have, and simply to recognize that uses of definite descriptions in ordinary language may be better understood as uses of 'ι_j' for some domain index j. Each such domain is determined by a situation that is salient. 'ι_j' can still be defined in terms of '$\exists_j$' and '$\forall_j$' as indicated above. This enables us to represent even the following monologue:[15]

> (16) The cat is in the carton. The cat will never meet our other cat, because our other cat lives in New Zealand. Our New Zealand cat lives with the Cresswells. And there he'll stay, because Miriam would be sad if the cat went away.

---

[15] From Lewis 1979; in Lewis 1983, 241.

Simplifying the key sentences to highlight the features of interest here, we could represent them as follows:

(16a) The cat is in the carton: $[\imath_1 x\colon Cx]\, Tx$

(i.e., $[\exists_1 x\colon Cx \land [\forall_1 y\colon Cy]\, y = x]\, Tx$)

(16b) The cat will not meet the other cat (we own):

$[\imath_2 x\colon Cx]\, [\imath_3 y\colon Cy \land y \neq x]\, {\sim}Mxy$

(16c) The cat will stay in New Zealand: $[\imath_4 x\colon Cx]\, Sxn$

This meets a couple of challenges. The most difficult is in (16b), where the definite description indexed by 3 must have a different domain than that of the definite description that immediately precedes it. This is a case of expanding the domain of the contextually available using the predicate 'our other cat', exploiting a relationship to the speaker and to the (index 2) cat under discussion. Having made this "other" cat contextually available, the speaker then narrows the domain for the next definite description, enabling reference to it as "the" (index 4) cat.

A fuller account might indicate the conditions under which domains can be identified. (For example, perhaps the 1 and 2 domains are identical. No other identifications are possible in this monologue.) Such identification will be needed if definite descriptions are to play much of a role in valid argument. Validity is hard to achieve if quantifier domains always shift.

The idea of multiple domains needs additional exploration, but it seems that the Russellian account of definite descriptions can continue to serve if we accommodate domain shifts in the way I have indicated. Definite descriptions seem to differ from other quantifiers in the way that they relate to context. Their domain shifts may be more strongly conditioned by context. Once we recognize that, our revised Russellian analysis fares well.

PROBLEM 1 RECONSIDERED

We briefly outlined the problem that many typical contexts for the use of definite descriptions do not contain predicates that can be used to uniquely specify a referent for the definite description. Examples like (3)–(5) involve use of a definite description that can be taken to uniquely specify an individual (or some individuals) only if we restrict ourselves to individuals that the speaker has in mind or that were the basis for what was said previously.

In the case of such "incomplete" descriptions, a predicate supplementation approach would force us to say that an ordinary description involves an implicit reference to the discourse. An expression of the form "the Fs" often needs to be taken as proxy for "the Fs that were the basis for what was just said" or "the Fs the speaker had in mind" or some such thing. However, the idea that an ordinary definite description (like 'the man', 'the jogger' or 'the students') includes such an implicit reference to semantic and/or pragmatic facts as a part of its meaning is implausible. It would seem to turn all uses of definite descriptions into discussions of conversations. That would be wrong.

As we have seen, though, the domain limitation approach also raises questions. In sentences like (3) and (4), nothing in the sentences themselves indicates how the domain is restricted. It seems that it is only the speaker's intention to speak about some things rather than others that limits what is referred to. Even if we allow that both processes, the predicate supplementation process and the domain limitation process, can be at play in interpreting definite descriptions, we are left with a question about even the simplest uses like in (3)–(5). Is there anything other than the speaker's intention to refer to a particular thing (some particular things) that makes that thing (those things) available as the referent(s) of a definite description? Even if we allow that a definite description has a special contextual sensitivity, that still leaves us with the fundamental problem raised by (3)–(5) – what makes one man rather than another the individual that the use of 'the man' refers to in (3)? Roberts requires a special conversational availability for definite descriptions, but it still seems that what makes something conversationally available is that the speaker intends to refer to that thing. What makes the referents of the definite descriptions available in (3) and (4)? Nothing in the sentences said or in the publicly available context, just the speaker's having some particular thing in mind. Example (5) is a pretty typical use of a plural definite description. The use of 'the students' does not require that what is said is true of all students, but only that it is true of the "significant" ones. We require totality (or uniqueness, in the singular case) only within this much more limited domain. But again, it seems that what is significant is largely determined by what the speaker has in mind and not by any more public feature of the conversation or its context.

The answer offered to this problem is that the definite description uniquely specifies something within a situation that the speaker is discussing. Is that an acceptable answer?

"PSYCHOLOGISM"

Apparently we have the problem of psychologism, if it is a problem.[16] In (3)–(5), nothing in the conversational text that precedes the definite description picks out a unique individual for reference. It seems that the only thing in the context that we can add to make the reference unique is that the individuals that are conversationally available for definite reference are whatever ones play the indicated role in a situation that the speaker had in mind.

There are two potential worries. The first has to do with the need for the description at all if we allow this psychologism. If reference is determined by what the speaker has in mind, then why can't the speaker just use 'it' (and maybe 'he' and 'she' and 'they') and get the right reference just by having the right thing(s) in mind? The second has to do with publicity. How can a use of a definite description in the public language get its semantic content from what the speaker has in mind, without the speaker's somehow making that explicitly available to the audience?

The first of these worries is relatively simple to answer. The speaker sometimes needs to differentiate among the things that s/he has in mind, and the definite description differentiates. We get uniqueness within the domain determined by the situation that the speaker has in mind. The monologue in (3) is typical, where more than one individual is relevant to the immediate situation (with a man, a boy, and a road), and the definite description differentiates among them. Use of the pronoun 'he' would not differentiate, and communication could be unsuccessful. In fact, simple use of pronouns would be fine if we had enough pronouns.

> (3*) One day, a man and his daughter were walking along a road, and he said to her: 'Would you like to be president?'

[16] Evans 1985, 128–31, discusses a related problem of psychologism raised by Geach. In Ch. 9 we criticize the specific details of the response that Evans gives. The answer here seems more apt and is in much the same spirit as the answer that Evans gives, though it improves on it. (The Evans–Geach exchange concerns the role of pronouns and does not directly concern definite descriptions.)

Definite descriptions enable us to uniquely specify the individuals within a situation that is under discussion even when the variety of pronouns is insufficient (as it normally is).

This pushes the psychologism back one step. If a speaker characterizes a situation but does not uniquely specify it, how does the conversation get to be about that situation rather than some other one to which the characterization applies? Suppose that a listener for (3) recalls a day when he and his father walked along a road talking about football. Why is this a totally screwy conversation?

> (3X) *Speaker1*: One day, a man and a boy were walking along a road, and the man said to the boy: 'Would you like to be king?'
>
> *Speaker2*: No he didn't. We just talked about football.

What makes Speaker1's definite description latch on to the ones he has in mind rather than to some others that fit equally well with everything set forth in the prior context?

That returns us to the publicity concern. I think that the response to that concern is that the definite description gets its unique reference as a part of a process of the speaker's familiarizing the audience with a situation. Within the situation being described in (3), there is just one man and one boy. Within the situation being described in (4) (the one the speaker has in mind), there is only one jogger who bumped into the speaker. The speaker uses the definite description in differentiating the individuals in that situation, and that is how the speaker describes the situation. In the course of a conversation the situation under discussion can be enlarged. Monologue (6), for example, must be understood as beginning with the discussion of a situation that includes the buying of some books. Then the books identified with respect to that situation (with the definite description) are placed in a larger situation that includes the (previous) buying of some other books (that are already on the shelf). Conversation may eventually produce enough to enable the hearer to identify a particular situation under discussion, but if it doesn't, maybe it doesn't matter. The hearer's epistemic difficulties are not necessarily the source of any referential difficulty for the speaker.

With this account, the "psychologism" in the account of definite descriptions seems less troubling. The situations the speaker wishes to describe are (in paradigm descriptions, at least) what the words are about. Definite descriptions indicate what differentiates individuals within these situations.

DEFINITE DESCRIPTIONS AS EXISTENTIALS

We analyze a definite description as an existential with a maximality clause (which amounts to an identity clause in the singular case). We must then provide for a special context that allows the maximality clause to be proper. We have identified that special context as reference to items within some contextually available situation that the speaker is discussing. A definite description is maximal relative to the domain of some such situation.

Recently some[17] have argued that definite descriptions should be understood more simply as existentials that have some special pragmatic restrictions that sometimes produce unique reference, but that uniqueness is not a part of the semantic content of definite descriptions. Indeed, the role we have given to the resource situation in the context might be thought to eliminate the need for a uniqueness or maximality clause in the analysis of the definite description. However, although such a view is difficult to refute when we consider only singular definite descriptions, it does not stand up well to examples involving plural definite descriptions.

Let's consider (3) again, our paradigm of a use of definite descriptions without uniqueness of applicability.

> (3) One day, a man and a boy were walking along a road, and the man said to the boy: 'Would you like to be king?'

We analyze that as a case of introducing a situation and then using definite descriptions to uniquely differentiate the individuals in that situation. The existential account would instead say that the illusion of uniqueness for 'the man' comes from the pragmatic fact that we have limited our discussion to that situation, and the word 'the' simply signals a pragmatic restriction to individuals already "given" in the conversation. Ludlow and Segal point out that many languages lack the rich system of determiners that English has, but that they can get by very well with something that we might represent in this way:

> (3a) One day, man and boy were walking along road, and man said to boy: 'Would you like to be king?'

---

[17] Ludlow and Segal 2004. See also Szabo 2000, 2003, and see Abbott 2003 for some criticisms of this approach. See Ludlow and Segal 2004 for further references.

There is no difficulty in understanding this (though it is not real English), and it says (or at least can say) what (3) says. Pragmatics alone does the work, and we don't really need determiners at all. In particular, no special determiner that carries uniqueness with it occurs in (3a), and so one might argue that there is no reason to think that there is a special determiner that carries uniqueness with it in the places where 'the' occurs in (3). The uniqueness is understood whether or not there is a determiner there.

This idea does not fare as well with similar examples involving plurals.

(5) Some students met together in the park, and now the students are playing well together.

(5a) Students met together in park, and now students are playing well together.

In the plural case, the interpretation of (5a) seems much more open to the two uses of 'students' having independent (possibly disjoint) references. Even if we interpret the second occurrence as being dependent on the first, nothing produces maximality for the second occurrence. In so far as we can interpret (5a) at all, there is nothing about it that would suggest that the second occurrence refers to all of the students in the situation under discussion.

(5b) **Contradictory:** Some students met together in the park, and now the students are playing well together and the students are not playing well together.

(5c) **Not contradictory:** Students met together in park, and now students are playing well together and students are not playing well together.

Although (5c) is not English, it seems to me that the natural understanding is one that is not contradictory, reading the later occurrences of 'students' as expressing what 'some (of the) students' would express in real English. This seeming contrast between (5b) and (5c) indicates that the word 'the' carries maximality in a way that is not, or at least not always, produced by the pragmatics alone. As our analysis in Chapter 7 indicated, when the definite description is singular, uniqueness is then just the special case of maximality.

The idea that the definite description is simply an existential, without a uniqueness clause, is difficult to refute if we look only at singular examples. Champions of this view identify the difference between the indefinite and definite descriptions in a *familiarity* principle that governs definite descriptions – that the referent is already contextually familiar. And our proposal that the referent is an individual in a contextually available situation is certainly similar. However, in the plural case, the pragmatic situation does not seem to be efficacious in guaranteeing the maximality (within the resource situation) that is a part of the definite description's reference to some individuals.

Thus I am not much tempted by the purely existential analysis of definite descriptions. Such analyses must in any case indicate what is pragmatically special about 'the'. Our account says what that special relation to a conversationally available situation is: the definite descriptions differentiate among the individuals in the situation by including specifications that are maximal (unique) within that situation. We differentiate the man from the boy in (3) and the students from other people in the park (and from the park and the trees) in (5). These definite descriptions seem always to be understood as carrying the maximality (uniqueness) interpretation, the pragmatic situation is not enough to guarantee that maximality is expressed, and so that must be understood as a part of what the definite description expresses. Uniqueness is then just the special case of maximality for the singular description.

What about the cases where uniqueness does not seem to be a part of the content of the definite description?[18]

(17) John was hit in the eye.
(18) John scribbled on the wall in the living room.
(19) We drifted towards the bank and tied our canoe to a tree.

Sentence (17) does not make us wonder whether John is a cyclops. And (18) and (19) raise serious concerns about the aptness of a uniqueness clause in the analysis of definite descriptions. Although it is easy to see 'the living room' (or 'our canoe') as being a unique specification within a contextually salient situation, it is hard to see how context would not automatically provide more than one wall (more than one bank) that is salient in the situation. One might regard (17) as a special idiom of some kind, especially since replacing 'the eye' by 'an eye' produces a

---

[18] These are adapted from examples in Ludlow and Segal. I have not included examples that have 'go to the dentist', 'go to the hospital', and 'go to the pub'. I think that they involve the same considerations as (18), and in any case, they might even more convincingly be argued to be special "idioms" (that can be treated as special cases rather than being subsumed under the general analysis of 'the').

sentence that is unidiomatic (though grammatical). In (18) (and (19)), however, replacing 'the wall' ('the bank') by 'a wall' ('a bank') seems to make no difference to the semantic content.

We could try to dismiss these problem cases as special idioms. If they are not widespread, that might be the best solution. In the end, though, it seems more apt to argue that the situations under discussion are cut very finely, so that these are like the case of Lewis's cats. (Known to us as 'the cat' and 'the other cat'.) If we consider continuations of (18) and (19), that seems like an attractive route.

> (18+) Fortunately, he did not scribble on the wall that was freshly painted.
> (19+) We saw an otter sitting on the other bank.

Different definite descriptions in a conversation can draw on different contextually available situations, and within a situation, an individual is uniquely specified by the predicative content of the definite description or some individuals are specified as all of those satisfying a certain condition. So in (18) (and (19)), only one wall (bank) is involved in the situation under discussion, making the definite description suitable. In those cases, we could have easily discussed a slightly broader situation, making the indefinite description also suitable. The continuations in (18+) and (19+) broaden the situation and identify other individuals within this broader situation relative to individuals already identified as a part of the included situation.

Can this deal with even the most challenging examples? Consider this situation, as described by Szabó (2003, 280):

> [S]uppose Sherlock Holmes deduces from general clues at the scene of a crime that six men entered the room, one of whom took off his hat and handed it over to another. He does not know whether another of the six also took off his hat and gave it to someone who entered the room with him; all he knows is that *at least one* of them did that.

Sherlock could go on to say, perfectly naturally:

> (20) A man entered the room with five other men. The man took off his hat and gave it to one of the other men.

This is a difficult example. Clearly there is no basis for predicate supplementation to produce uniqueness of specification for 'The man', the domain of quantification in the second sentence must include more than one man, and with respect to the resource situation, 'man' is not uniquely applicable, and so it is a bit of a mystery how 'The man' manages to uniquely denote. Although '*familiarity*' may be an inapt choice of terminology, the idea that 'A man' singled out someone in the first sentence who is then available for specific reference in the second sentence seems to be on target. Consider this variant:

> (20X) Six men entered the room. *The man took off his hat and gave it to one of the other men.

However, specific reference in (20) does not require a unique specification even within the resource situation; the felt linkage of 'A man ... The man' is enough. He is 'A man ... The man' and they are '(five) (other) men ... the (five) (other) men'. We differentiate in terms of which man is the subject of the previous sentence.

This might seem desperate. But it seems that every theory is here going to have to say something similar. Even if one gives only a simple existential analysis of the definite description, one must appeal to familiarity as a basis for explaining why the definite description is appropriate and how it is semantically associated with one man (the one introduced by 'A man ...') rather than one of the others. What makes one man more *familiar* than the others? Simply the fact that he is the subject of the preceding sentence.

This also indicates that the sense of "having a situation in mind" that is required for something to be an available resource situation is very weak. Sherlock is sure that a (at least one) situation of a certain kind exists, and that at least one such situation has the additional features that he will go on to predicate of it. No greater "acquaintance" than that is required. If Sherlock is wrong, and if his meager evidence derives from a situation in which two men and a woman entered the room and both men put their hats on the table, then it is unclear whether Sherlock is misdescribing the actual situation or just not describing any actual situation at all. On the other hand, if two situations of the type that Sherlock describes occurred, and if his evidence is not especially derived from one rather than another, then Sherlock is right. It is as if there were an existential quantification with respect to the situation:

> Some (at least one) situation of the following kind occurred: six men entered the room, one of whom took off his hat and handed it over to another.

If the definite description is itself within the scope of an event or situation quantifier, then it needs to pick out an individual relative to at least one situation of the relevant kind, but there is no sense in which it refers to a particular individual.

A PROBLEM FOR ANOTHER PROPOSAL

It should be noted that approaches to maximality problems that rely on the idea that definite descriptions are somehow referential seem to be non-starters. That idea will be useless in the following case.

(21) Each student bought some books and put the books on the shelf next to some other books s/he bought.

(22) Each jogger bumped into a bicyclist yesterday, and the bicyclist injured him/her.

Because of the initial universal quantification, these cannot be referential uses of a definite description. We do not refer to any particular books or any particular bicyclist. The account we have offered in terms of special quantifier domain restrictions provides the resources needed.

(21a) $[\forall x: Sx]$ $([\exists Y: BY]$ x bought $Y \wedge [\imath_1 Z: BZ \wedge x$ bought $Z]$ $[\exists W: BW \wedge x$ bought $W \wedge [\forall w: wAW] \sim wAZ]$ x put Z among $W)$

The domain for '$\imath_1 Z$' must differ from the domain for '$\exists W$' in the ways we have indicated. Furthermore, the definite description '$[\imath_1 Z: BZ \wedge x$ bought $Z]$' will refer to different things relative to different assignments to 'x'. This raises a question of whether the domain for '$\imath_1 Z$' also varies relative to different assignments to 'x' or whether '$\imath_1 Z$' has some single (large) domain that includes all of the conversationally available books that any student bought. We can leave that issue unresolved; it seems that either approach would work.

EVENTS

Event approaches may also seem attractive for dealing with cases like these. If sentences involve implicit quantification over events, then we can say that the first clause of (21) involves event quantification that is carried into the second clause. Using obvious abbreviations:

(21b) $[\forall x: Sx]\ [\exists e]\ ([\exists Y: BY]\ x$ bought Y in $e\ \wedge$

$[\exists e1]\ [\imath Z: BZ \wedge x$ bought Z in $e]\ [\exists W: BW \wedge [\forall w: wAW]$

$(\sim wAZ \wedge [\exists e2]\ x$ bought w in $e2)]\ x$ put Z among W in $e1)$

If a systematic event semantics was independently motivated and yielded this kind of result, it would remove some of the seeming arbitrariness in the way that a description is completed or a domain is limited. We would still need the phenomenon of contextual completion of descriptions (witness the insertion of 'that he bought' in our glosses on (6) and (21)), and we would probably need to recognize implicit domain limitation as well. But perhaps a systematic event semantics could be made to yield the results that are achieved by our limitation to situations "that were the basis of what was just said" in the account suggested above. It is better if a systematic, independently motivated process (and one that is not metalinguistic), such as a process based on event semantics, supersedes such an insertion.

I am skeptical that an event semantics could yield results of just the right kind, but that is in any case a project that we cannot take on here.[19] For now we must simply stand pat with the idea that context plays an important role in limiting the existence and uniqueness claims associated with definite descriptions. In large part, this is like other quantifiers[20] – context provides predicates that can be understood as implicit parts of the predicative content of the quantifier phrase, and context limits the domain for quantification. In addition, though, examples like (6) suggest that immediate conversational context may play a special role in the limitation of the domain for definite descriptions by making some situations especially conversationally available. Definite descriptions enable us to make distinctions within those situations.

A PROBLEM FOR THE MAXIMALITY ACCOUNT

We are now in a position to consider a *prima facie* difficulty for the maximality account of plural descriptions.[21] We have said that 'the Fs'

---

[19] We will discuss events in the semantics of plurals in Ch. 10. We won't develop the systematic semantics envisioned here, though.

[20] The importance of treating descriptions like other quantifiers is a major theme in Neale 1990, e.g., see p. 98.

[21] Byeong Yi pointed out this problem. Yi 2005 offers a different account of definite descriptions. It deals with the problem case described below but fails in many other cases.

can be understood as 'some Fs such that all (any) Fs are among them'. Thus if some students form a circle around a building, we use 'the students who form a circle around the building' to refer to all of them, even though all of them with one excluded might also be students who form a circle around the building. The description will be improper when there are no such all-inclusive Fs – if no one is forming a circle around the building or if two separate groups satisfy 'X form a circle around the building' (the little circle and the big circle, for example).

However, there are cases in which the definite description seems improper even though there are some all-inclusive Fs. Suppose that some students X (including Betty and Carla) formed a circle around Adams Hall on Tuesday, that X–Betty formed a circle around Adams Hall on Wednesday, and that X–Carla formed a circle around Adams Hall on Thursday. On my account, the description 'the students who formed a circle around Adams Hall' would be a proper description, since X satisfy and include all students who satisfy 'Y formed a circle around Adams Hall (last week)'. However, it might be argued that it is not a proper description in such a case, because no students are the students who formed a circle around Adams Hall – X formed a circle around Adams Hall, X–Betty formed a circle around Adams Hall, and X–Carla formed a circle around Adams Hall, and so it is unclear which students are meant by 'the students who formed a circle around Adams Hall.'

It seems that the solution to this is to recognize that the event of forming a circle around Adams Hall must be maximal as well as the people who do so. More explicitly:

> E is a uniquely maximal F-ing within E' iff E is a part of E', E is an F-ing event, every F-ing event within E' is a part of E.

> In a context in which E' is the maximal event under discussion, 'the Fs' refers to some individuals X iff there is an event E in E' such that E is a uniquely maximal F-ing within E, and X include all individuals who are F within E (X are the agents of E).

This solves the problem at hand. It also introduces a need for a clear account of event inclusion for full adequacy, but the intuitive idea is pretty clear in application to our example. If we are discussing only Tuesday's events, then 'the students who formed a circle around Adams Hall' is a proper description, even though, on Tuesday, both of these are true:

> X formed a circle around Adams Hall (on Tuesday).
> X–Betty formed a circle around Adams Hall (on Tuesday).

The latter event is a proper part of the former, so it is not maximal. On the other hand, if we are considering the events of the whole week, then there is no uniquely maximal F-ing; there are three F-ings (Tuesday, Wednesday and Thursday) that do not overlap. Wednesday's event had the same personnel as a sub-event of Tuesday's demonstration, but it is a different event and not a part of Tuesday's event. The definite description 'the students who formed a circle around Adams Hall (together)' will be improper.

This refinement of the account of definite descriptions would require a more thoroughly articulated theory of events, event "discussion", and event containment. That must be left for another occasion. It appears, though, that such an account might also fill out some details for our pragmatic requirement that a definite description relates to a resource situation (event) within which it makes distinctions.

9

Pronouns

There has been much discussion of the use of definite descriptions and plurals in representation of the semantic content of so-called *E-type* pronouns. Gareth Evans identified these pronouns "whose antecedents are quantifiers, but which are not naturally interpreted in the way that would result if the pronouns were bound by those quantifiers."[1] Often such a pronoun seems to be faithfully paraphrased by a definite description, and adding plural definite descriptions extends our capacity for such paraphrases. Although I will not develop a full theory of pronouns here, the representation of cross-reference relations is central to the logic of quantifiers, and so the consideration of sentences involving pronouns will help to clarify our project.

Fundamentally, taking account of plurals does not affect the picture with respect to the correct understanding of pronouns. The considerations that go into a theory of pronouns are parallel for singular and plural pronouns and for distributive and non-distributive predication. Still, because we have a fuller range of expression when we allow non-distributive predication and quantifiers, we can deal more securely with a wider range of examples.[2] Evans used many plural definite descriptions in his discussion of these pronouns, and we now have the resources for representing plurals that enable us to be clearer about what is going on in such cases.

[1] Evans 1985, 109. This is from Evans 1977, and all page references to Evans 1977 and Evans 1980 will be to the reprinted version in Evans 1985. See Neale 1990, chs. 5 and 6 for discussion of the use of definite descriptions in representing the semantic content.

[2] Evans discusses examples involving plural reference and non-distributive predication, e.g., pp. 120–1, but he never introduces the formal resources to accommodate this. His ultimate formal semantics, pp. 150–2, deals with singular pronouns only.

USES FOR PRONOUNS

There seem to be many *prima facie* distinct uses for pronouns. One key issue here is when these can be viewed as manifestations of a single underlying phenomenon. Pronouns can:

(A) Refer to a contextually specified individual or individuals.

> **He** is tall
> **They** are coming this way

There is a demonstration or other contextual factor that indicates who is being referred to.

(B) Repeat reference to someone or some ones first referred to by a name or names.

> John loves **his** mother.
> John knows where it is. **He** can help you.
> John and Alice went to Chicago. **They** saw a wonderful comedy.

(C) Act like bound variables; a pronoun within the scope of a quantifier is like a variable bound by that quantifier.

> Every man loves **his** mother (on the reading where **his** is not a pronoun of type (A).)
> Some students are discussing **their** teachers.

(D) Act like bound variables even though not within the scope of a quantifier.

> Every man loves his mother when he is young. **He** vows to always care for her, but others get **his** attention eventually.
> Any insurrectionists who meet together pose a threat to public safety. Security forces should monitor **their** activities.

(E) Function as E-type pronouns. These are not within the scope of a quantifier, they refer back to the things that the quantifier phrase singles out, but they do not behave like variables that are bound by that quantifier.

> John bought some donkeys, and **they** were very noisy.
> Most farmers bought several donkeys. **They** vaccinated **them**.
> Every farmer who buys a donkey vaccinates **it**.
> Every dealer who shows cars washes **them**.

Every great tenor finds a soprano he can work with. **She** must accept all his eccentricities.

More than one great tenor has found a soprano he especially likes to work with. **She** inevitably suffers from the relationship.

Many schools have faced the problem of dealing with students who surround the administration building. The school's plan to disperse **them** is always a matter of great concern.

(F) Function as pronouns of laziness, standing in for the words of a prior definite noun phrase, but in a case in which the definite NP does not fix the reference of the pronoun.

A person who cashes his paycheck is smarter than one who burns **it**.

Armies that nurture their soldiers fare better than armies that mistreat **them**.

I think that categories (A) (referential) and (C) (bound-variable) are the two paradigm types of pronouns. Category (B) divides between those two, category (D) is an extension of (C), and categories (E) and (F) should be assimilated to category (A), but require the recognition of an additional phenomenon of *relative reference*.[3] E-type pronouns that can be paraphrased by definite descriptions should be viewed as one end of a continuum of unbound pronouns, with paradigm demonstrative pronouns at the other end. In the middle are uses of pronouns whose reference is partially indicated by linguistic features of context and partly by other features of context.

PRONOUNS AS BOUND VARIABLES

In our formal language, a quantifier phrase binds from the head of a clause, and the variables associated with that quantifier phrase indicate the argument positions that it binds. Pronouns can be used like such variables, and those pronouns are represented well by our quantificational apparatus.

(1) Every man loves **his** mother.
   $[\forall x: Mx]$ (x loves x's mother)

---

[3] I have defended some aspects of this view in McKay 1991 and 1994. I will here recognize relative co-reference relations, to deal more adequately with some examples that cannot be viewed as simple reference.

(2) Every tenor wants **his** audience to appreciate **him.**
$[\forall x: Tx]$ (x wants x's audience to appreciate x)

Such a pronoun corresponds to a bound variable.[4] We have many
assurances from linguists that our standard approach, in effect "moving"
the quantifier phrase to the head of the clause, is well-motivated from a
linguistic standpoint.

We have already indicated that our use of plural variables corresponds
to similar uses of singular variables. The one additional issue is whether
the variable occurs in a distributive or non-distributive argument place,
i.e., whether there is a distributing universal.

(3) Some students are discussing their teachers.

$[\exists X: SX_D]$ X are discussing $X_{(D)}$'s teachers.

Distributive ambiguity here. Each student's teachers or the
teachers of **them,** however that might be interpreted.

(3a) $[\exists X: SX_D]$ $[\forall z: zAX]$ X are discussing z's teachers.

(3b) $[\exists X: SX_D]$ X are discussing X's teachers. (Where X's
teachers might be the teachers they have in common, those
that teach any one of the students, or whatever else is indicated
by context.)

(4) Several students want their dean to address them.
[Several $X: SX_D$] X_D want $X_{(D)}$'s dean to address X.
(4a) [Several $X: SX_D$] $[\forall z: zAX]$ z wants z's dean to address X.
(4b) [Several $X: SX_D$] $[\forall z: zAX]$ z wants X's dean to address X.

Examples of type (D) indicate that the binding of a quantifier
phrase can extend beyond a sentence boundary. Indisputable cases are
impossible to get with 'some' as the quantifier or with a plural universal
quantifier (such as 'all'), because in such cases the pronouns are also
interpretable as unbound (E-type or referential) pronouns. A universal
quantifier such as 'each' or 'every', where the syntactic number (singular)
differs from the semantic (universal, thus normally plural) does enable
us to produce convincing examples, however.[5]

---

[4] In our representation, there is also a bound variable in the argument position that
is occupied by the quantifier phrase in English and a bound variable use within the
quantifier phrase.
  [5] Neale 1990, 233–4, has several other examples of this sort. (His (23), (24), (27)
and (28₁) can all be read this way.) He would not accept my characterization of this as
cross-sentential binding, however.

(5) Every man loves his mother when he is young. **He** vows to always care for her, but others get **his** attention eventually.

Interestingly, there are other quantifiers that have differing semantic and syntactic number. For example, 'more than one' is syntactically singular and semantically plural. Bound variable pronouns are singular, but unbound pronouns are plural.

(6a) More than one student is failing the course.

(6b) *More than one student are failing the course.

(7a) Professor Adams failed more than one student, and so they appealed their grades to the dean.

(7b) Professor Adams failed more than one student, and so *he appealed his grade to the dean.

Because of this, it seems that we should be able to construct examples of cross-sentential binding with 'more than one'.

(8a) More than one great tenor is eccentric. **He** needs someone to pamper him.

Such cases are perhaps less felicitous than the examples with 'every', but they seem to be acceptable. However plural unbound pronouns are often much better in the case of 'more than one'.

(8b) More than one great tenor is eccentric. **They** need people to pamper them.

This may simply indicate that this phenomenon of cross-sentential binding has very limited scope. It is certainly robust, however, with the quantifiers 'each' and 'every', and there is no reason that we should hesitate to acknowledge it. A quantifier phrase can structurally command a finite sequence of sentences as well as a single sentence. We can view this as silent conjunction if we feel that we need to make all binding intra-sentential.[6]

---

[6] If we take the view that (8a) is not acceptable, then another path might seem to be open to us. With a universal, we have the following equivalence:

$$[\forall x: Tx] (Ex \wedge Nx) \text{ is equivalent to } [\forall x: Tx] Ex \wedge [\forall x: Tx] Nx$$

The corresponding equivalence does not hold if we substitute 'more than one' for the universal quantifier. So in (5), each pronoun can be understood either as a bound variable (in a case of cross-sentential binding) or as standing in for a recurrence of the quantifier. That is not possible in (8a), because the two different treatments of the pronoun would

Plural examples support the idea of cross-sentential binding in another way.

(9) Any insurrectionists who meet together pose a threat to public safety. Security forces should monitor **their** activities.

Although we will discuss E-type pronouns as a way of interpreting unbound pronouns related to a quantifier phrase, it is difficult to interpret (9) as an E-type pronoun. E-type pronouns can generally be replaced by definite descriptions, and that does not work in (9). If we try to paraphrase 'their activities' by 'the activities of **the insurrectionists who are meeting together**', then we are employing an improper definite description (assuming an adequate supply of insurrectionist cells). We do better if we take this as a case of inter-sentential binding.

Ultimately Evans wishes to argue that even bound pronouns[7] are interpretable by an extension of the method for interpreting referential pronouns, and we will look briefly at the considerations for that in our discussion of relative reference.

REFERENTIAL PRONOUNS

We have not made any special provision for referential pronouns in our formal semantics (Chapter 2 and 3). Paradigmatically (as in category A in our typology), they are like proper names, items that refer directly to an individual or some individuals. In natural language, context provides resources for singling out a referent, perhaps including an explicit demonstration associated with the referential expression. In a context-free formal language of the kind we developed in Chapters 1–7, we expect no similar devices. It will be useful to look at some of the things that need to be considered in developing an account of pronominal reference, to see how our approach might be extended.

---

yield non-equivalent results. This should not lead us to simply take the view that the pronoun in (5) is a stand-in for a recurrence of the quantifier, though, since that would leave us with the problem of explaining why no similar interpretation is available for (8a). Clearly we cannot interpret (8a) in the following way:

[more than one x: Tx] Ex $\wedge$ [more than one x: Tx] Nx

So this view would still leave us with a bit of a puzzle.

7 Evans 1985, 89.

The paradigm of a referential pronoun is a demonstrative accompanied by a suitable demonstration.

(10) **He** stole my wallet.

(11) **They** took my hubcaps.

But context can provide cues other than an explicit demonstration. When two detectives reach the scene of a death, they might look around for a while and then begin their conversation:

(12) **He** didn't fall, he was pushed.

(13) **They** didn't waste any time in getting out of here.

An individual is salient or some individuals are salient even without an explicit demonstration. No linguistic antecedent is needed.[8]

In what follows we will explore the extent to which unbound pronouns can be viewed as instances of referential uses of pronouns. With the introduction of the concept of relative reference, this can take us pretty far. However, there are cases of scope relations and scope ambiguities, pointed out by Soames and Neale, that seem to require that in at least some cases we must take the view that unbound pronouns go proxy for definite descriptions rather than having a referential role.

E-TYPE PRONOUNS

Gareth Evans identified E-type pronouns, a class of pronouns that are not within the scope of any binding quantifier, though they make reference to things that verify previous quantified clauses. The quantifier phrase seems to be an antecedent for the pronoun even though the pronoun is not functioning like a bound variable and the syntactic relations make binding impossible. Although Evans's examples all involve a quantifier phrase and a pronoun within a single sentence, we will also consider examples in which the quantifier phrase and the pronoun are in separate sentences. When a pronoun is not within the scope of a binding quantifier, there is no important difference between its being in the same sentence as the quantifier phrase and its being in a separate, following sentence.[9]

---

[8] Roberts 2003 says that the referent of a pronoun must be "weakly familiar" and "maximally salient".

[9] See McKay 1994 for further discussion of this.

(14) Only a few students studied hard, and they got As in the course and were happy.

(15) John knows some students who studied hard. They were happy that they got As.

(16) Any man who owns several cars washes them.

These contrast with simple bound variables.

(17) Only a few students studied hard and got As and were happy.
[Only a few x: Sx] ($Hx \wedge x$ got an A $\wedge x$ was happy)

(18) John knows some students who studied hard and were happy that they got As.
[$\exists x$: $Sx \wedge Hx \wedge x$ was happy that x got an A] Kjx

(19) Every man washes every car he owns.
[$\forall x$: Mx] [$\forall y$: C$y \wedge$ Oxy] Wxy

In (14)–(16), the scope relations do not make binding possible; the pronouns in (14)–(16) are not within the scope of any appropriate quantifier phrase. As should be clear, (14) does not mean the same thing as (17). (14) says that only a few students studied hard and that all of the students who studied hard got As, but (17) says neither of these things. (15) says that all of the students John knows who studied hard were happy that they got As, but (18) does not say or imply that. In (16), the pronoun 'them' is not within the syntactic scope of the quantifier 'several cars', so there is no way for it to be bound by that quantifier, even though it is within the same sentence. (The quantifier is within a relative clause within the other quantifier phrase, and it cannot bind a variable outside of that relative clause.) Like the pronouns in (14) and (15), the pronoun in (16) seems to refer back to previously identified individuals and to function in a clause that predicates something of all of them; and this behavior is very different from the behavior of a bound variable.

Evans argued that the reference for these E-type pronouns is fixed by definite descriptions. "Pronouns are often used as referring expressions, and it is not particularly surprising that some of them should have their reference fixed by a description recoverable from the antecedent quantifier-containing clause." Thus these are similar to pronouns of our class (A), referential pronouns, and not to bound variables. "There is not a single class of pronouns for which we must find a unitary explanation. There are two kinds of pronouns [referential and bound-variable], which are sharply distinguished by their grammatical position, and which function in quite different ways."

Evans's key idea is that a pronoun that is not a bound variable and is not simply a demonstrative pronoun has its reference fixed by what has been said. Furthermore, if something said – rather than demonstrations or other features of context – "fixed the reference" for the pronoun, then we can recover that in a definite description, and for E-type pronouns there is a systematic grammatical process for recovering this description (according to Evans).[10]

The description Evans associates with a pronoun will often be a plural description, and the semantics for non-distributive plurals and plural restricted quantifiers that we have developed provides a formal framework for a full implementation of such a proposal. The definite description that fixes the reference of the pronoun will be based on the predicates in the entire quantified clause that is the antecedent for that pronoun. If we construct a plural reference-fixing description of suitable scope and have it bind a variable put in place of the pronoun, we will get a sentence that retains the content of the sentence with a pronoun. We must keep it in mind that definite descriptions are subject to scope ambiguities in a way that pronouns often are not, so that this can be misleading in English.[11] The qualifier "of suitable scope" is needed.

(14) Only a few students studied hard, and they got As in the course and were happy.

(14a)[12] [Only a few x: Sx] Hx. [$\imath X$: $SX_D \wedge HX_D$] AX_D

(14b) [Only a few X: SX_D] HX_D. [$\imath X$: $SX_D \wedge HX_D$] AX_D

(15) John knows some students who studied hard. They were happy that they got As.

(15a) [$\exists x$: $Sx \wedge Hx$] Kjx. [$\imath X$: $SX_D \wedge HX_D \wedge KjX_D$] AX_D

(15b) [$\exists X$: $SX_D \wedge HX_D$] KjX_D. [$\imath X$: $SX_D \wedge HX_D \wedge KjX_D$] AX_D

The analysis of E-type pronouns applies in the same way with non-distributive predications, confirming the approach that employs plural definite descriptions.

[10] e.g., Evans, p. 111, where he indicates that E-type pronouns are "singular terms whose denotation is fixed by a description recoverable from the clause containing the quantifier antecedent."

[11] See Evans, pp. 131–4.

[12] A fuller analysis, indicating the distributions explicitly: $\neg$ [More than a few X: [$\forall Y$: $IY \wedge YAX$] SY] [$\forall Y$: $IY \wedge YAX$] HY. [$\imath X$: [$\forall Y$: $IY \wedge YAX$] $SY \wedge$ [$\forall Y$: $IY \wedge YAX$] HY] [$\forall Y$: $IY \wedge YAX$] AY

(20) John knows several students who study hard. They are meeting together now.

    (a) [Several x: $Sx \wedge Hx$] Kjx. [$\imath X$: $SX_D \wedge HX_D \wedge$ KjX_D] MX

    (b) [Several X: $SX_D \wedge HX_D$] KjX_D. [$\imath X$: $SX_D \wedge HX_D \wedge$ KjX_D] MX

(21) John knows several students who are fraternity brothers. They are meeting together now.

    [Several X: $SX_D \wedge FX$] KjX_D. [$\imath X$: $SX_D \wedge FX \wedge$ KjX_D] MX

In addition, some cases in which it is not clear whether the predication is distributive are also readily represented in either way.

(16) Any man who owns several cars washes them.

(16a) [$\forall x$: M$x \wedge$ [Several y: Cy] Oxy] [$\imath Z$: C$Z_D \wedge$ OxZ_D] W$xZ_{(D)}$

The washing of the cars in (16) may be distributive – he washes each one separately – or not (he washes them together from a low-flying helicopter, perhaps), so there may be a distributing universal or not, depending on the reading. Or we can substitute a more clearly non-distributive predication such as "arranges them in a circle" for "washes them".

(22) John criticized few philosophers, but their replies troubled him.

    [Few x: Px] Cjx, but [$\imath Z$: [$\imath W$: PW$_D \wedge$ CjW$_D$] Z_D are W's replies] T$Z_{(D)}$j

Again there is a distributive ambiguity. It is not clear whether each reply troubles him, or (more likely) whether it is the totality of the replies that troubles him.

DONKEY SENTENCES

As the representation of (16) should make clear, we have here a proposal for a solution to the problem of representing "donkey" sentences.

(23) Every man who owns a donkey vaccinates it.

(23a) Every man who owns a donkey vaccinates the donkey he owns.

    [$\forall x$: M$x \wedge$ [$\exists y$: Dy] Oxy] [$\imath z$: D$z \wedge$ Oxz] Vxz

It might be thought that (23a) presumes too much, in supposing that for each man there is just one donkey he owns. There is a plural version of it as well.

(23b) Every man who owns (one or more) donkeys vaccinates them (the donkeys he owns).

$[\forall x: Mx \wedge [\exists y: Dy]\, Oxy]\, [\imath Z: DZ_D \wedge OxZ_D]\, VxZ_{(D)}$

$[\forall x: Mx \wedge [\exists Y: DY_D]\, OxY_D]\, [\imath Z: DZ_D \wedge OxZ_D]\, VxZ_{(D)}$

The ambiguity about whether the last argument place is distributive or not is perhaps clearer with a slightly different example.

(24) Any person who owns bees takes good care of them.

$[\forall x: Px \wedge [\exists y: By]\, Oxy]\, [\imath Z: BZ_D \wedge OxZ_D]\, CxZ$

$[\forall x: Px \wedge [\exists Y: BY]\, OxY]\, [\imath Z: BZ_D \wedge OxZ_D]\, CxZ$

We are pretty certain to take the final argument non-distributively in this case – a good colonial environment rather than care of each bee is what it takes. Similarly, if a man owns many donkeys, then he may vaccinate his donkeys even though he does not vaccinate each one.[13] (A good vaccination program does not always require universal inoculation.)

This practice, though, of inserting the definite description is slightly misleading. In the sentence we have a pronoun, and, as Evans argued, we cannot simply insert a definite description in its place, since that will introduce scope ambiguities that do not exist with the pronoun.[14]

(25) John owns a donkey and it likes carrots, though it might not have been the case that it liked carrots.

(26) John owns a donkey and it likes carrots, though it might not have been the case that the donkey John owns liked carrots.

Sentence (26) has readings that are not available for (25). Pronouns do not just go proxy for descriptions. Rather, according to Evans, the pronoun is a device of direct reference, and that reference is fixed by the

---

[13] This analysis does not explain how the English sentence (23) can have a singular pronoun and get the interpretation in (23b). With the resources we have, we can represent the various possible meanings of sentences like these; we will not be able to explain all of the features of the English itself. That is a larger project. Having plural quantifiers enables us to do what Neale does with the "whatever" quantifier in his discussion of this in Neale 1990, 46, 234–52.

[14] Evans, p. 132. Neale and Ludlow have argued that we should take the view that pronouns stand in for definite descriptions. There is further discussion of that later in this chapter.

description. Thus we cannot see the sentence with a description inserted as unambiguously representing the referential aspect of the use of the pronoun.

This is a very weak argument that the definite description does not stand in for the description, since we can get the referential effect by simply stipulating that the pronoun must stand in for a wide-scope description. Later we will reconsider the idea that pronouns "go proxy" for definite descriptions. For now, we will fall in line with Evans and look at the extent to which we can interpret pronouns as referential.

RELATIVE REFERENCE

In evaluating (23) and (16),

(23) Every man who owns a donkey vaccinates it.
(16) Any man who owns several cars washes them.

we identify the pronominal referent(s) *relative to* another individual. There is quantification "over" people as well as cars or donkeys, and the semantics involves the consideration of multiple assignments of people who might satisfy the indicated conditions. We do not just refer to a donkey, but rather for each person S who owns a donkey, we evaluate the claim that S vaccinates **it** relative to an assignment that assigns a donkey that S owns to 'it'. We do not just refer to some cars, but for each person S who owns some cars, we evaluate the claim that S washes **them** relative to an assignment that assigns the cars that S owns to 'them'.

(23′) $[\forall x: Px \wedge [\exists Y: DY_D] OxY_D] Vx$ it
(16′) $[\forall x: Px \wedge [\text{several } Y: CY_D] OxY_D] Wx$ them

It would be misleading to represent such a pronoun by a free variable, because a free variable is ordinarily understood as receiving an assignment that is independent of the quantifier clauses that structurally command it (but which do not bind it). In cases of relative reference like these, however, two features conspire to cause consternation. One is that the pronominal reference is constrained by the prior discourse – we are considering the donkey that x owns as the referent for 'it'. The other is that the constraint itself is in a quantified clause and so must be evaluated with respect to an assignment to the variables. For each assignment i to 'x', we must consider a donkey that i owns. So the assignment of an individual to a pronoun that has this kind of "relative reference" is constrained by the conversational context and by the assignment of an individual to the variable of the commanding quantifier phrase. Thus in a formal language it would be better to introduce another notation for such pronouns.

Let's use Greek letters, with α, β, γ for singular pronouns and A, β, Γ for plural (with subscripts if we need more).

(23″) $[\forall x: Px \wedge [\exists Y: DY_D] OxY_D] Vx\alpha$

(16″) $[\forall x: Px \wedge [\text{several } Y: CY_D] OxY_D] Wx\beta$

Nothing in our notation indicates the contextual source of reference for these pronouns. Since both linguistic and non-linguistic resources can be a part or all of the basis for the reference, it is difficult to see how to implement any notational indication of the source.[15] The possibility of referential dependence is indicated by the fact that the pronoun is within a clause with a bound variable.[16] In evaluating these sentences, we are free to vary the assignment to the pronoun as we vary the assignment to the variable. We are also free to keep the same evaluation for the pronoun as we consider different assignments to the variable, if the source of pronominal reference is independent of the clauses containing the bound variable. The examples we are considering illustrate this, since they also have interpretations where the pronominal reference is fixed independently, by demonstration, for example. In these particular cases, the interpretation would be strange, requiring some single individual, perhaps one pointed to when the pronoun is said, to get vaccinations from all of the donkey-owners, and requiring some particular individuals to get washed by all of the people who own cars. For a more natural example to illustrate the ambiguity, consider the interpretation of the following sentence in which 'it' refers to the Dow-Jones industrial average.

Anyone who owns a stock portfolio checks it regularly.

---

[15] As I understand Alan Berger's proposal (Berger 2002*b*), it tags sentences with the linguistic constraints that apply to the pronouns. However, if we are to regard linguistic and non-linguistic constraints on a par, then this gets only part of the picture with regard to pronouns. (Berger seems to have only part of the picture with regard to plurals as well, since he makes no provision for non-distributive predication.)

[16] Speaking of the sentence "Every man who owns a donkey beats it," Evans says (1985, 119): "Since the 'every man' quantifier has a wider scope than that of the E-type pronoun, we do not begin evaluating the sentence by inquiring into the denotation of the pronoun." Also that such pronouns "have a scope less than that of the main quantifier, and can (and need) only be interpreted relative to some substitution instance of the main quantifier."

In the plural (car-wash) example, consider how the evaluation of an E-type interpretation of a pronoun with relative reference will need to work. Each person owns different cars, and so we wish to identify the reference of 'β' in (16″) relative to an assignment of an individual to 'x'. Given any such assignment of an individual i to 'x', if i satisfies 'Px ∧ [σY: CY_D] OxY_D', then there are some cars (the cars that i owns) that are salient for 'β' to refer to relative to that assignment to 'x'. We use the situation described in the previous clause as the basis for associating referents with the unbound pronoun (or a single referent with a singular pronoun). So this does not function the way a free variable ordinarily does. The assignments to the variable are constrained by the context – in this case constrained to the things verifying[17] the clause '[σY: CY_D] OxY_D' relative to an assignment of an individual to 'x'.[18] Some things J verify that clause if and only if J satisfy CY_D and OxY_D. The central point is that in evaluation we must consider an assignment for 'x' before we can evaluate all of the clauses containing the pronoun.

Evans's use of the terminology 'fixing reference' does not square well with the fact that such pronouns do not have a fixed reference. (Evans himself recognizes and discusses this issue.)[19] When a bound variable is involved, a singular unbound pronoun may have a relative referent, as in the donkey sentence (and a plural unbound pronoun may have relative referents) even though the pronoun has no referent *simpliciter* (or no referents *simpliciter*). Expressing the general idea of E-type pronouns in terms of fixing reference is at least misleading on this score. The most we can say is that unbound pronouns are associated with descriptions that fix reference – either *simpliciter* or relative to an assignment to associated variables in the description.

The reference of an unbound pronoun can be related to a bound variable in the same way that it is related to a name in a similar sentence. And in some cases it will make little difference whether the pronoun is treated as a bound variable or an unbound pronoun.

(27) John loves a soprano and lives with her.
(27a) [∃y: Sy] (Ljy ∧ Vjy)
(27b) [∃y: Sy] Ljy ∧ Vjα

---

[17] This is Evans's terminology. See, e.g., Evans 1985, 119.
[18] There is a maximality question here. Instead of 'washes them' we could have 'arranges them in a circle'. This makes it clear that the plural pronoun must be assigned those verifiers of the clause such that all verifiers of the clause are among them.
[19] Evans 1985, 117–20 and 236–7.

For (27a) to be true, some individual must satisfy the clauses 'Sy' and 'Ljy ∧ Vjy'. For (27b) to be true, some individual must satisfy 'Sy' and 'Ljy', and α must be assigned an individual that satisfies 'Vjy', under the constraint that it also satisfy 'Sy' and 'Ljy'. Ultimately, those come to the same result. Some quantified sentences fare similarly:

(28) Many tenors love a soprano and live with her.
(28a) [Many x: Tx] [∃y: Sy] (Lxy ∧ Vxy)
(28b) [Many x: Tx] ([∃y: Sy] Lxy ∧ Vxα)

To evaluate (28b), we consider assignments to x that satisfy

Tx
[∃y: Sy] Lxy

The assignment to α can be constrained to individuals who satisfy the following, relative to such an assignment to x:[20]

Sy
Lxy

The evaluation of the whole sentence requires determining whether the individuals satisfying

Tx
[∃y: Sy] Lxy
Sy
Lxy
Vxy

are many tenors, where 'y' is assigned a value that is fixed by the description

[ıy: Sy] Lxy.

In this case, this is equivalent to the evaluation of (28a).

In the case of donkey sentences, though, bound-variable interpretations do not work, but unbound pronoun interpretations are still available.

(29) If John now loves a soprano, then he lives with her.

---

[20] We say 'can be constrained' because it is always possible to use the pronoun in conjunction with a demonstration to indicate some other individual who is salient in the context.

It is impossible to interpret this sentence as an existential quantification (governing the pronoun's position), but we can take 'her' as an unbound pronoun.

(29a) If [∃y: Sy] Ljy, then Vjα

As before, the interpretation of α is constrained to individuals satisfying the sub-clauses of the existential clause. And this works similarly in the quantified donkey sentences, where the interpretation of the pronoun is restricted to individuals satisfying the sub-clauses of a contextually available quantifier clause (though the position of the pronoun is not within the scope of the quantifier) relative to each relevant assignment of an individual to the other variables in those clauses:

(16) Any man who owns several cars washes them.

(16″) [∀x: Px ∧ [σY: CY_D] OxY_D] Wxβ

Relative to any assignment of an individual i to '*x*', the interpretation of β is fixed on individuals satisfying the clauses of the contextually available quantifier clause (i.e., satisfying 'CY_D' and 'OxY_D') relative to i.

CAVEATS

I believe that Evans's analysis of these examples may be fundamentally correct and that we can see definite descriptions as fixing the content of E-type pronouns in most of the examples that we have discussed so far. However, there are important caveats to record concerning this view and there are other important examples to consider. Ultimately, I will have to leave unresolved the matter of whether these caveats require abandoning Evans's approach or merely revising it. But it will be valuable to face these issues and see what difference our introduction of non-distributive predication and our discussion of definite descriptions will make.

Caveat 1: The description that encodes the content of the pronoun cannot always be read off from prior clauses in the simple way that Evans's remarks suggest.

Caveat 2: Pronouns like those that provide examples of E-type pronouns are sometimes used in a way that does not carry the uniqueness claim that Evans's E-type analysis requires.

Caveat 3: Pronouns like those that provide examples of E-type pronouns sometimes refer to individuals that are not correctly characterized by any substantive description recoverable from the linguistic context.

Caveat 4: In some cases, pronouns seem to be involved in scope ambiguities, *contra* Evans, and this argues that we should return to the idea that unbound pronouns can sometimes go proxy for definite descriptions.[21]

The first of these caveats is a difficulty for Evans, though perhaps one that would not be very deep on its own. The second and third caveats raise issues recognized but little discussed by Evans. I believe that these three caveats together have a significant consequence, suggesting that Evans's examples of E-type pronouns are just one end of a continuum of examples of referential (and relative-referential) unbound pronouns.

The fourth caveat suggests that we could take a different direction in the analysis of unbound pronouns, giving definite descriptions an even more prominent role. This makes our incorporation of plural definite descriptions, and the connected incorporation of non-distributive predication, more significant. There are strong arguments that we must go in this direction.

Caveat (1)

There is a question about the uniformity of the rule that Evans suggests for generating definite descriptions that "fix the reference" of pronouns. He says that the appropriate description can be "recovered" from the antecedent clause, and he always uses the full clause as the basis for the description. The description that represents the E-type pronoun contains the content from the predicative portion of the clause as well as from the quantifier phrase. However, contrary to his claim of uniformity, it sometimes seems that it is less obvious than that just what description should be recovered. For example, one might regard (15) as ambiguous, with the reading (15b) in addition to (15a).

(15) John knows some students who studied hard. They were happy that they got As.

(15a) $[\exists x\colon Sx \wedge Hx]\ Kjx.\ [\imath X\colon SX_D \wedge HX_D \wedge KjX_D]\ AX_D$

(15b) $[\exists x\colon Sx \wedge Hx]\ Kjx.\ [\imath X\colon SX_D \wedge HX_D]\ AX_D$

---

[21] Neale 1990 and Ludlow and Neale 1991 argue for this.

In both cases, a description recovered from the linguistic context is the source of a definite description that indicates the reference of the pronoun, but the description in (15b) uses less of the predicative material in the antecedent clause.

It seems that Evans would say that the interpretation indicated by (15b) does not treat the pronoun as an E-type pronoun. He wants to hold that E-type pronouns are associated with a uniform grammatical rule for generating the definite description that fixes their reference or relative reference. He would have to regard (15b) as either an incorrect interpretation of (15) or as an interpretation that is of type (A), referential, but not of type (E), relying in a somehow more direct way on contextual salience as the basis for a reference to some individuals.

Evans believes that the recognition of a rule for E-type pronouns is necessary, because reference fixing is impossible unless there is a clear rule for generating the reference-fixing definite description, especially since the definite description is not explicit. In cases of relative reference, where no particular thing or things are being referred to, this becomes especially important. Consider:[22]

(30) John owns some donkeys and feeds them at night.

(31) Every villager owns some donkeys and feeds them at night.

Evans says,

Now, it plainly does not make sense to ask which group of donkeys the pronoun in [(31)] refers to. Once the proper name *John* has been supplanted by the quantifier *Every villager*, there is no determinate answer to such a question. Hence, since it is not referring to anything in [(31)], a pragmatic account of E-type pronouns in sentences like [(30)] would leave this pronoun unaccounted for.

He argues instead for the Fregean treatment (relative reference) we have considered and for the claim that there is a systematic rule for recovering the definite description that fixes the reference of a pronoun. He evaluates quantified sentences in terms of truth-values of possible substitution instances.

Provided we give an account of the E-type pronoun in a sentence like [(30)], the pronoun in [(31)] – of which [(30)] is a substitution instance – will take care of itself. However, once again, the Fregean treatment presupposes that there is an interpretation of the pronoun in [(30)] on which its reference is determined by a linguistic rule, and not by 'considerations relating to situation, communicative intention, and the like'.

[22] Evans 1985, 237.

Evans's theory and arguments generate a prediction. It should be impossible to have relative reference without relying on a grammatical rule to do it. If there is relative reference for a pronoun, then either that pronoun will be an unbound, E-type pronoun with a reference generated by the Evans rule (i.e., generated by constructing a definite description based on the quantified clause that is the base for the pronoun) or it will be a bound variable. This prediction is not correct, however.

(32) Every doctor knows that some of her patients who need to lose weight will not succeed, and so the doctor is happy when **they** try hard, because she knows that all of the patients who try hard will succeed.

The bold-face pronoun seems to have only relative reference, it is a not a bound pronoun, but it is impossible to interpret it by Evans's rule for E-type pronouns, since that would make (32) inconsistent. However, (32) is consistent. We must and can interpret the pronoun as referring (successively in the stages of evaluation) to each doctor's patients who need to lose weight rather than (as Evans's rule would predict) to each doctor's patients who need to lose weight and will not succeed.

It is easy to construct examples of the kind of ambiguity at issue here without relative reference:

(33) Few students liked him, but they admired his intelligence. (The students who did not like him or all students?)

(34) Many students John knows are chemistry majors. They had a party last night. (The students John knows, the chemistry majors, or the students John know who are chemistry majors?)

(35) More than one student carried a banner. They marched to the Chancellor's office. (All of the (contextually relevant) students or the students carrying banners?)

These ambiguities indicate that there is no absolute rule concerning the scope of the definite description that we use to represent unbound pronouns. These unbound pronouns have all of the unclarity that contextual saliency brings. Definite descriptions can often stand in their place, based on the descriptive content that the context provides. Example (32) indicates that this flexibility about the definite descriptions that give content to pronouns is not a phenomenon solely of referential pronouns. It also applies to relative-referential pronouns. Since the pronouns in these examples are not within the syntactic scope of the quantifier phrases or clauses that provide the predicative material that constrains reference or relative reference, it seems unlikely that we could expect any tighter relationship.[23]

Caveat (2)

There is another important qualification on Evans's view. In Evans 1980, he argues as follows:[24]

If it is the role of E-type pronouns in general to refer to the object or objects which verify the antecedent clause, and if an E-type pronoun is singular, then we would predict that the use of that pronoun will convey the implication that there is *just one* object verifying the antecedent clause – an implication which is not carried by the use of existential quantifiers themselves. When a pronoun is in a clause coordinate with the clause containing the quantifier, as in [(36)],

[(36)] Socrates owned a dog and it bit Socrates.

there is a clear implication that Socrates owned just one dog.

Certainly he is wrong about (36); (36) carries no uniqueness implication. Imagine (36) in an Athenian police report, with the continuation, "It has been destroyed, and his other dogs are being watched for signs of similar tendencies." There is nothing out of the ordinary there. Also note that one does not need to inquire about what other dogs Socrates owned before deciding whether it is acceptable to use (36) to open a conversation about a dog that bit him.

Many conversations begin with existentials that carry no uniqueness claim and then proceed to refer to a particular individual who has the properties mentioned in the existential. This is just the kind of issue that we discussed in connection with definite descriptions in Chapter 8, leading us to amend the account there on the basis of the idea that definite descriptions are special among quantifiers in having a (potentially) smaller domain consisting only of items that have a special conversational availability. If we add this special indexing of definite descriptions, then we can associate E-type pronouns with definite descriptions so understood.

Let's consider a very basic example that does not involve plurals. (I am numbering the conjuncts separately for ease of reference.)

---

[23] I have also discussed these issues in McKay 1994, though I no longer accept all aspects of the view offered there.

[24] Evans 1985, 222.

(37) John bumped into a woman who was jogging yesterday, and
(38) she was wearing a Yankees' cap.

I think that the representation of (37) is unproblematic.

(37a) $[\exists x: Wx \wedge Jx]\, Bjx$

The representation of the content of (38) is more difficult if we do not introduce the kind of context-sensitivity of domains for definite descriptions that was discussed in Chapter 8. None of the following are entirely correct if we are employing insensitive descriptions:

(38a) $[\imath x: Wx \wedge Jx]\, Cx$
(38b) $[\imath x: Wx \wedge Jx \wedge Bjx]\, Cx$
(38c) $[\exists x: Wx \wedge Jx \wedge Bjx]\, Cx$

(38a) is incorrect because the speaker of (37)–(38) is not committed to the claim that only one woman was jogging yesterday. Similarly, (38b) is incorrect because the speaker of (37)–(38) is not committed to the claim that John bumped into only one woman who was jogging yesterday (contrary to what Evans claims about similar examples). The speaker uses the pronoun referentially, to refer to the individual who was the basis for the claim in (37). Thus the speaker says more than what is expressed in (38c); (38c) fails to capture the unique reference of (38). The speaker does not just say that John bumped into some woman yesterday who was wearing a Yankees' cap; the speaker says that John bumped into a woman yesterday, and then the speaker goes on to refer to the very woman who was the basis of the first claim and say that she was wearing a Yankees' cap.[25]

If we incorporate the idea of a conversationally restricted domain, however, that takes us a long way towards solving the problem:

(38d) $[\imath_1 x: Wx \wedge Jx \wedge Bjx]\, Cx$

As we said in the discussion of definite descriptions, a subscript will indicate a restriction of the domain of the quantifier to the individuals of a conversationally available situation; definite descriptions will ordinarily distinguish among individuals within a domain determined by a conversationally salient situation. This gives our representation of (38) an appropriate special relation to (37), the context that introduces a

---

[25] Cf. Lewis 1983, 243. He says that although indefinite descriptions "are not themselves referring expressions, they may raise the salience of particular individuals in such a way as to pave the way for referring expressions that follow."

situation. The uniqueness condition is then restricted to the domain of this situation and can be satisfied.

Similar remarks apply to plural examples. If Alice looks out the window and says:

(41) Some students are playing together in the park, and

(42) Now they are moving towards your car.

we cannot represent the pronoun in (42) with an insensitive definite description that is based on the predicates in the prior clause (i.e., it cannot be 'the students who are playing together in the park'), since there might be many students playing together in the park other than the ones under discussion. Taking the discourse as a sentence with a single existential quantifier will not be fully adequate either, since it will miss the referential aspect of the use of the pronoun in (42). However, if we take the existential in (41) to introduce a situation and some individuals into the conversation, with the pronoun in (42) functioning like a definite description that is restricted to the individuals in that situation, then the uniqueness condition falls into place again. As we argued in Chapter 8, this approach requires that an existential like (41) introduce into a conversation the individuals that play a role in a situation that the speaker has in mind.

Caveat (3)

Another way to see what is wrong with (38c) is to consider a situation in which the speaker of (38) changes her mind. Suppose that she says that it was not a Yankees' cap, it was a Mets' cap. Suppose also that John bumped into a woman who was jogging yesterday and who was wearing a Yankees' cap, though John thought it was a man, didn't notice the cap, forgot about the incident, and didn't tell anyone, and thus that incident plays no role in producing the speaker's claim (37)–(38). Notice that (38c) is true in such a situation. But that would not show that our speaker was wrong when she changed her mind. Because of the domain limitation, the pronoun in (38) refers to the individual who is the basis for asserting (37), not merely to a woman who happens to make (37) true. Consider

(39) She was wearing a Mets' cap.

If the woman who was the source of the claim in (37) was wearing a Mets' cap, then (39) is true and (38) is false, despite the truth of (38c).

It might seem more promising in some ways to continue the quantification in (37), representing the whole discourse as follows:

(40) $[\exists x: Wx \wedge Jx]$ (B$jx \wedge Cx$)

But (40) is equivalent to (38c), and it too fails to represent the referential aspect of (38).

The plural case (41)–(42) fares similarly. Suppose that Alice realizes that it is not your car that she sees and goes on:

(43) Oh, I was wrong. They are moving towards a different car.

(43) would not be falsified because, out of sight somewhere, some students who had been playing in the park were moving towards your car. They are not the students Alice referred to in her use of (42) and (43).

We seem to be at a problematic point in the representation of (37)–(38). It seems that the pronoun may refer even if insensitive definite descriptions in (38a) and (38b) are wrong. By understanding that a definite description can be taken to be limited to what is conversationally available, we can preserve the connection between pronouns and definite descriptions in the simple version of this. However, in the elaboration of the case that is under consideration now, the prior conversational context provides predicates that do not correctly identify the referent of the pronoun, and so it might seem that the pronoun cannot be explained in terms of any available description based on those predicates. But that is too hasty. The pronoun does not need to stand in for a description any more detailed than *the woman*, once we recognize that the description itself can be understood to be restricted to conversationally available individuals. The speaker's having a particular situation in mind in which only one woman is involved is enough to make it possible to use a pronoun to refer to her.

Some other examples might help to illustrate.

(44) In the 1770s, a woman played an important role in the founding of the US. Well, I guess not really, but at least she made a nice flag.

A speaker of (44) might have Betsy Ross in mind. Though he changes his mind about the importance of her role, he uses the pronoun to refer to her. The speaker refers to the woman who was the basis for uttering the first sentence, the one woman in the situation he was beginning to describe. The definite description *the woman*, where that is limited to the conversationally available individuals, will do.

This approach preserves the connection of pronouns to definite descriptions, but at the cost of allowing descriptions to carry almost no descriptive content. We can always get *the female*, *the male*, and *the thing* for *she*, *he*, and *it*. But we are not just falling back on these as our general form for descriptions associated with pronouns. Those descriptions are suitable only when there is a unique female (unique male or unique thing) conversationally available for reference. Otherwise we must associate some fuller description or provide other resources in the context (such as pointing) in order to get the required uniqueness.

However, we should not suppose that there is just one thing that is going on with pronouns. Consider a variation on (44).

> (45) By 2030, a woman will walk on Mars. Well, at least she will be a part of the mission that goes there, even if she is not among those who walk on the planet.

(45) is problematic, especially if we imagine (as is most likely) that the speaker does not have any particular woman in mind, so that no one is the speaker's referent or the basis for the utterance of the first sentence. We cannot say that this involves reference to a particular woman, and so it seems that we must view it as relative reference of some kind.

The essential content is:

> (45a) $[\exists x: Wx]$ x will be on a mission to Mars by 2030.

Commitment to the stronger conjunct (that she will walk on Mars) has been withdrawn. We do not have the referential element that we had for (38c).

However, since our analysis really says that the speaker uses a pronoun to single out an individual in a situation that the speaker is discussing, (45) is not as problematic as it might first appear. (45) does something that we might paraphrase in this way:

> (45b) By 2030, some mission to Mars m is such that in m a woman will walk on Mars. Well, at least α will be a part of m, even if α does not walk on Mars.

The occurrences of 'α' in the second sentence of (45b) might correspond to unbound pronouns with a relative reference (relative to the bound variable m). If sentences typically involve implicit quantification over events, as some have argued, then something along these lines may be an especially attractive approach.[26]

Whatever analysis we pick, it seems that we must reach out in ways that differ from Evans's approach.

A CONTINUUM OF LINGUISTIC INFORMATION

Interestingly, Evans recognizes our third caveat himself (Evans 1977, Evans 1985, 129–1), that for some uses of pronouns the context provides a quantified antecedent for an unbound pronoun but does not provide the resources for a proper definite description.

> [T]here does not seem to be any great harm in liberalizing the account we give of the truth conditions of sentences containing E-type pronouns with a dash of psychologizing, in the interests of greater realism. For, when the speaker is manifestly *talking about something*, for example, in narrating an episode, it is acceptable to continue with the use of an E-type pronoun even when the antecedent containing sentence or clause has not provided the basis for a unique specification. One might begin a story:

> > One day, a man and a boy were walking along a road, and the man said to the boy: 'Would you like to be king?'

> One does not want to be committed, by this way of telling the story, to the existence of a day on which just one man and a boy walked along a road.

Ultimately he concludes this discussion: 'I shall ignore the wrinkle produced by this liberalization. I hope that it is obvious how it can be incorporated into the final product.'[27]

I believe that once we back away from the idea that an unbound pronoun must have a reference-fixing definite description, recoverable in a routine way from context, we have adopted a new view. We need a different picture. Like Evans, I would assimilate unbound pronouns to A-type, referential, pronouns. However, I would argue that there

---

[26] We will consider the role of events in more detail in Ch. 10. Ludlow and Neale 1991, 546, propose an event semantics as one possibility in the analysis of donkey sentences.

[27] Evans 1985, 131. This sentence ends a section of Evans's paper. Oddly, the first sentence of the next section is, "It appears that any treatment of E-type pronouns that does justice to all the considerations we have mentioned will involve recovering the description from the sentence containing its antecedent." He is exceedingly prompt in keeping his promise to ignore the "wrinkle" in his theory.

is really a continuum. Simple demonstrative uses of pronouns (and other uses that refer without any linguistic support) are at one end of the continuum. Paradigm cases of E-type pronouns, where the linguistic context provides a proper definite description that applies to the referent of the pronoun, are at the other end. In the middle are the cases of pronouns where the linguistic context cannot produce a uniquely specifying description but where what is said still plays a role in indicating the referent of the pronoun.

In these middle cases, the linguistic context alone is not enough to single out a referent; there is no way to construct a reference-fixing insensitive definite description based on the explicit background linguistic material.

> (46) Yesterday I saw a woman jogging. She greeted me, but I didn't recognize her.

> (47) Some teenagers are headed towards my car. I think that they are going to take my hubcaps.

In these cases, there might be more than one woman that the speaker saw jogging yesterday, and the speaker may know of other teenagers headed in the direction of his car without malicious intent. The descriptive material helps in focusing on a particular referent or some particular referents for the pronoun only within some situation that the speaker is describing. We can find appropriate definite descriptions only if we recognize the enhanced context sensitivity of definite descriptions that we discussed in Chapter 8.

Evans himself liberalizes his account of the sources for the definite description, to maintain the view that a definite description always fixes the referent of an unbound pronoun. "In order to effect this liberalization we should allow the reference of the E-type pronoun to be fixed not only by the predicative material explicitly in the antecedent clause, but also by the material which the speaker supplies upon demand." This response has at least two problems. First, it gives over too much to speakers' ability to be articulate about what they are referring to. In many cases, pointing, not describing, may be a speaker's only way to fully specify the referent. Second, this undermines the "rule-governed process" that Evans associates with E-type pronouns.

Recognition of the sensitivity of definite descriptions to available situations and recognition of their role in individuating within such contextually available situations provide a much better basis for liberalizing the account of unbound pronouns. We do not have a rule-governed process of the kind proposed by Evans, and we need not limit ourselves to insensitive definite descriptions in identifying the reference-fixing content of unbound pronouns. Whether we regard this as a liberalized account of E-type pronouns or as a supplement to E-type pronouns is a matter of terminology that we need not decide.

The domain indexing that we introduced for definite descriptions relates pronominal reference to what is conversationally available for reference by a definite description. This again raises the question of what is conversationally available. The sketch of an answer is that the things available are the individuals involved in some situation that is being characterized.

CATEGORIES OF PRONOUNS AGAIN

Let's return to the list of types of pronouns that we mentioned initially, (A)–(F). We have identified the referential (A) and bound-variable (C) as the two major types of pronouns. Evans suggests that we should also view bound-variable uses as a special case of (A), based on a Fregean account of quantification. [Qx: Ax] Bx is evaluated by considering, for each member of the domain of quantification, the truth-values that Ax and Bx would have if x were a name referring to that individual (and then seeing whether the As that are Bs are Q As). That reduction is neither necessary nor problematic from our standpoint.

Category (B), pronouns that co-refer with proper names, are split between types (A) and (C). In some cases (such as "John nominated himself" or "John loves his mother"), the pronoun can or must be viewed as a variable that is involved in constructing complex predicates (*x nominated x* and *x loves x's mother*). In others ("John knows where it is, and he can help you") the pronoun is a referential pronoun that can rely on the prior occurrence of the name as a contextual resource for securing reference.

As we indicated, at least with the quantifiers 'every' and 'each', though not so clearly for other quantifiers, there appear to be cases of inter-sentential binding. Such cases must be seen as working like long strings (or conjunctions) with a common dominating quantifier. Thus our category (D) is assimilated to (C).

Our main argument has been to suggest that unbound pronouns (including our category (E)) are referential. Some are pure (A)-type referential pronouns that do not use anything in the linguistic context as a basis for reference (relying instead on demonstrations or other non-linguistic cues from context to secure reference); others use a relation to linguistic context to limit the possibilities for pronominal reference, but without there being a fully specifying description available in any sense; and still others, the paradigm E-type pronouns of Evans, refer to something that is specifiable by a proper definite description that can be constructed from contextually available predicative resources.

In connection with these unbound pronouns, we needed also to recognize the phenomenon of relative reference.

Finally, "pronouns of laziness," pronouns that "stand in" for definite descriptions within a quantified context, illustrate relative reference and our more liberal attitude toward the relationship between linguistic context and pronominal reference.

> (48) A person who cashes his paycheck is smarter than one who burns **it**.

> $[\forall x: [\imath z : z$ is x's paycheck] x cashes $z]$ $[\forall y: y$ burns $\alpha]$ x is smarter than y

We must evaluate

> $[\imath z: z$ is x's paycheck] x cashes z
> y burns α
> x is smarter than y

The interpretation of α is constrained to satisfying the following, relative to w:

> w is v's paycheck

The sentence is ambiguous in that v can be assigned the same interpretation as x or as y. (The ambiguity may be clearer with 'paints his house' in place of 'cashes his paycheck'.) We get the salient interpretation by making the same assignment to v and y and using that as the constraint on α. This requires that the constraint on α is quite abstract – *being v's paycheck*, where v is contextually salient – and requiring a further resolution of the ambiguity concerning which contextually salient individual is assigned to v.

Caveat (4): D-type pronouns
It is possible to maintain a slightly different view of all of this. Instead of taking the view that unbound (E-type) pronouns are referential, we

might instead hold that they stand in for (or can be "treated as")[28] definite descriptions, at least in the vast majority of cases. Neale calls pronouns that are proxies for definite descriptions "D-type pronouns". Evans rejected this idea on the grounds that there is a difference in the scope properties of pronouns and definite descriptions. We have already indicated that this is a very weak argument, since we can account for what is observed by simply stipulating that the pronoun must stand in for a wide-scope description. However, it is not even so clear that we wish to make that scope restriction an absolute rule, because sentences with pronouns seem to have some of the scope ambiguities that occur in sentences with definite descriptions.

For example, using Evans's own example, Neale points out that non-referential readings of pronouns are at least available in the following sentence:

(49) Boston has a mayor. He used to be a Democrat.

And this is even clearer in the variation:

(50) Right now the Mayor of Boston is a Republican, but next year he'll be a Democrat.

These, however, are inconclusive examples, since they can also be explained in terms of shifting temporal parameters. That is, the pronoun in (50) is ambiguous because it might rely on 'x is now mayor of Boston' as the contextual source for its reference, or it might rely on 'x is mayor of Boston at t', with 'used to be' introducing a new value for t in the second sentence of (49). Similarly for 'next year' in (50). So there may be an account of temporal reference in sentences that make these tractable on a reference-fixing approach like Evans's.

Neale also cites the following examples against the idea that pronouns are used referentially.[29]

(51) *The inventor of the wheel* was a genius. I suspect that *s/he* ate fish on a daily basis.
(52) *An insurance agent* is coming to see me today. I'm sure *s/he* just wants to sell me a policy.

Since there is no intent to express a singular proposition, these are not referential uses of the pronouns (or the descriptions they are based on),

---

[28] Ludlow and Neale 1991, 543 in Ludlow 1997. Further page references will be to this reprinted version.
[29] Neale 1990, 178.

in Donellan's sense of *referential*. This is a very successful argument against proponents of certain kind of referential – attributive distinction who want to argue that pronouns are referential. However, I am not a proponent of that distinction, and I see no problem in an account of pronouns that says that the pronouns in (51) and (52) refer to contextually salient individuals. Thus I am not yet persuaded that this consideration requires that we regard pronouns as proxies for definite descriptions.

Scope effects also seem to be at play in other cases, however.[30]

> (53) A man has killed Alice. Charlene hopes that he can be found.

If we use a definite description, there is a scope ambiguity:

> (53a) A man has killed Alice. [$\imath x$: x killed Alice] Charlene hopes that x can be found.

> (53b) A man has killed Alice. Charlene hopes that [$\imath x$: x killed Alice] x can be found.

(53a) can be true even if Charlene does not know that Alice is dead (and even if Charlene has never heard of Alice). There merely needs to be a unique man who killed Alice such that Charlene has the hope (for whatever reason) that that man can be found. (53a) accords with the analysis we have developed, where 'he' in (53) is an unbound pronoun with an interpretation that is constrained by the first sentence. On the other hand, (53b) can be true even if Charlene has no idea who killed Alice, as long as she wants the unique killer (whoever he is) to be found. Both readings are available for the pronominal sentence (53), and in more complicated situations, there can be multiple possible scopes.

> (54) A man has killed Alice. Betty believes that Charlene hopes that he can be found.

Here there are three scope possibilities, representing different attributions to Betty and Charlene. It seems that we can interpret the pronoun as having any of the three scopes that the definite description can have.

> (54a) A man has killed Alice. [$\imath x$: x killed Alice] Betty believes that Charlene hopes that x can be found.

> (54b) A man has killed Alice. Betty believes that [$\imath x$: x killed Alice] Charlene hopes that x can be found.

---

[30] This is a variation on an example in Neale 1990, 187, example (20).

(54c) A man has killed Alice. Betty believes that Charlene hopes that [ɪ*x*: *x* killed Alice] *x* can be found.

Thus it does seem that the scope ambiguities that exist for definite descriptions can also exist for pronouns.[31] When the pronoun is interpreted by a description that does not take maximal scope, the pronoun has neither a bound-variable nor a referential use, as we have understood those categories.

This scope argument makes a convincing case that we must treat at least some pronouns as proxies for definite descriptions, as long as we are convinced that there is a real ambiguity in sentences like (53) and (54). These are not merely cases of an available definite description fixing reference for a pronoun; there is scope variation within the sentence that contains the pronoun, and we account for that by varying the scope of the description within that very sentence.

One might think that it is still open to hold that (53) is not ambiguous and that we can use (53) in two different kinds of situations. First, where the speaker refers to the man who killed Alice and Charlene need not know that he killed Alice but does hope (*de re*) that he can be found. Second, in a situation in which the speaker believes that Charlene hopes that whoever killed Alice can be found. This looks like a standard *de re–de dicto* ambiguity, but on this proposal we would not take it that way. We say instead that in either situation, the pronoun 'he' refers to the unique killer of Alice (if there is one). Whether Charlene has a *de re* hope about that individual or merely a general hope about finding the killer of Alice would be regarded as something that is not indicated in (53). It is simply extra information. Similarly, the differences in the situations in which (54) is true would not be regarded as differences in meaning for (54).

I do not find that approach promising, however. Like other sentences involving *de re–de dicto* ambiguities, (53) seems to involve either one or another attribution of a hope to Charlene. Either her hope involves an object-directed proposition or it is of a general kind. There is no way to attribute a hope to her and to remain neutral about which of these hopes it is. Thus I find scope considerations to be decisive in favor of the idea that, in at least the *de dicto* readings of this kind of sentence, the pronoun must be understood as a proxy for a definite description.

---

[31] The fact that multiple scopes are possible also makes it clear that no binary semantic ambiguity (referential *vs.* non-referential, for example) can make the appropriate distinctions. Cf. Kripke 1977, Soames 1989, Neale 1990, 187.

If we take the view that pronouns stand in for definite descriptions, we can handle our caveats (2) and (3) in a different way.[32] As we indicated in Chapter 8, definite descriptions are restricted to what is conversationally available. So the pronoun can be seen to stand in for a definite description, where context may limit the domain of interpretation in the usual way for quantifiers, and the description may also be limited to what is conversationally available, and context may also provide additional descriptive content for the definite description in ways that provide for the satisfaction of the uniqueness requirement.[33] With all of this, I think that the view that unbound pronouns are generally D-type (proxies for definite descriptions) can be successfully defended.

One might suspect that a similar defense would work for Evans as well. The definite description that fixes the reference of a pronoun on Evans's view can be found in the same way as the description the pronoun goes proxy for on the Neale–Ludlow view. However, once we admit that the domain for the definite description is so delimited by context, it becomes hard to distinguish this version of the Evans view (that the pronoun's reference is fixed by a contextually delimited description) from the plain view that these are referential pronouns and context limits what they can refer to.

---

[32] The view that pronouns stand in for descriptions requires another qualification, in light of some differences in the behavior of descriptions and pronouns. Consider these contrasting pairs:

> Most baritones are married. ?She must be very tolerant.
>
> Most baritones have a spouse. She must be very tolerant
>
> Most baritones are married. The woman must be very tolerant.
>
> A woman entered, and then another woman entered from the other direction. She was carrying a bunch of flowers.
>
> A woman entered, and then another woman entered from the other direction. ?The woman was carrying a bunch of flowers.

There is a clear deficiency in the naturalness and perhaps even the acceptability of the questioned sentences. Roberts suggests that the difference can be explained by the fact that a pronoun requires maximum saliency for its referent (in addition to the conversational availability that the definite description requires). Roberts 2003, esp. 321–6 and 335–7.

[33] Ludlow and Neale, 544–5, Neale 1990, 200, 241. Using the terminology 'D-type pronoun' for a pronoun that stands in for a definite description, Neale 1990, 241, says, "I suggest that quite general contextual considerations must play a role in spelling out the descriptive content of D-type pronouns in exactly the same way that such considerations play a role in spelling out the contents of overt definite descriptions and quantifiers."

As long as the scope phenomena in (53) and (54) are regarded as genuine ambiguities, we should allow that in some cases we must understand the pronoun as a stand-in for a definite description. Reacting to such cases, Ludlow and Neale say that "perhaps the rules of language dictate only that an unbound pronoun anaphoric on a quantifier must be interpreted as a referring expression *or* a description. It would then be a question for pragmatics exactly how any particular unbound anaphor is interpreted."[34]

[34] Ludlow and Neale 1991, 543.

10

Plurals and Events

Donald Davidson, Terence Parsons, and others have developed the semantics for English with a central role for quantification over events.[1] Their principal arguments for this relate to semantic and inferential connections involving adverbs, but there are also arguments based on other features of English. Many of these are strong arguments, and so it is of some interest that we have so far been able to develop our semantics for plurals without introducing a major role for events. This may relate to the "sub-atomic" character that Parsons identifies for event quantification; event quantification is part of verb and verb-phrase meaning, and so, at least in its principal function, it may not be visible at a semantic level that takes verbs and verb phrases as unanalyzed elements. The possible role for events in the semantics of definite descriptions (mentioned at the end of Chapter 8) may be unrelated to the role for events in the semantics developed by Davidson and Parsons.

The fact that these event quantifications have not played a major role in our semantics for plural quantifiers may seem especially striking to those who are familiar with the literature on the semantics of plurals. Some of the principal work, such as that of Schein and Landman, makes events central characters in the semantics of plurals. So I want to look at some of the phenomena that might tempt one to give events this central role. I believe that our approach is adequate without the introduction of event quantification as a part of the semantics of plurals.

It is important to be able to develop the logic of plurals without relying in a general way on an event analysis. Oliver and Smiley have shown how a general reliance on event paraphrases will inevitably lead to paradox (analogous to the set-theoretic paradoxes).[2]

---

[1] See esp. Davidson 1967 and Parsons 1990.
[2] Oliver and Smiley 2001, 298–305.

In closing this discussion of the relations between plurals and events, I will note an argument due to C. Brisson[3] that makes a case for recognizing a role for event quantification if we are to understand some features of the use of the particular quantifier word 'all'. In this case we can see how this particular plural quantifier seems to behave differently with different types of verbs, and Brisson offers the internal event structure of these verbs as the account of this. Using our formalization of plurals and plural quantification, we can put together a very clear picture of what is going on here. Thus we can perhaps find a place where our treatment of distribution interacts with the internal, event structure of some complex verbs.

The fact that we have not so far employed quantification over events does not reflect any animus towards the idea that events are central in the meaning of English sentences. In fact, I think that arguments like those that Davidson and Parsons have developed are very strong. However, it is useful to separate that from the treatment of plurals and non-distributive predication; then we can better understand what features of language really bring about the need for event quantification.

DISTRIBUTIVE AMBIGUITY AND EVENTS

Let's look at an idea that might occur to anyone familiar with the Davidson and Parsons approaches to events in the semantics of English. Once we have introduced events in the semantics, it might appear attractive to use a scope distinction to account for the difference between distributive and non-distributive readings of some ambiguous sentences. In this way, the ambiguity in a sentence like

(1) Lisa and Frank read *The Cat in the Hat* to Molly.

might be treated as a scope ambiguity:

(1a) [∃e: e is a reading of *The Cat in the Hat* to Molly] (Lisa is an agent of e ∧ Frank is an agent of e)

This would contrast with

(1b) [∃e: e is a reading of *The Cat in the Hat* to Molly] (Lisa is an agent of e) ∧ [∃e: e is a reading of *The Cat in the Hat* to Molly] (Frank is an agent of e)

---

[3] Brisson 2003.

The relative scopes of the event quantifier and the conjunction would seem to indicate the difference between a non-distributive interpretation (1a) and a distributive interpretation (1b). In quantified cases, the difference would show up as a difference in relative quantifier scope.[4]

(2)   Three students lifted 200 pounds.

(2a) [∃e: e is a lifting of 200 pounds] [∃x: x is a student] x is an agent of e

(2b) [∃x: x is a student] [∃e: e is a lifting of 200 pounds] x is an agent of e

The idea is that (2a) would represent the non-distributive reading and (2b) the distributive. So far we have not needed the apparatus of plural quantification.

However, this does not quite work, since in each of these cases, the (b) (distributive) sentence follows from the (a) (non-distributive) sentence, but a distributive reading of a sentence should not follow from the non-distributive reading.[5] To avoid this problem, we need to say that Lisa and Frank are *the* agents of the event, not just that each is an agent; and we need to say that the three students are *the* agents of the event, not just that each is an agent. Without using plural quantification and non-distributive predication to say this, we would presumably need to try this:

(1c) [∃e: e is a reading of *The Cat in the Hat* to Molly] (Lisa is an agent of e ∧ Frank is an agent of e ∧ [∀y: y is an agent of e] (y = Lisa ∨ y = Frank))

(1d) [∃e: e is a reading of *The Cat in the Hat* to Molly] (Lisa is an agent of e ∧ [∀y: y is an agent of e] y = Lisa) ∧ [∃e: e is a reading of *The Cat in the Hat* to Molly] (Frank is an agent of e ∧ [∀y: y is an agent of e] y = Frank)

This is much better, but it reinstates a problem that we got ourselves out of in Chapter 2. On the event-based approach being considered here, the non-distributive analysis of (1) will be importantly different from the non-distributive analysis of:

(3)   Lisa, Frank and Ned read *The Cat in the Hat* to Molly.

---

[4] We leave aside the question of whether 'S being an agent of e' refers to an event. Obviously we cannot require a full "expansion" of event analyses if this is an event.

[5] Cf. Landman's criticism of Schein, Landman 2000, 79.

(3c) [∃e: e is a reading of *The Cat in the Hat* to Molly] (Lisa is an agent of e ∧ Frank is an agent of e ∧ Ned is an agent of e ∧ [∀y: y is an agent of e] (y = Lisa ∨ y = Frank ∨ y = Ned))

The monadic, non-distributive predicative construction:

(3*) ───── read *The Cat in the Hat* to Molly.

gets analyses with a different logical structure in the two cases; a different number of agents requires a different logical structure. The importance of this shows up most clearly when we consider quantified cases. We can make (2) work as well as (1) and (3) did, because it is numerically specific:

(2c) [∃e: e is a lifting of 200 pounds] [∃x, y, z: x is a student ∧ y is a student ∧ z is a student] (x is an agent of e ∧ y is an agent of e ∧ z is an agent of e ∧ x ≠ y ∧ x ≠ z ∧ y ≠ z ∧ [∀w: w is a student ∧ w is an agent of e] (w = x ∨ w = y ∨ w = z)))

(2d) [∃x: x is a student] [∃e: e is a lifting of 200 pounds] (x is an agent of e ∧ [∀w: w is an agent of e] w = x) ∧ [∃y: y is a student ∧ y ≠ x] [∃e: e is a lifting of 200 pounds] (y is an agent of e ∧ [∀w: w is an agent of e] w = y) ∧ [∃z: z is a student ∧ z ≠ x ∧ x ≠ y] [∃e: e is a lifting of 200 pounds] (z is an agent of e ∧ [∀w: w is an agent of e] w = z)

But we are not able to do that with quantifiers that are not numerically specific.

(4) Several (or some) students lifted 200 pounds.

We cannot construct sentences like (2c) and (2d), because we have no basis for determining how many conjuncts are needed. This is just a symptom of the problem already noted in Chapter 2, that we have not really given a unitary analysis for

(2*) ───── lifted 200 pounds.

As we argued there, we should always prefer a unitary analysis of such a predicate over one that analyzes it as a family of predicates with differing polyadicity. Cases that are not numerically specific make that need clear.

The appropriate solution to this problem seems to be to go to our account of definite descriptions and employ plural quantification. The non-distributive reading involves a plural definite description, and we can differentiate the two readings as follows:

(1e) [∃e: e is a reading of *The Cat in the Hat* to Molly] [ɿX: X are agents of e] $X \approx$ ⌊Lisa, Frank⌉

(1f) [∃e: e is a reading of *The Cat in the Hat* to Molly] [ɿx: x is an agent of e] $x =$ Lisa ∧ [∃e: e is a reading of *The Cat in the Hat* to Molly] [ɿx: x is an agent of e] $x =$ Frank

(1e) involves non-distributive predication, since the analysis of it involves *among*, which is non-distributive in its second argument place.

(1e′) [∃e: e is a reading of *The Cat in the Hat* to Molly] [∃X: X are agents of e ∧ [∧Y: Y are agents of e] YAX] $X \approx$ ⌊Lisa, Frank⌉

Once we allow non-distributive predication, however, we do not need to introduce event quantification in order to distinguish the distributive and non-distributive readings. The difference lies in the presence of a distributing universal.

(1f) ⌊Lisa, Frank⌉ read *The Cat in the Hat* to Molly.

(1g) [∀x: xA⌊Lisa, Frank⌉] x read *The Cat in the Hat* to Molly.

(4a) [Several X: X are students] X lifted 200 pounds.

(4b) [Several X: X are students] [∀y: yAX] y lifted 200 pounds.

This is a simple and intuitively satisfying account of the difference without the introduction of events.

Ultimately we have not found any way in which the introduction of quantification over events in the semantics improves the treatment of the distributive–non-distributive ambiguity.[6] We need plural reference and quantification in any case, and once we have that, we can develop a satisfactory treatment of the ambiguity without the introduction of event quantification.

---

[6] James Higginbotham 2000, (94–6) also includes arguments that we must use plural quantification even if we introduce an event analysis. "The term 'is one of' is the plural ersatz for membership, and in the presence of plural quantification and plural variables it is not going to be eliminable." But he goes on. "However, we do not lose the advantage of Schein's fundamental thesis, that undistributed plural reference may involve, not group agency, but multiple agency of single events." Since we have been able to account for non-distributive predication and plural reference and quantification without that, though, it is difficult to see what the advantage of the Schein thesis would be in the context of a semantic account of plurals.

EVENTS AND PARADOX

Oliver and Smiley 2001 show that there is a serious problem in any attempt to use event paraphrases (like those that we have just considered) in a fully general way. Let's consider the method used in generating paraphrases like (1e) and (1f). We turn a sentence 'FY' into a sentence '[∃e: e is an F-event] [ɿX: [∀y: yAX] y is an agent of e] $X \approx Y$'.

(5) FY → [∃e: e is an F-event] [ɿX: [∀y: yAX] y is an agent of e] $X \approx Y$

Now one might think that this has promise for a singularist account of plural predication if we instead use a set-theoretic relationship. All predication will be distributive in the set-theoretic version of (1e):

(1e*) [∃e: e is a reading of *The Cat in the Hat* to Molly] $\{x: x$ is an agent of e$\}$ = $\{$Lisa, Frank$\}$

Ordinary set-theoretic identity begins to work for us again. The general method is:

(6) FS → [∃e: e is an F-event] $\{x: x$ is an agent of e$\}$ = S

Where S is an expression that refers to some set of things. So if we could understand plural predications as predications of sets, then we could go back to singularist logic and set theory. Thus the introduction of events would serve an important purpose after all.

However, Oliver and Smiley have shown that the introduction of events as a basis for such general paraphrases is problematic whether we take (1e) or (1e*) as our paraphrase.[7] In other words, whether we use the set-theoretic or non-set-theoretic account of plural predication, we will encounter paradoxes if we adopt these as general methods of paraphrase.

To see this, first note that the notion of event used in making such paraphrases must be very extended if it is to serve the purpose of providing a general method for paraphrase. Whenever some things have a property, there must be a way of associating an event, in this extended sense, with the property.

Consider now the fact that some events play a part in themselves and some don't. For example, "if the events are many, then there is

---

[7] They consider something like (1e*), but the argument applies equally to (1e).

an *are-many* event in which all and only events play a part."[8] It plays a part in itself. But typical events do not play a part in themselves. In particular, they are not agents of themselves. In fact,

(7) The events that are not agents of themselves are many.

According to our method of paraphrase, that is:

(8) $[\imath Z: [\forall y: yAZ]$ y is not an agent of $y]$ $[\exists e: e$ is a being many] $[\imath X: [\forall y: yAX]$ y is an agent of e] $X \approx Z$
(9) $[\exists e: e$ is a being many] $\{x: x$ is an agent of e$\} = \{x: x$ is an event that is not an agent of $x\}$

But now if we ask whether e (this particular event of being many) is an agent of e, we have a paradox. e must be among or be a member of one side of the identity but not the other (no matter which paraphrase we like); e is an agent of itself if and only if it isn't. Thus it appears that this kind of event paraphrase cannot be a general method for representing plurals.

Happily, we have other methods. To illustrate, it will be worthwhile to look at some of the kinds of sentences that Landman and Schein see as central in motivating an event treatment, to see how we represent those.

UNSCOPED QUANTIFICATION AGAIN

In Chapter 2 we developed an account of unscoped quantification, readings of multiply quantified sentences that do not interpret one of the quantifiers as having scope over the other.

(10) Five doctors treated thirty patients.

The conclusion there was that we can use non-distributive predication and plural quantification to provide an adequate representation of the various meanings of such sentences. In the case of simple, non-distributive plural readings with our most fundamental quantifiers, the quantifier scopes do not matter; we get an equivalent sentence no matter what the order of the quantifiers is. So we can use:

(10a) $[5 X: DX_D]$ $[30 Y: PY_D]$ TXY

---

[8] Oliver and Smiley 2001, 301.

As we indicated in Chapter 4, the most general treatment of the special unscoped reading, applying even to non-basic quantifiers, follows a pattern like this:

(10b) $[5X:DX_D] [\forall x:xAX] [\exists V:VAX] (xAV \wedge [\exists Y:PY_D] TVY)$
$\wedge [30Y:PY_D] [\forall y:yAY] [\exists W:WAY] (yAW \wedge [\exists X:DX_D] TXW)$

This allows that doctors might treat patients together or individually and that patients might be treated together or individually. If, in the context, distribution of either argument is possible, then some simplification can occur. Obviously the relative scope of the two main quantifiers, '[5 X: DX_D]' and '[30 Y: PY_D]' does not matter, and of course the order of the conjuncts in the conjunction doesn't matter. If we use defined quantifiers like 'at most 5' and 'at most 30', then we must rely on (10b) for the unscoped analysis. (See Chapter 4, 93–6, for the full discussion.)[9]

Fred Landman makes these examples central to his case for events in the semantics of English. But the analysis that we have given provides an alternative to that, and there is no evident advantage to be gained from the introduction of quantification over events in the representation of the meaning of sentences of this kind. (There could be an advantage from the standpoint of linguistics if the recognition of the role of events provided a systematic way to generate something like (10b) from the syntactic form of the natural language sentence. I don't see that as a factor here, though.)

SCHEIN'S COMPLEX EXAMPLES

Barry Schein argues that we must instead introduce quantification over events that uses, as its only polyadic predicates, predicates that indicate functional roles in relation to events. He presents some examples that he says pose insurmountable problems for any approach like ours that uses polyadic (distributive and non-distributive) predicates in the general representation of relations, and he argues that we cannot get the predicates and arguments properly understood so that all cases, distributive and non-distributive and scoped and unscoped, can be represented correctly. Schein's examples are quite complex, and rather than laying out in full the arguments he presents, it will suffice to show

---

[9] We haven't included any discussion of the distributive readings of (5), since those are not at issue here.

how we would represent the semantic content of the difficult readings that he considers. These contents can be generated systematically from procedures of interpretation developed in Chapter 4.

Consider the following sentence:

(11) Three ATMs gave two new clients (each) exactly two passwords.

Suppose further that the situation diagrammed below is the situation being described by (11). Using 'ti' for the ith ATM, 'pi' for the ith password and 'ni' for the ith new client:

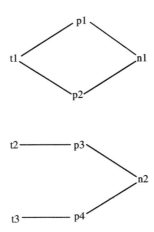

Here we have a combination of complicating phenomena that we discussed in Chapter 4: the first two quantifiers (*three ATMs* and *two new clients*) are unscoped with respect to each other, but the third quantifier is within the scope of a distributing universal (*two clients each*) and is an *exactly* quantifier. We need to identify a number of processes (also employed in Chapter 4) that are relevant in generating a representation of the semantic content of (11). First is our general pattern for unscoped quantification in $[nX: DX]\ [mY: PY]\ TXY$:

(12) $[nX: DX]\ [\forall x: xAX]\ [\exists V: VAX]\ (xAV \wedge [\exists Y: PY]\ TVY)$
$\wedge\ [mY: PY]\ [\forall y: yAY]\ [\exists W: WAY]\ (yAW \wedge [\exists X: DX]\ TXW)$

Second is the general procedure for representing 'Exactly n F are G', when the relevant argument positions in F and G are distributive:

(13) $[nY: [\forall y: yAY]\ Fy]\ ([\forall y: yAY]\ Gy \wedge [\forall y: Fy \wedge Gy]\ yAY)$

Finally there are some relevant equivalences that enable some simplifications, the most noteworthy being this:

$[\exists W: WAY] [\forall y: yAW] \ldots y \ldots$ is equivalent to
$[\exists y: yAY] \ldots y \ldots$

Our sentence is this:

Three Ts gave two Ns (each) exactly two Ps.

Because the passwords are given distributively, we can represent the target sentence in the following way:

(11a) $[3X: TX][\forall x: xAX][\exists V: VAX](xAV \land [\exists W: NW][\forall y: yAW][2Z: PZ]([\forall z: zAZ] GVyz \land [\forall z: Pz \land GVyz] zAZ)) \land [2Y: NY][\forall y: yAY][\exists W: WAY][\forall y: yAW](yAW \land [\exists V: TV][2Z: PZ] ([\forall z: zAZ] GVyz \land [\forall z: Pz \land GVyz] zAZ))$

Because of the distribution of clients (the 'each' in the example sentence), some simplification is possible (in accord with the relevant equivalence cited and the reduction of some subsequent redundancy):

(11b) $[3X: TX][\forall x: xAX][\exists V: VAX](xAV \land [\exists y: Ny][2Z: PZ]([\forall z: zAZ] GVyz \land [\forall z: Pz \land GVyz] zAZ)) \land [2Y: NY][\forall y: yAY][\exists V: TV][2Z: PZ] ([\forall z: zAZ] GVyz \land [\forall z: Pz \land GVyz] zAZ))$

This gives the logical content of the sentence. We have given a set of rules for constructing such an interpretation of the English sentence, though we have not given an account of why natural language semantics should permit such a reading.

Relating the formal language to English examples is an important help for understanding the formal language, and I hope that linguists will see some value in the kind of formal language I develop. To that end, it is important that we see what can be semantically represented, but it is not part of my project to do the systematic syntax and semantics of natural language that would fully indicate how to derive every semantic representation from the surface syntax of English. Getting clear about the semantic content of the sentences is a preliminary to developing a full theory of how natural language syntax systematically represents that content.

We should acknowledge, though, that if the events approach provides a better way to relate the natural language syntax to the semantics, that would be an argument in its favor. I present something that provides a basis for an alternative to the semantic interpretation of plurals based on events, and I hope that linguists can evaluate whether the events approach to plurals provides a more systematic semantics. That would be an interesting finding, but in the current state of things, it is not evident that it does.

Although Davidson and Parsons have made a case for thinking that events play an important role in the semantics for English, so far we have not seen any reason to think that the account of plurals provides any additional reason for incorporating events into semantics. Looking at this another way, these preliminary considerations give us no reason to think that an account of plural predication and quantification will require reference to events, and Oliver and Smiley present a powerful reason for avoiding any very general employment of events in the account of plural predication.

We have developed several resources that enable us to provide an analysis of sentences involving plurals without requiring that events play a role: we take non-distributive predication and quantification as basic, and we recognize that distributive predications involve distributing universals. We have argued that those resources are needed in any case for the semantics of plurals, and once we have them, we seem to have the resources for dealing with unscoped quantification and for making the kinds of distinctions that Schein requires.

LANDMAN'S OBJECTION TO THE MULTIPLE ROLE APPROACH

Fred Landman (79–80) has put forward another important objection to Schein's approach to the semantics of plurals. We need to see what the objection is and see that it does not apply to our approach to plurals.

Schein's approach can be called a "multiple role" approach; when some boys surround a building or touch the ceiling, each of them is an agent of the surrounding or the touching. Landman objects that meaning constraints on verbs that apply to singular uses of those verbs cannot be carried to plural cases if we adopt such a multiple-role approach. Landman considers:

(12) a. John touches the ceiling.

b. The agent brings part of himself into physical contact with the theme.

(12b) formulates a general semantic constraint on the verb in (12a), expressing it in terms of thematic role. But now consider:

(13) The boys touch the ceiling.

On Schein's account, each of the boys is an agent of the event. But it is not required that each boy touch the ceiling, if touching the ceiling is here a group activity. (If they are surrounding a building, it is even clearer that we cannot say that each is an agent without considerable revision of our usual way of talking about such examples.) Thus, according to Landman, the multiple role (Schein) approach must require that *touch* has different meanings in singular and plural cases (since there are different requirements on agency).

Landman says that instead we must regard a single object, the sum of the boys, as the agent in order for the constraint to apply.

(13a) The sum of the boys brings a part of itself into physical contact with the theme.

But it seems that we can also recognize the correct thematic relations with a non-distributive plural constraint:

(13b) The agents bring (part of) themselves into contact with the theme.

(12b) is then just the special case of this where there is only one agent. (The words 'part of' in Landman's (12b) are gratuitous in both singular and plural cases.)

A similar case is made based on a different example:

(14) a. John sings *Rock of Ages*.
       b. The school boys sing *Rock of Ages*.

Landman notes that, "As is well known, collective noun phrases have very weak involvement conditions: we all know that some of these boys are faking it ...." Thus he argues that we would not wish to regard each of these boys as an agent, though the group that includes them is an agent (p. 81).

> If we assume that in the collective interpretation, what is the agent is not every school boy, but the plural object which is the sum of the school boys, then we assume that we have an event which has a single, collective agent.

If we assume that the sum is a "plural object", this is right; but if we allow non-distributive predication, then we can say that they are the agents of the singing without being thereby forced to say distributively that each is an agent. This will be an especially apt result in variations such as

(15) The school boys sing *Rock of Ages* in three-part harmony.

These examples remind us that singularism provides no special advantage here. If we start with singular, distributive predication as our only kind of predication, we can only get collective predication by making it singular predication of collections. Landman's criticism of Schein builds on that. But if we instead take non-distributive predication as the general case and introduce distributing quantifiers, then we get both non-distributive and distributive predication, without requiring that non-distributive predication is predication of a sum individual.

ALL

C. Brisson may have located a way in which the semantics for the quantifier term 'all' interacts with an underlying event structure for verbs that she identifies as *accomplishment* terms.

The introduction of the quantifier term 'all' often disambiguates a sentence that would otherwise have both distributive and non-distributive readings.

(16) The bottles are too heavy to carry.
(17) The bottles are all too heavy to carry.[10]
(18) The senators voted for the tax cut.
(19) The senators all voted for the tax cut.

Sentences (17) and (19) all strongly favor a distributive reading, whereas either reading is readily available for (16). (Brisson's claim that (17) "can only be interpreted distributively,"[11] is perhaps a bit too strong.) Thus one would be initially tempted to take distributivity as an element

---

[10] There are perhaps subtle differences among these:

> The bottles are all too heavy to carry.
> All the bottles are too heavy to carry.
> All of the bottles are too heavy to carry.

However, those differences don't seem to be relevant to the issues here.

[11] Brisson 2003, 172. Brisson has a number of arguments for her treatment of 'all' that are outside the scope of our discussion here.

in the meaning of 'all'. However, in many other cases the introduction of 'all' does not disambiguate as it does with (16) and (18).

(20) The students carried the piano.
(21) The students all carried the piano.
(22) The girls built a raft.
(23) The girls all built a raft.

(21) and (23) preserve the ambiguities of (20) and (22). So it appears that 'all' does not always have the power to favor a distributive reading.

Brisson argues that 'all' carries distributivity as a feature when it can, but that the event structure of some verbs provides multiple locations for 'all', and so the ambiguity is persistent with those verbs. She contrasts *achievement* and *state* verbs with the *accomplishment* and *activity* verbs that have this richer structure. (16) involves a state verb, and (18) involves an achievement verb, but (20) and (22) involve accomplishment or activity verbs.

According to Brisson, the special structure of an accomplishment or activity verb is that it involves two quantifications over events rather than just one. The inner quantification relates to an inner "Doing" verb that is a part of the meaning. For example:

(24) Alice moved the piano.

On the kind of event treatment that we have already discussed, along the lines that Davidson or Parsons would propose, this would be interpreted in the following way (leaving out irrelevant details):

(25) $\exists e$ (e is a moving $\wedge$ Ag(e, Alice) $\wedge$ Th(e, the piano))[12]

But Brisson argues that this is an accomplishment verb with a richer structure. Alice does something that is a part of the event that is the piano's moving. Thus:

(26) $\exists e$(e is a moving $\wedge$ Th(e, the piano) $\wedge$ $\exists e'$(e' is doing $\wedge$ e' $<$ e $\wedge$ Ag(e', Alice)))

The symbol '$<$' is used here to represent a parthood relation among events. Then the universal 'all' in a sentence like (21) can still be

---

[12] Here we use 'Ag(e, Alice)' for 'Alice is an agent of e' and 'Th(e, the piano)' for 'the piano is a theme of e'.

associated with distribution and yet be ambiguous, because there is an additional location for the distributing universal:[13]

(27) [The X: X are students] [$\forall x$: xAX] $\exists e$ (e is a moving $\wedge$ Th(e, the piano) $\wedge$ $\exists e'$(e' is a doing $\wedge$ e' $< e \wedge$ Ag(e', x)))

(28) [The X: X are students] $\exists e$ (e is a moving $\wedge$ Th(e, the piano) $\wedge$ [$\forall x$: xAX] $\exists e'$ (e' is a doing $\wedge e'$ $< e \wedge$ Ag(e', x)))[14]

In both cases there is a distributing universal associated with 'all', and yet we still get the two readings for the sentence as a whole. In (27), we have distribution with respect to moving, so that each student may be an agent of a different moving. In (28), each agent is said to do something that contributes to the one moving.

As elaborated thus far, this has a problem. (28) entails (27), but the non-distributive reading of the natural language sentence does not entail the distributive reading.[15] We need to add a uniqueness clause in order to correct these readings of the English examples.

(27') [The X: X are students] [$\forall x$: xAX] $\exists e$ (e is a moving $\wedge$ Th(e, the piano) $\wedge$ $\exists e'$(e' is a doing $\wedge$ e' $< e \wedge$ Ag(e', x) $\wedge$ [$\forall y$: Ag(e', y)] $y = x$))

(28') [The X: X are students] $\exists e$ (e is a moving $\wedge$ Th(e, the piano) $\wedge$ [$\forall x$: xAX] $\exists e'$ (e' is a doing $\wedge$ e' $< e \wedge$ Ag(e', x) $\wedge$ [$\forall y$: Ag(e', y)] yAX))

With that amendment, we have a way to make the requisite distinction correctly. It is a bit more than just a scope distinction.

This raises many issues that go beyond what we can do here, but if the requisite distinctions among verbs are robust, then this may be

---

[13] Brisson has a different treatment of distribution, based on Schwarzschild, but her use of that relates to a separate set of issues concerning the *nonmaximality* of some uses of 'all' and of plural definite descriptions. I think that these issues are better handled in pragmatic ways (as in, e.g., Lasersohn 1999). Those issues can be separated from the arguments being considered here concerning the employment of an event semantics in conjunction with the semantics for 'all'.

[14] Whether there is a fully non-distributive reading:

[The X: X are students] $\exists e$ (e is a moving $\wedge$ Th(e, the piano) $\wedge$ $\exists e'$ (e' is a doing $\wedge$ e' $< e \wedge$ Ag(e', X)))

seems to depend on whether the agent role in a "doing" can be non-distributive. This would be a third reading for (20). It is hard to know how to distinguish this from (28) without more work in doing-theory.

[15] This problem also exists for Brisson's analysis. Cf. p. 168, sentences (131) and (132).

a useful application of an event semantics for English in conjunction with the semantics for plurals to give an account of the particular quantifier word 'all'. A complex internal structure for 'moved the piano' provides multiple places for a distributing universal, and so our account of distribution interacts with such an internal structure. I have not attempted an analysis with that kind of linguistic specificity, but rather have tried to give an analysis of non-distributive plural predication in a formal language. I hope that the analysis will be useful for linguists, but I have no doubt that natural language has many features that my starker focus on plurality has not uncovered. What I can hope is that I have shown how recognition of non-distributive predication's role in language and metalanguage is a strong basis for insight into the fundamental features of the semantics of plurality.

Bibliography

Abbott, Barbara 2003. "A Reply to Szabo's 'Descriptions and Uniqueness'," *Philosophical Studies* 113: 223–31.

Benardete, José 2002. "Logic and Ontology: Numbers and Sets," in *Blackwell Companion to Philosophical Logic*, Dale Jacquette (ed.), Blackwell, 351–64.

Bernays, Paul 1976. "On the Problem of Schemata in Axiomatic Set Theory," in G. Müller (ed.), *Sets and Classes: On the Work of Paul Bernays*. North Holland, 121–72. This is a translation of a paper first published in German, 1961.

Barwise, Jon and Robin Cooper 1981. "Generalized Quantifiers and Natural Language," *Linguistics and Philosophy* 4: 159–219.

Berger, Alan 2002*a*. "A Formal Semantics for Plural Quantification, Intersentential Binding and Anaphoric Pronouns as Rigid Designators," *Noûs* 36: 50–74.

—— 2002*b*. *Terms and Truth*. MIT Press.

Boolos, George 1984. "To be is to be the value of a variable (or to be some values of some variables)," *Journal of Philosophy* 81: 430–49; reprinted in Boolos 1998, 54–72.

—— 1985*a*. "Nominalist platonism," *Philosophical Review* 94: 327–44, reprinted in Boolos 1998, 73–87.

—— 1985*b*. "Reading the *Begriffschrift*," *Mind* 94: 331–44; reprinted in Boolos 1998, 155–70.

—— 1998. *Logic, Logic and Logic*. Harvard University Press.

Bricker, Philip 1989. "Quantified Modal Logic and the Plural *De Re*," *Midwest Studies in Philosophy* 14: 372–94.

Brisson, C. 2003. "Plurals, *All*, and the Nonuniformity of Collective Predication," *Linguistics and Philosophy* 26: 129–84.

Brown, Mark A. 1984. "Generalized quantifiers and the square of opposition," *Notre Dame Journal of Formal Logic* 25: 303–22.

Burge, Tyler 1977. "A Theory of Aggregates," *Noûs* 11: 97–117.

Burgess, John P. 2004. "*E Pluribus Unum*: Plural Logic and Set Theory," *Philosophia Mathematica* 12: 193–221.

—— and Gideon Rosen 1997. *A Subject without an Object*. Oxford University Press.

Carlson, Greg 1998. "Thematic roles and the individuation of events," in *Events and Grammar*, ed. by Susan Rothstein, 35–51. Kluwer Academic.

Cartwright, Helen 1996. "Some of a Plurality," in *Philosophical Perspectives* 10, ed. by James E. Tomberlin, 137–57. Blackwell.

—— 2000. "A Note on Plural Pronouns." *Synthese* 123: 227–46.

Cartwright, Richard 1994. "Speaking of Everything." *Noûs* 28: 1–20.

—— 2001. "A Question about Sets," in *Fact and Value*, ed., by Alex Byrne, Robert Stalnaker and Ralph Wedgwood. MIT Press, 29–46.

Cochiarella, Nino 2002. "On the Logic of Classes as Many." *Studia Logica* 70: 303–38.

Davidson, Donald 1967. "The logical form of action sentences" in N. Rescher (ed.), *The Logic of Decision and Action*, 81–120. University of Pittsburgh Press.

Dowty, David. 1986. "Collective predicates, distributive predicates, and *all*." *Proceedings of the 1986 Eastern State Conference on Linguistics*, 97–115. Ohio State University.

Drake, Frank R. 1974. *Set Theory*. North-Holland Publishing Co.

Evans, Gareth 1977. "Pronouns, Quantifiers and Relative Clauses (I)." *The Canadian Journal of Philosophy* 7: 467–536, reprinted in Evans 1985.

—— 1980. "Pronouns", *Linguistic Inquiry* 11: 337–62, reprinted in Evans 1985.

—— 1985. *Collected Papers*. Oxford University Press.

Frege, Gottlob 1914. "Logic in Mathematics," in *Posthumous Writings*, 203–50, University of Chicago Press, 1979, ed. by Hans Hermes, Friedrich Kambartel, and Friedrich Kaulbach, and trans. by Peter Long and Roger White.

French, Peter A., Theodore E. Uehling, and Howard K. Wettstein 1977. *Contemporary Perspectives in the Philosophy of Language*. University of Minnesota Press.

Goldstein, Laurence 2002. "The Indefinability of "One"," *Journal of Philosophical Logic* 31: 29–42.

Gomez-Torrente, Mario 2002, "The Problem of Logical Constants," *Bulletin of Symbolic Logic* 8: 1–37.

Graff, Delia 2001. "Descriptions as Predicates," *Philosophical Studies* 102: 1–42.

Groenendijk, Jeroen, Theo M. V. Janssen, and Martin Stokhof (eds.) 1981. *Formal Methods in the Study of Language, Part 2*. Mathematisch Centrum, Amsterdam.

Hart, W. D. (ed.) 1996. *The Philosophy of Mathematics*. Oxford University Press.

Hawthorne, John 2003. "Identity," in the *Oxford Companion to Metaphysics*, Oxford University Press, 99–130.

Hazen, A. P. 1993. "Against Pluralism," *Australasian Journal of Philosophy* 71: 132–44.

Heim, Irene, Howard Lasnik, and Robert May 1991. "Reciprocity and Plurality," *Linguistic Inquiry* 22: 63–101.

Higginbotham, James 2000. "On Second-Order Logic and Natural Language," in Sher and Tieszen 2000, 79–99.

Hossack, Keith 2000. "Plurals and Complexes", *British Journal for the Philosophy of Science* 51: 411–43.

Krifka, Manfred 1999. "At Least Some Determiners Aren't Determiners," in *The Semantics/Pragmatics Interface from Different Points of View*, ed. by K. Turner, 257–91. Elsevier Science Ltd.

Kripke, Saul 1977. "Speaker Reference and Semantic Reference," in P. A. French *et al.*, 1977, 6–27.

Kurtz, Charles 1996. "Generalized Quantifiers and Measure Theory," Ph.D. dissertation, Syracuse University.

Landman, Fred 1989. "Groups I," *Linguistics and Philosophy* 12: 559–605.

—— 2000. *Events and Plurality*. Kluwer Academic.

Lasersohn, Peter 1996. *Plurality, Conjunction and Events*. Kluwer.

Lewis, David K. 1983. *Philosophical Papers*, vol. 1. Oxford University Press.

—— 1998. *Papers in Philosophical Logic*. Cambridge University Press.

—— 1991. *Parts of Classes*. Blackwell.

—— 1979. "Score-Keeping in a Language Game," *Journal of Philosophical Logic* 1979, 8: 339–59, reprinted in Lewis 1983.

Lindenbaum, A., and Alfred Tarski 1934–35. "On the Limitations of the Means of Expression of Deductive Theories," in Tarski 1983, 384–92.

Link, Godehard 1998. *Algebraic Semantics in Language and Philosophy*. CSLI Publications.

Linnebo, Øystein 2003. "Plural Quantification Exposed," *Noûs* 37: 71–92.

—— "Plural Quantification," *Stanford Encyclopedia of Philosophy*, http://plato.stanford.edu/.

Ludlow, Peter, and Gabriel Segal 2004. "On a Unitary Semantic Analysis of Definite and Indefinite Descriptions," in Marga Reimer and Anne Bezuidenhout (eds.), *Descriptions and Beyond*, 420–36. Oxford University Press.

Massey, Gerald J. 1976. "Tom, Dick and Harry, and all the King's men," *American Philosophical Quarterly* 70: 340–61.

McKay, Thomas J. 1984. Review of Michael Devitt's *Designation, Noûs* 18: 357–67.

—— 1989. *Modern Formal Logic*. Macmillan (New York); revised version, 2005, Thomson.

—— 1991. "Representing *de re* Beliefs," *Linguistics and Philosophy* 14: 711–39.

—— 1994. "Plural Reference and Unbound Pronouns," in *Logic and Philosophy of Science in Uppsala*, 559–82, ed. by Dag Prawitz and Dag Westerstahl. Kluwer Academic, 559–82.

Moltmann, Friederike 1997. *Parts and Wholes in Semantics*. Oxford University Press.

Mostowski, Andrzej 1957. "On a Generalization of Quantifiers," *Fundamenta Mathematicae* 44: 12–36.

Neale, Stephen 1990. *Descriptions*. MIT Press.

Oliver, Alex 2000. "Logic, Mathematics and Philosophy," *British Journal for the Philosophy of Science* 53: 857–73. (This is a review of Boolos 1998.)

—— and Timothy Smiley 2001. "Strategies for a logic of plurals," *The Philosophical Quarterly* 51: 289–306.

Parsons, Charles 1990. "The Structuralist View of Mathematical Objects," *Synthese* 843: 303–46; reprinted in Hart 1996.

Parsons, Terence 1990. *Events in the Semantics of English.* MIT Press.

Plantiga, Alvin 1974. *The Nature of Necessity.* Oxford University Press.

Quine, Willard van Orman 1960. *Word and Object.* MIT Press.

Rayo, Agustín 2002. "Word and Objects," *Noûs* 36: 436–64.

—— and Gabriel Uzquiano 1999. "Toward a theory of Second-Order Consequence," *Notre Dame Journal of Formal Logic* 40: 315–25.

Resnik, Michael 1988. "Second-order logic still wild," *Journal of Philosophy* 85: 75–87.

Roberts, Craige 1990. *Modal Subordination, Anaphora and Distributivity.* Garland Publishing.

—— 2003. "Uniqueness in Definite Noun Phrases," *Linguistics and Philosophy* 26: 287–350.

Rouilhan, Phillippe de 2002. "On What There Are," *Proceedings of the Aristotelian Society* 102: 183–200.

Russell, Bertrand 1903. *The Principles of Mathematics.* Allen & Unwin Ltd.

—— 1905. "On Denoting," *Mind*, 14: 479–93.

Scha, Remko 1981. "Distributive, Collective and Cumulative Quantification," in Groenindijk *et al.* (eds.), 483–512.

Schein, Barry 1993. *Plurals and Events.* MIT Press.

Schwarzschild, Roger 1996. *Pluralities.* Kluwer Academic.

Shapiro, Stewart 1991. *Foundations without Foundationalism.* Oxford University Press.

Sharvy, Richard 1980. "A more general theory of definite descriptions," *Philosophical Review* 89: 607–24.

Sher, Gila 1991. *The Bounds of Logic.* MIT Press.

—— and Richard Tieszen (eds.), 2000. *Between Intuition and Logic: Essays in Honor of Charles Parsons.* Cambridge University Press.

Sider, Theodore, ms. "Parthood." http://fas-philosophy.rutgers.edu/sider/

Simons, Peter 1982*a*. "Number and Manifolds," *Parts and Moments. Studies in Logic and Formal Ontology*, edited by Barry Smith, 160–98. Philosophia Verlag.

—— 1982*b*. "Plural Reference and Set Theory," *Parts and Moments. Studies in Logic and Formal Ontology*, ed. by Barry Smith, 199–260. Philosophia Verlag.

—— 1982*c*. "On Understanding Lesniewski," *History and Philosophy of Logic* 3: 165–91.

—— 1987. *Parts.* Oxford University Press.

Simpson, Stephen G. 1999. *Subsystems of Second Order Arithmetic.* Springer-Verlag.

Stanley, Jason, and Timothy Williamson 1995. "Quantifiers and Context-Dependence," *Analysis* 55, 291–5.

Szabó, Zoltán 2000. "Descriptions and Uniqueness," *Philosophical Studies* 101: 29–57.

—— 2003. "Definite Descriptions without Uniqueness: A Reply to Abbott," *Philosophical Studies* 114: 279–91.

Tarski, Alfred 1983. *Logic, Semantics, Metamathematics*, trans. by J. H. Woodger; 2nd edn. edited by John Corcoran. Hackett Publishing.

Uzquiano, Gabriel 2004. "The Supreme Court and the Supreme Court Justices: A Metaphysical Puzzle," *Noûs* 38: 135–53.

van der Does, Jaap 1993. "Sums and Quantifiers," *Linguistics and Philosophy* 16: 509–50.

van Inwagen, Peter 1990. *Material Beings*. Cornell University Press.

Wallace, Megan. "On Composition as Identity." http://www.unc.edu/~megw/PapersAndIdeas.html

Williamson, Timothy 2003. "Everything," *Philosophical Perspectives* 17: 415–65.

Winter, Yoad 2000. "Distributivity and Dependency," *Natural Language Semantics* 8: 27–69.

—— 2002. "Atoms and Sets: A Characterization of Semantic Number", *Linguistic Inquiry* 33: 493–505.

Yablo, Stephen 2000. "Apriority and Existence," *New Essays on the apriori*, Paul Boghossian and Christopher Peacocke (eds.), 197–228. Oxford University Press.

Yi, Byeong-Uk 1999*a*. "Is Mereology Ontologically Innocent?" *Philosophical Studies* 93: 141–60.

—— 1999*b*. "Is two a property?" *Journal of Philosophy* 95: 163–90.

—— 2005. "The Logic and Meaning of Plurals Part I," *Journal of Philosophical Logic* 34: 459–506.

—— 2002. *Understanding the Many*. Routledge.

—— "Is There a Plural Object?" ms.

Index

Abbott, Barbara 198 n. 17
all 252–5
among 15, 56–7, 135–9
  as logical constant 160–1
  axiomatization 121–35
at least 79–80
at most 80–1
axiom of choice 155–6
axiom of heredity 158
axiom of reflection 159–60
axiom of replacement 155, 158–9
axiom of separation 158

Ben-Yami, Hanoch 73 n. 26
Berger, Alan 219 n.15
Bernays, Paul 159, 160
Boolos, George 1 n., 16, 28 n., 32
  n.28, 139, 143–5
Bricker, Philip 4, 177–81
Brisson, C. 241, 252–5
Burge, Tyler 7, 33
Burgess, John 142–3, 156–60

Cartwright, Helen 165 n. 8, 166–7 n.,
  170 n. 15, 176
Cartwright, Richard 32 n. 29, 146 n.
  29
class as many 24, 36, 146–7; *see also*
  set
Cochiarella, Nino 36 n. 36
common noun 9 n. 13
compactness 140–1
completeness 141
composition 42
  anti-realism 42–5
  as identity 36–45
  compositionalism 42–5
  unrestricted 33
comprehension 129–30
conjoined terms, *see* conjunctive terms
conjunctive terms 11–12, 57–8,
  97–9, 112
cumulative predicate, *see* predicate,
  cumulative
cumulative quantification, *see*
  quantification

Davidson, Donald 2 n., 240
de re 177–81
de Rouilhan, *see* Rouilhan, Pierre de
definite description
  as existential 198–203
  domain restriction 185–7
  improper 167–9
  mass 173–7
  peculiar 170
  plural 162–70
  predicate supplementation 185–7
  psychologism 196–7
  referential 163, 203
  singular (as special case) 171–3
distribution
  intermediate 88–92
  see also predicate, quantifier, relation
distributive correlate 78–79
distributive predicate, *see* predicate,
  relation
donkey sentence 216–22
Dowty, David 9 n. 12, 12 n.

Evans, Gareth 187 n. 6, 207–39
events in semantics 203–4, 240–55
everything 147–59
exactly 81

Fara, Michael 46 n. 53
first-order plurals 15–16
Frege, Gottlob 11 n.15, 38 n. 42
fusion, *see* mereology

Geach–Kaplan sentence 15–16, 27–9,
  31
generality absolutism 147–54

Hawthorne, John 41 n.46
Hazen, Allen 46, 51–2, 137–9, 141,
  142–3
Higginbotham, James 146–7, 244 n.
Hodes, Harold 46 n. 53
Hossack, Keith 1 n., 6 n. 4, 17

identity 122, 127–9
involved in, *see* distributive correlate

Kaplan, David 15 n.22

Landman, Fred 1 n., 2 n., 6 n. 4,
   87–8, 90–2, 240, 247, 250–2
Lasersohn, Peter 6 n. 4
Lewis, David 17, 28 n. 17, 33–4, 36,
   41 n. 47
limitation of size 160
Lindenbaum, Adolf 160
Link, Godehard 6 n.4, 34–5, 36, 38 n.
   42, 40 n. 45
Linnebo, Øystein 29–31
logical constant 160–1
Ludlow, Peter 198 n. 17, 200 n. 18,
   217 n. 14, 223 n. 21, 235–9

mereology 33–42, 122, 124
Moltmann, Friederike 12 n.
multi-grade relation 21–2
multiple relations idea 19–22

non-distributive predicate 6, 13–14,
   81–8
non-proportional quantifier, *see*
   quantifier
numerical quantification, *see*
   quantification

Oliver, Alex 1 n., 17 n. 24, 23 n., 240,
   245–6
one of 27, 57, 135–7

pairs 141–2
paradox 28, 31–2, 148–51, 245–6
Parsons, Charles 29, 143–5
Parsons, Terence 2 n., 240
part 124
Peano axiom 16, 140
perplural 46–53, 137–9
plurally plural, *see* perplural
predicate
   cumulative 7, 14
   distributive 5, 13–14, 81–8
   distributive ambiguity 11–12,
      84–8, 98–9, 241–4
   distributive correlate 78–9
   non-cumulative 7–8
   non-distributive 6
   strongly distributive 8
pronoun
   bound variable 208
   E-type 207–9, 213–39
   laziness 209

referential 208–9
relative reference 218–22
proportional quantifier, *see* quantifier
psychologism 196–7

quantification
   multiple 15, 92–6; cumulative
      (unscoped) readings 93–6,
      256–7
   numerical 79–81
   restricted 6
   second-order, *see* second-order logic
   unrestricted 6
quantifier
   distributing universal 83–8, 99–100
   dual 74–7
   existence entailments 71–3
   numerical 79–81
   proportional 61–3, 70–1, 110–11
   semantics 70–1

Rayo, Agustín 1 n., 7 n. 5, 28 n. 17, 63
   n. 11, 85 n. 7
referential definite descriptions 163,
   203
reflection 159–60
relation
   distributive 13–14
   in semantics 64–6
Resnik, Michael 28
Roberts, Craige 186, 189
Rouilhan, Pierre de 145
Russell, Bertrand 146, 163

Scha, Remko 6 n. 4, 86, 181–4
Schein, Barry 80 n., 240, 247–52
Schwarzschild, Roger 6 n. 4, 7 n. 6,
   88–90
second-order arithmetic 141
second-order logic 15–16, 32,
   139–46, 147–54
Segal, Gabriel 198 n. 17, 200 n. 18
semantic anomaly 61–3, 69–70
semantic role 22, 26–7, 87–8, 118
semantics 60–71
   quantifiers 70–1
   set-theoretic 103–18
set
   as many 24, 36, 146–7
   semantics 103–18
   see also paradox, singularism
set theory 154–60
Sharvy, Richard 163, 165, 173–7

Sher, Gila 160
Sider, Ted 38
Simons, Peter 35–6 n. 36, 145
singularism 19, 22–45, 137, 143–5
   mereological 22, 23, 24–5, 33–42
   paraphrase principle (SPP) 34
   set theoretic 22–32
Smiley, Timothy 1 n., 23 n., 240,
   245–6
sortal relativity 38–42
Stanley, Jason 191–2
Szabó, Zoltan Gendler 198 n. 17,
   201–2

Tarski, Alfred 160
thematic roles, *see* semantic roles
theta roles, *see* semantic roles

universal quantifiers
   two types 74–6
Uzquiano, Gabriel 42 n. 48, 50 n. 58,
   67 n. 17

van Inwagen, Peter 17
variable polyadicity 20
variables 13, 14

Wallace, Megan 38 n. 42
Williamson, Timothy 147–54,
   191–2

Yi, Byeong-Uk 1 n., 6 n. 4, 21 n. 1,
   23 n. 5, 34 n. 34, 38, 123,
   204 n. 21